A Cry from the Heart

A Cry from the Heart

THE LIFE OF EDITH PIAF

Margaret Crosland
contributions by Ralph Harvey

ARCADIA BOOKS

Arcadia Books Ltd
15–16 Nassau Street
London W1W 7AB

www.arcadiabooks.co.uk

First published in the United Kingdom 1985
Revised edition published by Arcadia Books 2002
B-format edition published 2007
Reprinted April 2008
Reprinted June 2008
Copyright © Margaret Crosland 1985, 2002
Copyright © Ralph Harvey 2002 (appendices)

A catalogue record for this book is available from the British Library

ISBN 978-1-905147-68-7

Typeset in Ehrhardt
Printed in the United Kingdom by Cox & Wyman, Reading

Editions Paul Beuscher: *Çe gueule ça, madame* (Bécaud, Piaf); *Les Amants*
(Dumont, Piaf); *A quoi ça sert l'amour* (Elmer); *Avant l'heure* (Monnot,
Achard); *Si, si, si* (Monnot, Achard); *Petite si jolie* (Monnot, Piaf); *Les Amants
d'un jour* (Monnot, Delécluse, Senlis).

Editions Raoul Breton: *Hymne à l'amour* (Monnot, Piaf); *Je t'ai dans la peau*
(Bécaud, Pills); *Couchés dans le foin* (Mireille, Nohain).

Editions Intersong: *Le Droit d'aimer* (Laï, Nyel); *Roulez tambours* (Laï, Piaf).

Editions Salabert: *Le Chemin des forains* (Sauguet, Dréjac); *Je me souviens d'une
chanson* (Moulin, Marten); *Escale* (Monnot, Marèze); *Il n'est pas distingué*
(Maye, Hély); *Opinion publique* (Monnot, Contet).

Editions S.E.M.I. (and Southern Music Publishing Co., London):
Mon Légionnaire (Monnot, Asso); *C'est peut-être ça* (Dumont, Vaucaire);
Cri du cœur (Crolla, Prévert); *Le Chant d'amour* (Dumont, Piaf).

Executors of Raymond Asso: *On danse sur ma chanson* (Asso, Poll). Executors of
René Rouzaud: *La Goualante du pauvre Jean* (Monnot, Rouzaud).

Arcadia Books supports English PEN, the fellowship of writers who work
together to promote literature and its understanding. English PEN upholds
writers' freedoms in Britain and around the world, challenging political and
cultural limits on free expression. To find out more, visit www.englishpen.org,
or contact English PEN, 6–8 Amwell Street, London EC1R 1UQ.

Arcadia Books is the *Sunday Times* Small Publisher of the Year

For my son
Patrick
just for the record

Contents

CONTENTS

List of illustrations

Acknowledgments

A great number of people have helped me with this book, in its original and newer versions, and it could not have been written without them. My colleague Ralph Harvey has continued his valued collaboration with an up-to-date discography of popular and accessible Piaf CDs plus a few related collections which include other singers. In addition to the checklist of songs in alphabetical order there are two detailed appendixes which provide absorbing accounts of the *chanteuses réalistes* whose lives and songs preceded or coincided with those of Piaf herself, while some of them have continued the tradition, even if Piaf herself has never had any serious rival.

I am especially grateful to my colleague Elfreda Powell who edited this version of Piaf's life. At the same time I would like to thank all those in France and Britain who have helped me, many of whom, sadly, are no longer there to assist further. I have learnt much from the conscientious work by Pierre Ducos and Georges Martin included in their book of 1993 and from recent books by Marc and Danielle Bonel and Marcel Cerdan Jnr. with their many moving recollections. I am also indebted to Denise Merlin, my Paris researcher, Bernard Marchois, Secrétaire-Générale of Les Amis d'Edith Piaf and Angelo Giannecchini, generous owner of a remarkable collection of Piaf documents, located in Italy.

The long list of people who have helped me with this book include:

Le Docteur Audouy, Jean-Christophe Averty, Lord Bessborough, Marcel Blistène, Madame Raoul Breton, Jacques Canetti, Alain Chamrobert, Stuart Collins, Henri Contet, André Couteaux, Lily Denis, Max and Mimi Denis, Charles Dumont, Janine and Jean-Marie Favinet, Herbert Gassion, Penni Harvey-Piper, John Haslam, Assistant Press Secretary to The Queen, Margery Hemming, Gilles Henry, Edith Hillyar, Carol Johnson, Monique Lange, Vic Lanza, Auguste Le Breton, Philippe Leroux, editor of *L'Eveil normand*, Marcelle Lallier, "Bunny" Lewis, Patricia Marne, Jean Mauldon, Benjamin A. McCormick, the late Henri Merlin, Olivier Merlin, John Mitchell, Cécile Mordecai of Pathé-Marconi, Paris, Marie-Christine Movilliat, Jean Holi, André Pousse, Isabelle de Préaumont of the Mairie de Paris, Daphne Richardson, Ginette Richer, John Rush, Vernon Scannell, André Schoeller, David Shipman, Guy-Charles Simonnet, Stanley Smith, Gérard Trimbach, Lucien Vaimber, Thomas J. Watson, Margory Whitelaw, Michael Williams, John Wilson, Donald K. Young.

Valuable help also came from the BBC Data Enquiry Service, *Boxing News*, the British Film Institute, EMI Records (U.K.), the staff of the Olympia Music Hall, Paris, the Phonothèque Nationale Paris, the S. A. C. E. M., and from the French music publishers who are listed separately.

M.C.

Prelude

'Others before me', said the chaplain, 'have told the story of Edith Piaf, and others will tell it again ...' The occasion was a Mass arranged by an admirer in the august church of La Madeleine in Paris, in 1983, twenty years after the singer's death. The congregation included a few stage personalities but it was a typical Piaf audience, men and women of all ages, from all walks of life, who wanted to remember their idol in some way that took them a little further than the sound of her voice on record. They would all know her famous song, the *Hymn to Love*, for which she wrote the words: in heaven there are no problems, God reunites those who love each other.

Others have indeed told the story, and Piaf herself told it twice, but her autobiography of 1958, *Au bal de la chance* (translated as *The Wheel of Fortune* in 1965), did not tell the whole story. It perpetuated one legend that was true but several others that were not. It omitted certain incidents and people crucial to her life and, of course, was written before her theatrical 'resurrection' of 1960 and her second marriage in 1962. Shortly before she died she dictated another very different 'autobiography', *Ma vie*, published first as a series of newspaper articles, edited by Jean Noli, which were to appear in *France-Dimanche* only after her death. In 1978 they were published in book form. Here she included a great deal about her early sensational life, but she was so ill and disorientated at the time, and seemingly resentful or revengeful about the circumstances of her teenage years that the 'facts' she gave may have been closer to fiction and suitable for tabloid journalism: but that was how she chose to remember them. In 1969 Simone Berteaut, claiming to be Piaf's half-sister, wrote a long book about her – with the help of a 'ghost' – in which she gives the impression that they had been extremely close all their lives. She was not Edith's half-sister. The two women were indeed close at various periods, notably when they were teenagers, but it is significant that Edith did not mention this 'sister' in either of her books. After *la môme* had become Edith Piaf her friends often resented Berteaut's intrusion into her life. The best thing she ever did for Simone was to forgive her a good deal of anti-social, even anti-Piaf behaviour.

Since 1963 her true half-sister Denise Gassion, friends and admirers in France and abroad have talked and written about Edith, usually in a subjective way, sometimes contradicting each other, while coffee-table books, documentaries for film, radio and television, feature films and plays have been put together. Pam Gems' play of 1978 had great success in Britain. By the start of the second millennium many of the people who had worked with the singer are dead, but her own reputation, thanks to the recordings, mostly now available on well-edited CDs, is totally alive. She herself wrote the words for over eighty of her songs and composed the music for many. The songs reflect her own story and also the changes in French life and taste from the mid-1930s to the early 1960s. It is impossible to imagine those years without her, for she both continued a long tradition and anticipated its vibrant future. She is still the icon that helps to explain the quality of other types of song, for instance, the Portuguese *fado*. 'Think Edith Piaf on downers', wrote *The Guardian* in August 2000, 'and you're half way there'. And how could Juliette Greco and Nana Mouskouri have sung as they did without Piaf among their ancestors?

The voice is the essential Edith. Where did that voice come from, how and why did it develop as it did, how did the two hundred songs come about and why have they lasted so well? Why are so many young people all over the world still discovering Piaf?

The French, wrote the film critic David Shipman, approach her like a religious ceremony. What can she and her songs mean to the rest of the world, and can those who remain outside the French language still experience the ritual, the mystery, the charisma, of Edith Piaf and her living legend?

Part One

Tempo de Java

1

Backgrounds and beginnings

'Who is that plain little woman, with a voice too big for her body?' asked Mistinguett. Out of jealousy, the great star would pretend to forget her name. The 'little woman' was in fact only four foot ten inches tall, her looks reflected no conventional glamour, but whenever she sang she grew beautiful. She had a solid neck and broad cheekbones, useful equipment for a singer. She did not dance or reveal million-dollar legs, she could never have been a rival to the queen of the Folies-Bergère, preferring a plain black dress to ostrich plumes and strass, just as she always chose a song with a story rather than a catchy music-hall number, and her own life had even more drama than anything she sang. Such was her commitment both to living and singing that other stars may glow and fade but Edith Piaf has never lost her vivid quality; her small-range but powerful voice can illuminate even a shadowy song. Memory may darken, the true story has merged into legend, just as words and music blend into a song. If, after forty years, reality has sometimes moved from black and white into full colour and back again, if the remaining image is far from *la vie en rose*, its outline, like a musical phrase or a line of verse, remains intact.

For the French, at least, the outline of this legend has been kept alive in one of those Paris faubourgs which have never attracted many tourists, although they have in the past fascinated novelists and poets, for they were densely populated and

3

lively. People worked hard if they had the chance and played hard even if they were broke. Go up to the steep section of the rue de Belleville, in the 20th arrondissement to number 72. Suitably, it was another entertainer from the faubourgs, *le gars de Ménilmontant*, Maurice Chevalier himself, who unveiled the plaque over the doorway which states: 'On the steps to this house there was born on 19 December 1915, in utter destitution, Edith Piaf, whose voice was later to shatter the world'. Inside the doorway a tiled passage leads to a small dismal courtyard and a notice requesting you not to spit.

This story gave Edith Piaf a start in life more suitable to a novel by Eugène Sue or Emile Zola, but there is one drawback: it has little, if anything, to do with fact. The birth certificate, signed by the midwife, for Edith Gassion, later Piaf, states that she was born at 4 rue de la Chine in the 20th arrondissement, which is in fact the address of the old-established Hôpital Tenon. Edith's half-sister, Denise, who was born there herself sixteen years later, maintains in her book, *Piaf ma Soeur* (1971), that their father told her about Edith's birth. However, the legend states that Edith's mother could not get to the hospital in time, that her father, on leave from the army, stopped for too many drinks on his way to join her, in order to prepare himself for fatherhood, that gendarmes acted as midwives under a convenient street-lamp, and it all adds up to a good story. Edith, who enjoyed drama, was delighted to keep up the fiction, and proved herself a true child of Sagittarius, spending her life in moving from one crisis to another.

Edith Gassion's parents had been married in Sens, about fifty miles south-east of Paris, in the Yonne area. The year was 1914. Louis-Alphonse Gassion, who was thirty-three at the time, had been called up into the army, and his life as a *poilu* must certainly have been a change from his existence so far. He had been born in Falaise, Normandy, and had started work in a travelling circus

4

at the age of ten, following the lead given by his father. Louis-Alphonse trained hard to become an acrobat and his physique gave him a good start: he was about five foot tall and weighed only eighty-eight pounds. He called himself a *contorsionniste-antipodiste*, presumably because in one of his numbers he would walk upside down on his hands. He would also tie a bandage round his eyes, put a sack over his head and perform an impressive long-jump. He was a good-looking man with brown hair and brown eyes, well-defined eyebrows and a broad forehead, who remained attractive to women all his life. He had no difficulty in attracting a girl called Anetta Maillard whom he met when she was sixteen, probably at one of the big fairgrounds in or near Paris, or possibly even in Italy. She earned a little money selling nougat, she also ran a small roundabout and when the takings were not good she would also sing, as many other people did, since there was always a potential audience at those places of entertainment, even if it was an ever-changing one. Her parents travelled round Europe and presumably her French father, Auguste-Eugène Maillard, also worked at some casual circus-type job.

Nobody seems to know where Anetta's mother, Edith's maternal grandmother, was born, but she had probably travelled a long way before she met Maillard. Emma Saïd ben Mohamed came from Kabylia, a mountainous region on the coast of North Africa in western Algeria. The villages there were so overcrowded that even in the mid-twentieth century their inhabitants were still emigrating to Algerian towns or France in search of work. In *The Wheel of Fortune* Edith allotted a few sentences to this side of her family. Her mother, she said, 'had show business in her blood; her parents had roamed Algeria with their small travelling circus'. Edith obviously was keen to promote the Maillards to the same level as the Gassions. Her grandmother, usually known at this period as 'Aïcha', carried out an act with performing fleas. Perhaps because the Maillard daughter was born in Leghorn, Italy, she was named Anetta Giovanna. She had been living with Louis Gassion in Sens, but in 1914 a soldier who got married could go on leave, perhaps a good reason for legalizing the arrangement. There could not have been much of a family party at the wedding on 14 September, so soon after the outbreak of war, for Anetta's father was dead and her mother had no work. Anetta and her mother went back to Paris and the newly married Gassion went back to the war.

Both sides of Edith's immediate family had been living a nomadic existence but this was a fairly recent development among the Gassions, whose history has been traced back to the seventeenth century. The name was probably of Spanish origin – Edith liked this touch of exoticism – coming into France originally through Béarn in the south-west. For a long time, however, the Gassions lived in the north, first in the Calvados region, working as ploughmen or masons. In 1780 or thereabouts the family went off to Falaise, in Normandy, a centre of the hosiery trade, where they took up specialized work as '*siamoisiers*', making the silk and cotton fabrics imitating those brought to the court of Louis XIV by the ambassadors from Siam. One generation later a Gassion worked as a toll collector because he had just married and wanted a safe job. He was the last member of the family to want that, for his grandson took a new turning: he joined a well-known circus, became a successful *écuyer* and from then onwards the Gassions were entertainers. Louis-Alphonse had three remarkable sisters: Mathilde and Zéphora (known as 'Zaza') who performed brilliant tight-rope acts until 1910, while Louise, with her husband and a partner, formed the internationally known 'Krag's Trio'. They visited the United States and China and were based in London for no fewer than eleven years. They were so famous that mail was addressed to them simply as 'Monsieur et Madame Krags, London', and they are known to have lived at number 11 Upper St Martin's Lane.

The Gassions were enterprising and mobile; nothing is known about the Maillards, but they were obviously mobile too, and it seemed unlikely that Louis and Anetta were going to settle down anywhere. For the time being they just waited for the end of the war. Anetta had presumably hoped to do more singing in Paris, but this was not the moment and she was soon pregnant. Their daughter was born two months after the Germans shot the English Nurse Cavell in Belgium, which is why, like many other young couples in France, they gave their baby the un-French name of Edith, adding one of her mother's names, Giovanna, which Edith never liked. Her mother longed to escape from the apartment into the streets as soon as she could, leaving the baby sometimes with her own mother, then known as 'Ména', who lived conveniently near. At what point Anetta Maillard Gassion called herself 'Line Marsa' is not clear, but there was a theatrical air about her, she was handsome and dark-haired. If her voice had inherited anything from her Kabylian ancestors it would probably have had a harsh, flamenco-like quality, produced well-forward and likely to carry in the streets or in the *boîtes* and *caveaux* where she is said to have sung. She herself had certainly inherited nomadic tendencies of a kind: she was a drifter, and very soon she drifted away from home, leaving her daughter behind.

The story goes that Louis Gassion removed the little girl from Ména's care, if that is the word, when he found she was being sent to sleep with the aid of red wine and was hardly ever washed, but he too would leave her alone in the Belleville apartment while he was out and away. His discharge from the army left him with no ambitions beyond a return to his acrobatic stunts. He had asked his sister Zéphora, 'Tante Zaza', if he could buy the caravan where she and her family had been living in Montreuil. He would pay later, he said, as money came in, but if it came he did not use it that way, and Madame Gassion senior, who had helped her daughter to buy this makeshift

7

home, did not see her money back. However, Louis Gassion could now tour the country in search of work though his daughter was still too young to be useful to him.

Tante Zaza had married, given up the circus act with her sister, and apparently worked as *ouvreuse*, or usherette in a Gaumont cinema at Versailles and also at the Gaîté-Montparnasse in Paris. One day she went in search of her brother Louis: 'I particularly wanted to see my niece, I had heard very little about her; I arrived ... and went up to the floor where my brother lodged with his daughter Edith; I went in, the rooms were empty, apart from the bedroom ... Edith was sleeping there, peacefully and calmly; she was about five then and there she was, abandoned, she had fair curly hair ... and she was on her own; I went downstairs again and asked the concierge if she knew why Edith was completely alone; she told me that "her mother had walked out" shortly before and she had no idea where she was. I thought that she was too young and could not possibly stay there in those conditions, and I decided to take her with me; a few days later she was with her grandmother in Bernay.'

Tante Zaza told this story to Gilles Henry of Caen, whose genealogical research has revealed endless details, all fascinating, about the Gassion family. It was a good thing that Edith's aunt went in search of her that day, for she was just in time: 'I learnt soon afterwards that the Assistance Publique were going to take charge of her.' Edith was in fact seven, not five when Tante Zaza found her. 'We had to clean her up thoroughly, for she had lice, poor thing.'

Bernay in Normandy is a pleasant, busy little town between Rouen and Alençon and Edith's grandmother Louise Gassion had a good job; she was the owner of the local *maison close* where she also supervised the cooking. There was plenty of room here for one extra little girl. The town apparently needed an establishment of this sort for an infantry regiment had been garrisoned there since before 1914 and they required female company. The soldiers left in 1945 but the handsome solidly built house is still there at number 7, rue Saint-Michel. The 'staff' in 1922 consisted of several ladies who were delighted to have a little girl on the premises and they apparently spoilt her, for a small child in a brothel is supposed to bring good luck. So Edith became used to well-dressed, attractive women, and men in uniform, determined to enjoy themselves: but the men never stayed very long. Background music was supplied by a mechanical piano which, although no longer in the house, is said to be somewhere in the Bernay region. No wonder so many of Edith's songs were to include the evocative sound of this individual percussive instrument.

She lived in this cheerful place for just about a year and at one point probably developed conjunctivitis. Legend has magnified this stay into several years and the eye-trouble has been turned into blindness. Edith invented or believed this story because it was dramatic, but people who knew her well later doubted very much if she was ever blind. However, Edith later talked about 'those years in the dark' and the 'miracle' which ended them, the trip to nearby Lisieux – a short distance from Bernay by train – where Saint Thérèse, who was not actually canonized until 1925, obligingly cured her. The miracle did not happen instantly, it appears, but a few days later. The whole incident has inevitably been compared with the well-known Maupassant story *La Maison Tellier* which had to be closed when the 'girls' went to take their First Communion. The girls from the rue Saint-Michel are said to have gone to Lisieux in a body, and the Saint, the writer of the masochistic *Story of a Soul*, who is now the patron of *les petites gens*, the humble people of the world, established a permanent relationship with Edith Gassion. Saint Thérèse helped Edith and her friends, we are told, through worldly and otherworldly life. Raymond Asso, later so important to Edith, insisted that the trip to Lisieux was not undertaken in search of miracles but as a gesture of gratitude.

Proprietors of *maisons closes* are practical people, and her grandmother, who had accepted the child – more from duty than from love – was not content with allowing her to be the household pet all the time, so she was sent to school, and the local curé, who did not approve of her presence in the house, was said to be pleased, although Edith was not. In 1985 the Ecole Paul-Bert still existed in Bernay. Her father apparently wanted her to go to school whenever possible, but of course he never stayed long enough in one place for this to be arranged. However, Bernay probably supplied most of the formal education Edith ever received. Louis Gassion would come to Bernay when he could and take her to see her many Normandy relations. He liked to visit his old home town of Falaise, where father and daughter were particularly fascinated by the château, the birthplace of William the Conqueror. Edith did not forget Bernay of which more later.

Edith was about eight when she left the comfortable life of Bernay in 1922 or 1923 and when not in Belleville she probably spent most of the time in her father's caravan, mainly touring in the north of France and Belgium. She was old enough to stand on a stool and stir the soup for him; food, money and would-be 'mothers' were picked up at random, whenever possible, and Edith spent more time on the road than Colette had done when she toured the provinces with a theatrical company soon after her first divorce. Colette extracted literary mileage from her experiences, Edith absorbed hers, remembered them and somehow translated them into her singing. On their travels she and her father would even sell goods, such as slippers, in local markets. 'Don't feel sorry for me', she said later, adding that she had learnt more about life that way than she had at school.

Street acrobats, however brilliant, were beggars, and Louis Gassion would do anything to draw a larger crowd round him. He soon tried to turn Edith into a performer and she is said to have started by singing *La Marseillaise*, the only song she knew by heart. Unfortunately she had not inherited the family talent for acrobatics, but if her mother had deserted her she bequeathed a voice to her, although obviously it was not identical to her own. The Gassions were a talented family, but they did not sing, and if all small girls can make some attempt at singing Edith must have realized, even before adolescence, that the type of singing her father encouraged was not merely 'natural', it was meant to have an emotional appeal, it was already performance, and it made her the centre of attention, if only for a few minutes at a time.

As far as can be judged, several years passed in this unsettled existence. The young Edith Gassion was about fifteen when her father brought her back to Paris. But she was not his only companion, for Louis Gassion, who was now forty-nine, had been feeling the need for adult female company on at least a semi-permanent basis; he was no longer satisfied by the short-term presence of endless 'aunts' for Edith, the women who were attracted by the lively middle-aged acrobat and touched by the large-eyed motherless girl who passed the hat or cap around, and sometimes sang a little. Gassion was rumoured to have at least thirty children, which may or may not be true, and the last of his temporary companions had just left him in order to get married. So there was no domestic life, only the bistrot or the café in the evening, and then the caravan.

Louis and Edith were in Nancy, that town of superb architecture and stirring historical associations, when he decided to do what solitary Frenchmen usually did, and still do: he advertised for a companion, hoping presumably to find someone rather younger than himself.

How many women responded to the few lines in the local newspaper is not known, but there is a good deal of information about one of them. Her name was Georgette L'Hôte, brought up by a domineering stepmother, her parents' former maid who had come from Luxembourg to live in Maxeville, a village a few kilometres outside Nancy. By the time she was twenty-two Georgette, known as 'Yéyette', had had enough of her situation and the long row of step-brothers and sisters who had appeared, for whom she was the hard-working unpaid nurse. She took to reading the *petites annonces* in the local newspaper and decided to follow up the one that suggested meeting on the steps of the Hôtel de Ville in the centre of the town, the splendid eighteenth-century Place Stanislas.

Again it is not known if she had any rivals, or whether Gassion compared one woman with another as he paused in his act. In any case he liked the look of Yéyette and the very next day they left for Paris, accompanied of course by Edith.

If the phrase *vue mariage* had been mentioned in the advertisement in Nancy, neither party acted upon it, for Louis Gassion never married his new companion. The trio lived together in the same part of Paris where Louis Gassion had lived with his wife, and where his daughter had been born, but this time he chose the small hotel at number 115 rue de Belleville. Yéyette, who was only seven years older than Edith, soon became pregnant. Her daughter Denise, from whose book this information comes, was born on 8 March 1931, and duly registered at the local Mairie by her mother who was listed in the birth certificate as '*sans profession*'.

In the margin of the certificate are the crucial words 'Recognized at the Mairie of the 20th arrondissement in Paris on 18 March 1932, by Louis-Alphonse Gassion'. The little girl's father had unaccountably waited just over a year before making the declaration. No doubt he was still working hard and travelling about, although he does not seem to have gone far from Paris during this period.

Edith was now nearly sixteen and according to her half-sister did not take too kindly to the appearance of this new baby. She had already been hurt more than she knew by her mother's absence, and later in life she was still bitter, sometimes violently so, about her own abandonment. She realized that she herself was no longer the human centre of her father's existence, and although she remained truly fond of him for the rest of his life, what teenage girl reaching Paris after a far from comfortable childhood would not be tempted to find her own way in the city, live her own life, and see something beyond the little world of street acrobatics and casual singing that her father had created for the two of them? Perhaps she would have waited a little longer had she not met a slightly younger girl named Simone Berteaut, who has been called her dark angel, her evil genius and many other names very much less polite. Simone, 'Momone', as she was often called, was only too close to Edith at crucial moments of her life, and more remarkably perhaps after Edith's death when, in 1969, she put her name to a book about her which became a bestseller and fared no worse for being bitterly contested, often through lawyers, by many of the people mentioned in it.

But all that lay far ahead. Simone always maintained that she was one of Gassion's many children, and therefore Edith's half-sister. Her maternal grandmother, she said, had come from Peru, which no doubt helped to explain why there was no physical resemblance between the girls although they were about the same height. When Simone's mother found herself pregnant she looked about for a legal father for her child and conveniently found Berteaut who agreed to marry her. Her daughter was born in Lyons in 1916, although Momone herself preferred to say 1918. The Berteaut family did not accept this story, but no matter: Simone maintained that she met Edith in a Belleville apartment where Louis Gassion's friend 'Alverne' was keeping an eye on the girl who, the men hoped, would carry on the Gassion tradition of acrobatic success. Simone reported that she found 'a shapeless creature' suspended from 'some rings hanging in an empty door-frame'. Edith's mother had apparently been afraid of the high wire, and her daughter had no talent as an acrobat.

The two girls had to find some way of earning their living, for nobody was going to support them. There was not much money about in their district and it was always said that if the inhabitants of Belleville were lucky enough to have jobs and get paid on Friday or Saturday, they had nothing left by Tuesday. In Paris, in the early 1930s, if you were young, poor, untrained and female there were not many worthwhile jobs open to you. For quick returns there was prostitution, one of the least uncomfortable types of work. Think of the girls who worked at 'Le Panier fleuri', described by Elliott Paul in *A Narrow Street*. If you wished to remain respectable you could learn to be a milliner, a dressmaker, a hairdresser. Or you could do the kind of job that Edith and Simone did, the latter assembling car headlights for the firm Pile Wonder, which remained a household name in France for decades. She claimed that she began work at the age of twelve and a half and that 'the conditions were criminal, but we accepted them without question'. Simone was often far from accurate, but she no doubt told the truth here, for she would have had no choice. Edith had a variety of jobs – she worked as a housemaid and was soon dismissed for several easily understandable reasons: she broke too much crockery, was lazy and insubordinate.

For three whole months, Edith said later, she worked for a firm which made army boots – a Belleville industry – and her job was to varnish them. Not surprisingly both girls were extremely keen to find jobs that would pay them reasonably well, but more especially employment that would be less destructive than factory work. They would have to look after themselves, for society would certainly do nothing for them. The urban working class in France was relatively small, and on the whole less important than the peasant class. The centre right, led by such unattractive figures as Laval and Daladier, basically held power and the parliamentary reforms suggested by Gaston Doumergue were rejected. There had been no shortage of violent incidents: the

President, Paul Doumer, had been assassinated in 1932, the Foreign Minister, Jean-Louis Barthou, was shot in 1934 along with the King of Yugoslavia as the latter arrived in Marseilles. The government failed to explain away the Stavisky swindle in which many leading political figures were implicated. The extreme right had more power than most liberal-minded francophiles would like to admit today, even in retrospect. Foreign visitors came to Paris in crowds and were delighted to find so much instant culture to admire, buildings and art galleries in particular. There was no shortage of entertainment and what is generally called glamour available at all prices. Tourists and expatriates were delighted also by the 'picturesque' and there was plenty of this in the poorer districts, for poverty has often formed a strong element in what is described as 'colourful'. Paris was also cheap, for pounds and dollars bought many, many francs and there were, of course, plenty of low-priced goods coming into France from the convenient colonies in Africa and further afield, where raw materials were cheap, and wages low.

Cultural life was still dominated by the old-school literary giants such as François Mauriac and Jules Romains, while Cocteau and Giraudoux were continually successful in their own specialized fields, and nobody trembled at the appearance of Malraux's *La Condition humaine (Man's Estate)* in 1933 and its questioning about individual and social life.

Edith Gassion, whose education had been minimal, read nothing beyond the romances of the prolific 'Delly' (actually a brother and sister writing under a pseudonym) or, to quote her own memories of the period, stories with melodramatic titles such as *Seduced at Twenty*, and she read them in her Belleville room as a joke, for she believed that reading was *un truc pour les bourgeois* – a pastime for the middle-classes.

She needed money for food and began to sing in the streets. She did not lose contact with her father, who also had to make a living, and he was helped and advised by a Belleville friend and neighbour, Camille Ribon, known as 'Alverne'. He would take Edith and various other teenage girls singing in army barracks, where there was obviously a captive audience only too ready to be entertained. Edith had already seen plenty of soldiers while she was living at Bernay, and at this stage of her life she was fascinated by them. When a girl lives a disorganized life, earning no more than a pittance whatever she does, a uniformed soldier represents order and perhaps some steady money. A soldier was also seen as an irresponsible solitary man who needed glamorous female companions but they must have no urge whatever to settle down. And there were also sailors on leave, always talking about faraway countries and always ready to say romantic goodbyes.

Edith had been under the public gaze, however small-scale, however provincial, as long as she could remember, ever since she first began to perform with her father as a child. Sometimes in the street she had to sing through a megaphone, and once at least her singing blocked a road in the faubourg Saint-Martin, so many people stopped to listen. Therefore she was used to attention and came to expect it, but when she was barely sixteen some instinct made her choose, or rather accept, a companion with no obvious glamour at all. He was the first man whose name she did not forget, and he first caught sight of her when she was actually singing.

She described herself at this age as not being '*très sentimentale*'. She thought she wanted attention as a person, not just as a performer. Her mother had given her none; her father, even if he loved her, made her work hard and was perpetually involved with a succession of women. The effect of this upbringing may have made her independent in some ways but it did nothing to reduce her primitive femininity. 'I thought that when a boy summoned a girl, the girl must never say no. I thought that this was what we women should do. So I didn't hesitate long when P'tit Louis signalled to me.'

2

Death of a child

'P'tit Louis' as Edith called him was not her first sexual partner, but he was a little older than she was and lived with his mother in Romainville, a community in the Seine-Saint-Denis area, north-east of Paris. Edith has described in *Ma vie* in some detail how they came together. She saw him for the first time at the Porte des Lilas one day when she was out singing with her father. The crowd in the street usually melted away as she began to walk round with a beret or a saucer: after all, most people regarded open-air entertainment as free. But P'tit Louis did not move away, 'he looked me straight in the eyes, gave a whistle of admiration, and then with a regal gesture placed a five-sous coin in my dish'.

For days on end, she said, he followed her round the faubourgs, and one afternoon when her father was not there, he came up to her, took her by the hand and said, 'Come with me. We'll live together'.

He was tall and fair, he smiled, and Edith Gassion confessed over twenty-five years later that she thought him handsome and strong, and she loved him. They moved into a furnished room in the rue Orfila.

What did they live on? Somehow they managed, but Louis Dupont, to use his correct name, did not earn very much. He was supposed to be a builder, but could not find any work, for the Paris of the early 1930s had very little to offer him. So he became an errand-boy. Edith was apparently still varnishing boots when she was not singing, but when the couple could not even afford to eat in the local cafés, Edith tried to cook in old food cans while Louis, like so many boys of his generation, simply stole what was needed, including cutlery and plates. Sometimes they could allow themselves a treat on Saturdays: they went to the local cinema, sat on wooden benches and saw films with Tom Mix and Charlie Chaplin.

Then one day at the boot factory Edith felt ill and at the local hospital she was told why: she was pregnant and was immediately sacked. '*C'était la règle.*'

In February 1933 a little daughter Marcelle was born to Edith at the Hôpital Tenon in the rue de la Chine, where she herself had been born less than eighteen years earlier. Her father came to see his daughter and granddaughter. Edith said later that she and Louis, children as they were, were delighted to have one of their own. The 'family' still lived in one room at the Hôtel de l'Avenir, 105 rue Orfila.

Their room, as described by Edith, was as 'picturesque' as any realistic French film could have made it: 'There were nappies and clothes hanging on a line across the window. Under my bed I had piled up suitcases, old papers, dirty linen and all the dust I had swept up.'

It was hardly surprising that they could not pay the rent for very long. The only solution to that problem was a moonlight flit, and the young parents, carrying their baby, crept out past the concierge's little *loge* by getting down on their knees and shuffling out on all fours. They had to live somewhere and found a room in the rue Germain-Pilon, off the Boulevard de Clichy but that arrangement did not last long either, because Edith could not tolerate such a life – no work, no money, no fun. She wanted to be out on the streets where there was always something going on; she wanted to be independent, and she knew that if she was lucky with her singing she could just manage, despite the competition. Yet she clung to her little daughter, Marcelle. What was she to do? She had left her father and the home that he and Yéyette had created. That dark angel Momone hovered about, even if Edith chose not to mention her except possibly in disguise, at this precise stage of her late memoirs. Louis Dupont still had no real work and one night Edith felt she could no longer tolerate this existence. She made a rope of sheets from the bed like any prisoner – for that is what she was – and lowered herself down from the window to the ground. She had escaped. Like her mother she had left her partner, but unlike Line Marsa she did not abandon her daughter. 'I entrusted my kid to one of my pals, and went off again to sing in the streets.' She did not go back to P'tit Louis, but she did not spend the next two years on her own: the streets were too dangerous, and she liked company.

Momone, according to her eager, untrustworthy recollections, gives the impression that the two girls were inseparable, singing in any street or courtyard which they knew to be worthwhile, and trying out a new place, waiting to see people pause as they walked by, or looking up to see curtains twitch, windows open, and small coins come rattling down on to the pavement in addition to those which dropped into the hat or saucer. Sometimes the baby was there too, somehow carried or pushed. She added pathos to the situation. Years later Edith described how for two and a half years she remembered the 'endless walk': they were continually moving round and begging and, of course, owing to the depression in France, there were plenty of other street singers.

Then there was Zephrine, whoever she was, who played a leading part in one melodrama which Edith remembered so vividly. Zephrine could have been a fictional memory of Momone, but if Edith's account is highly exaggerated it is unlikely that she invented the whole incident, which might have provided a starting point to Georges Simenon for one of his Paris-based stories. She describes how with two companions she sang in the streets, in military barracks and at fairs. They earned just enough 'not to die of hunger'. But they were often very frightened, for the police were looking for them. Zephrine and a boy called Jean were both in trouble for stealing from counters outside shops, while Edith herself was wanted for a different reason: her father, concerned about his wayward daughter, had been to the Commissariat de Police in the Place des Fêtes, and asked them to find her. He seemed to think she was a missing person and did not realize she often walked a long way in search of an audience, and did not always have the energy or the wish to get back to her Belleville lodgings late at night. Undoubtedly Louis Gassion cared about his daughter, and the two of them remained close for the rest of his life.

As for little Marcelle, Louis Dupont often looked after her. Although he had fallen in love with Edith while she was singing, he had not anticipated that she would go on singing, especially now that she had a daughter. He would have preferred a more respectable occupation for his girlfriend, such as making funeral wreaths out of bead flowers, a job which both Simone and Edith actually did for a time. But Edith could only live dangerously, and she had had enough of P'tit Louis. She wanted a 'stronger, harder man', and she did not have to look far. She chose a Legionnaire, a member of that romanticized, ruthless army, the Foreign Legion without which France may not have had, or kept, a colonial empire. But there are two versions of the story, both from Edith herself. One says that the Legionnaire, Albert, was put on a charge after a fight in the guardroom. Edith managed to see him and later told him she could not go to live with him. After which he was reported killed in the colonies but turned up several years later wearing a cloth cap. She did not recognize him at first. He was glad she had been successful, said it had been nice meeting her again, and disappeared. The other version, set out in *Ma vie*, is shorter. She took her baby and went to live with the soldier. But Louis Dupont did not let them go so easily. He took the baby away one evening when she was out and left a message with the concierge: if Edith wanted to see Marcelle again she would have to come back to him. Edith says she spent one last night with her lover and then went back.

In the meantime there were more incredible adventures. A generation later Algiers-born Albertine Sarrazin was to write novels culled from her experiences in prison and on the run. Edith Piaf, in a strange way, was one of her precursors. When she and her friends could not get home at night they would often sleep rough behind the dustbins in the entrance to a courtyard. The dustbins stank, and there were rats, but there was no choice, even during one week when Zephrine caught measles. Edith described her as a 'gypsy girl of eighteen, horribly ugly', but at least she and the boy Jean were in love with each other. One night, when Edith was keeping watch, she fell asleep, and suddenly they were all awakened by a light shining on their faces. Their worst fears had come true, three gendarmes had found them.

But then, as usual *le hasard fait bien les choses*. The sergeant fell for Zephrine, measles and all, and events took a possibly hopeful turn. If Zephrine accepted the sergeant's advances then they would all three escape the threat of prison. 'Jean and I looked beseechingly at our friend, but she loved Jean and Jean loved her. The sacrifice was hard.' However, sacrifice there was. Zephrine disappeared into the darkness with her conquest, Edith and Jean were told to beat it. Later Zephrine had a row with Jean and went back to her gypsy family who lived in caravans at Pantin, to the north of the city. But Jean still loved her and asked Edith to help him: would she find Zephrine and beg her to come back to him? Edith went, found the family, who immediately attacked her with all the anger they felt for the gringos of Paris. She escaped, swore revenge, ran down to Belleville and collected a crowd of supporters from the cafés and street corners. With knives and sticks they battled with the gypsies until suddenly they found themselves surrounded by police. They were all prisoners.

Jean decided to make a dash for it. They must somehow get away or they would both be in prison. They hurtled over the rough ground, and Edith remembered how the brambles tore her bare legs, as she heard the police firing shots over their heads. Through the fog the houses at Pantin looked like a pasteboard set, and she added that it was as good as the cinema. Thanks to Jean and maybe to the mist and rain they escaped, but the story was not over yet. Somehow they reached Belleville, soaking wet, and hid in the back room of a café. Edith decided she must swallow her pride and go back to P'tit Louis. They reached his mother's house where he had returned with little Marcelle, but they had reckoned without his mother, Madame Georgette.

At the sound of the creaking door she appeared, 'carrying a paraffin lamp … with a black shawl round her shoulders'. She had to hold on to the door because she was blind drunk. She hated Edith and shouted insults at her. She picked up the poker and would have hit her but she was too drunk to stand; she fell flat on the floor, knocked her head against a stray bucket, blood ran down on to her face and she choked. Edith did not dare move to help her. 'Then P'tit Louis came in. He looked at Madame Georgette's body, then he looked at us and said, "Get out." ' He loved the drunken woman who had brought him up, and now he hated Edith whom he thought had tried to kill his mother. Edith left.

Family life, obviously, was not for her. Already, at eighteen, professional life, if it could be called that, mattered more, and not just because she had to earn her living. She in fact found a way of climbing out of the streets occasionally, fighting her way through heavy competition into small bars and clubs in the Montmartre-Pigalle area, one of the great amusement centres. The club called

Les Juan-les-Pins was run by a woman who would now be described as a butch lesbian, Lulu, who always dressed as a man, '*un vrai Jules*', Edith called her. Club-goers were always looking for a new atmosphere, new entertainment that would somehow pass the time for them until about three in the morning, and club-owners were looking for young performers who would accept the smallest amounts of pay and unmentionably bad conditions. The clients would listen to singers with half an ear, but at least the girls who were always around as sexual entertainers were friendly, and the waiters would feed Edith and the other performers in secret; it was a good way of using up the left-overs. At the same time Edith did not escape from washing the glasses or sweeping the floor.

Since the French, and the British come to that, were not much worried by international events, and remained practically deaf to the ever-louder voice of Hitler, Paris itself was a great centre of entertainment, and in fact one travel agency in London would take parties of tourists there for less than £1 a day. While Edith Gassion was trying to make her voice heard over the racket in the little clubs, and going back to the streets during the afternoons, there was plenty of grand style entertainment in the city. The great classical actress Cécile Sorel retired from the Comédie-Française in 1933 at the age of sixty, and then, very soon afterwards, made a comeback: dressed entirely in silver, she would descend the golden staircase at the Casino de Paris just as Mistinguett had been doing for years. And even the very hypocrisy of the authorities added to the fun. 'Marlene Dietrich's Paris visit', wrote Janet Flanner in that same year in the *New Yorker*, 'which began with the Prefect of Police asking her to leave town in trousers, is ending with her being asked everywhere in skirts'. It is fascinating to think that years later Dietrich would be a great admirer and true friend of the girl who was then struggling to survive not very far away in Montmartre, while she herself was staying at the Trianon Palace Hotel in Versailles with her husband and daughter.

Nothing good seems to have happened in 1934, when the people of Paris were so infuriated by the government's behaviour and the Stavisky scandal that there were serious anti-Republican riots. Stavisky shot himself: or did the police shoot him? Perhaps nobody knew, or remembered, that back in 1906 Alexandre Stavisky had tried to be a singer, but failed in his attempt. In the same year John Dillinger and Dr Dollfuss were shot too. Madame Curie died and Emile Zola's middle-aged children sued Sam Goldwyn because they disapproved of the way he had filmed the novel *Nana*. Hitler organized the Night of the Long Knives while the British public were even more impressed by the trunk murders than they were by Sir Oswald Mosley. However, in Paris, show business flourished, and everyone who cared about *la chanson* fell in love with Tino Rossi.

La chanson – this simple but evocative word recalls a whole long chapter in the history of music, a whole encyclopedia of singers, musicians and, crucially, the writers who were never far away. When Jean-Jacques Rousseau published his *Dictionnaire de musique* in 1768 he gave a precise and pleasing definition, typical of the times, now modified after two centuries by transfer of *la chanson* into the streets and then into the music-halls: 'A kind of very short lyrical poem, normally dealing with pleasant subjects, to which is added melody to be sung on familiar occasions, such as when at table, with one's friends, with one's mistress and even when alone, to pass a few moments of *ennui* if one is rich, and to tolerate poverty and work more pleasantly if one is poor.' Voltaire said that nobody had more delightful songs than the French and Pierre Jean de Beranger, the popular nineteenth-century poet, wrote accurately that 'in France, *la chanson* is a native plant'.

Edith Piaf and her contemporaries were all innovators in their way, but these singers had inherited a long and rich tradition.

Some of their fascinating and picturesque ancestors and contemporaries would be well known even to the young Piaf and are described by Ralph Harvey in Appendix 2.

By 1935 Edith's adventures were not yet over, in fact they never were, but there was a final chapter in what can be called the pre-Piaf story. One night when she was working at Le Tourbillon, a *bal musette* in Pigalle, she was told that Louis Dupont wanted to see her. He was white with anxiety, for little Marcelle had been taken to the children's hospital with meningitis. He feared she would die. In those days there was very little treatment available for this illness, which was only too common. The doctors merely gave a lumbar puncture and waited nine days. For eight days Edith believed in miracles. 'Just before the ninth day, in the middle of the night, driven by some kind of presentiment I started to walk from my place in Belleville, for I was completely broke, to the hospital.' An old nurse told her the child had recovered consciousness, there seemed to be some hope. 'Marcelle's big blue eyes were open and for the first time since her illness she recognized me ...' She begged her mother to stay with her. Edith wept, kissed her and stayed until five in the morning.

At noon that day she came back with Louis Dupont, but the child was dead. The doctor told them that they had brought her in too late. There was nothing he could do. In the morgue Edith cut off a lock of Marcelle's hair with a borrowed nail-file. The parents had no money for a wreath. 'We separated without a word and I went back to Pigalle.'

There had to be a funeral, and there was no money for that either. Edith's friends at Le Tourbillon helped her, one of the *entraineuses*, whose job was to entice men into the bar, collected for her, but when the money was counted she still had to find ten francs. How? In desperation she picked up a man who saw her walking slowly along the pavement, for this was a quick way of earning money. About twenty-five years later a 'good' Piaf story became an even better one. Jean Noli, editing her recollections for his newspaper, suggested that her women readers might be shocked by this incident. She asked him if he had any ideas.

"'Why not say", he suggested, "that in the bedroom you burst into tears, he asked why, you explained. He understood, put down ten francs and left at once."

"'You're right," Edith agreed. "It's nicer and it's moral.'"

A few days later, according to Noli, Edith referred to this incident again and recounted it with the conclusion he had suggested. 'And the man didn't touch you?' he asked innocently.

'In no way. He was a gentleman'.

Maybe both versions of the story were invented. Nobody will ever be able to prove either of them. Marcelle Dupont was buried in the paupers' cemetery of Thiais and later, when Edith bought the customary 'concession' at the cemetery of Père Lachaise, Marcelle and her grandfather Louis-Alphonse Gassion were brought there to share eternity.

3

Love and war, but not all fair

In the summer 1935, there was no shortage of bad news, for Italy invaded Abyssinia. Pierre Laval has not gone down in history as a great French leader but, to quote Janet Flanner, 'he was the only man in France behind the enforcement of sanctions against Italy; every other Frenchman is eating spaghetti and drinking chianti in Italian restaurants to show where his heart and stomach are'. However, since both France and Italy were in low water, the currency in both countries was devalued.

Home, to Edith at this juncture, was a room at the Hôtel au Clair de Lune in the Pigalle area, for there was more paid work – barely paid – to be found there than in the streets of Belleville and beyond. She had seen her daughter die, and the child's father disappear. She did not lose touch with her own father, but contact was probably not too close. She may have known that her handsome, unstable, alienated mother, with her impressive yet wasted voice, could also be heard singing in the streets and various dives in the faubourgs, under the name of Line Marsa, but if she knew she would in any case have avoided her. *She* had never totally abandoned her own daughter and her loss had only made her more conscious of being alone. There were two ways of forgetting it all, one was to work, and she had to work in any case, and the other, now that she was totally free, was of course to have a good time.

When she had started to sing she naturally had to choose songs that everyone knew, the hits – *les tubes*, as the French call them. There was no shortage of these, there were a great many popular singers and composers, and lots of cheap entertainment in the *bals musettes*, where there was nearly always some accordionist liable to be playing a *java*, that cheerful quick waltz that asked to be danced to. The origin of the word, according to the song writer Bernard Dimey, does not go back to 'some native of the southern seas who happened to find an accordion on a wrecked ship'. The accordions came from Auvergne, where they were very popular, and the Auvergnats brought them to Paris when they went there looking for work. They started to play them in the streets, more especially in the bars; they began to run the bars, and when they greeted their customers they would say in that inescapable accent which is still a perpetual joke in France, not *ça va?* but *cha va?* – 'how are things?' – and that was the start of it all (see Appendix 1). Among the older *java* songs that Edith probably knew was *La Valse brune*, still sung by the popular Mouloudji in the 1980s, then there was *La java de cézigue* which in Parisian argot means 'his' *java*, and *La java bleue*; there were songs about *les mauvais garçons*, of whom there was no shortage, *Le Dénicheur*, for instance, and the sentimental *Le Chaland qui passe*, made popular by Lys Gauty in 1931. (For more details, see Appendix 2.)

Edith's father had even taken her to music publishers in the hunt for new songs, which obviously she could only 'borrow'. She could not read music but if she heard a song three times at the most, then she knew it. Inevitably too, she met other singers; some of them were already successful, and one of these, known as 'Fréhel' (see Appendix 2), had by no means forgotten the faubourgs, for the drink was cheaper there.

The meeting that put Edith on the road to professionalism and thence to stardom is the third of the six or so much publicized melodramatic incidents in her early life. Her supposed birth on the pavement and the miracle cure from blindness were surely apocryphal, but the encounter with Louis Leplée, although the reported details vary a little, obviously happened, and nobody has contested it. The time was October 1935, the place was the corner of the avenue Mac-Mahon and the rue Troyon in the 17th arrondissement, not far, in a north-easterly direction, from the Etoile and the Arc de Triomphe, and a little further from the Place des Ternes. Edith chose this moment, not surprisingly, as the starting point of her 1958 autobiography *Au Bal de la chance*. 'I was pale and unkempt. I had no stockings and my coat was out at the elbows and hung down to my ankles. I was singing a song by Jean Lenoir ...' This was *Comme un moineau*, an amusing piece in which a sparrow recounts how he lives, an old song dating from 1927. Jean Lenoir's most famous song, *Parlez-moi d'amour*, closely associated with Boyer, is still remembered as a big international hit. It has also been said that Edith was singing *Reste*, a song which, like many she sang later, included words more spoken than sung. The theme is one that returns in many Piaf songs: the lover tells his/her partner to stay so that they can talk a little about the times when they were happy. Years later the piece was included in the *enregistrement intégral*, an early so-called complete recording of all Piaf's songs. However, on this occasion, the vital element was the singer, not the song.

Louis Leplée, who stopped to listen to her as he walked past, knew a good deal about voices, singers and performers generally. Originally he had been an entertainer himself, and there was a well-known theatrical personality in the family, namely his uncle, the singer-entertainer Polin. Polin, who died in 1927, had been an immense success wearing a railway-man's uniform, standing totally still and waving a large checked handkerchief whenever he included an obscene phrase. He even sang an early version of that Josephine Baker hit *La Petite Tonkinoise*. Photographs of Polin and Leplée showed a distinct family likeness. Leplée had been a café-concert entertainer but had left the stage after 1918, because a war wound had caused him to limp slightly.

He decided instead to present other artists, and his own homo-sexuality, plus the entertainment fashion of the time, led him to join other gay personalities in Montmartre, the amusement centre. It was in the rue Montmartre in 1932 that he took over a cabaret from one Dufresne, also gay, who was shot. The cabaret was in the basement of Le Palace. However, Leplée soon moved to Pigalle and directed a cabaret called Liberty's where he performed with a partner, both of them in drag, while the other acts included women singing 'obscene songs that would make a guardsman blush'. A few years later Leplée opened Gerny's Club in a much smarter area between the Champs-Elysées and the avenue Georges V, where dinner was served from 9 p.m., and the sophisticated cabaret went on until the small hours.

To continue with the well-worn but inevitable story: the well-dressed man looked at the ragged girl and listened. Then he told her not to ruin her voice by trying to sing so loudly, and she riposted with Parisian-type banter. He persuaded her with some necessary bribery to come to Gerny's for what we now call an audition. Edith is supposed to have arrived at the rue Pierre Charron an hour late, and he is said to have remarked, 'Whatever will you be like when you're a star?'

Stardom was not instant, for she had to rehearse every day for a week. Leplée had not been too impressed by her repertoire, and refused to hear her sing an aria from Gounod's *Faust* – which was surely not the Jewel Song? For her first appearances at least she would have to sing songs that most people knew, and Leplée realized that she could not go wrong with *Les Mômes de la cloche*, a song with words by Decaye and music by the extremely successful Vincent Scotto who wrote at least 4,000 songs: this one dates from the 1920s, and is about the poor girls who may sell their love for a night but will never know real love, will never have any money, and nobody cares. Very much a song from the streets, a song for times of high unemployment, and a song for the idle night-club audiences to listen to and think that, perhaps, they ought to shed a tear. Kiki of Montparnasse was still singing it, for her supper, in 1950.

One of the greatest problems for Edith was learning how to sing to a piano accompaniment, for in the streets or the small clubs she had nothing beyond a banjo. She had some idea of how to play one, but the few photographs showing her holding a banjo, an accordion, or a guitar, or sitting at the piano, are unconvincing. One fascinating thing about her earliest records is the way she hesitates very slightly now and then in matching her words to the music. Another song which seemed in some ways right for her was *Je me sens dans tes bras si petite*, for nobody was more *petite* than she was. Edith said later that she had difficulty in remembering the words, but this may be because the song was associated with Mistinguett, and that would be another good reason for her objections to it. Mistinguett never had a good word to say about Edith, and the jealous Fréhel had already warned her off Gerny's.

There were two other problems, neither of them important in principle, but in the event they both turned out to be crucial. First, the new young singer must have a name, and it could not be Gassion, which sounded 'common', or any of the pompous little names she had used in the Montmartre clubs. Leplée remembered the song he had heard her sing: *comme un moineau*, but he could not call her '*La Môme Moineau*' – another singer was already using that name. *Moineau* means a sparrow, and Parisian slang for a sparrow is *un piaf*: so Edith would be '*La Môme Piaf*'. Second, had she any clothes to wear? Her black skirt was tolerable and yes, she had almost finished knitting a black pullover – it would be finished in time for the performance. Like everything else Edith knitted, it was never finished. It was like the last coat of nettles knitted by the Hans Christian Andersen princess for her brothers who had been turned into swans: one sleeve, intended for the younger brother, was not complete, but Edith's equivalent of the swan's wing was concealed by a white evening scarf given to her by no less a person than the wife of Maurice Chevalier, Yvonne Vallée. Usually the *chanteuses réalistes* appeared on stage with a red one. So the singer was nearly complete: she was still *la môme*, not yet Edith Piaf, and was wearing black, if not yet a black dress. The skirt fortunately had pockets, for Edith did not know what to do with her hands. To complete the street-singer look Edith wore no make-up and she appeared under the spotlight just as Louis Leplée had found her. He exploited the situation skilfully in his introductory remarks and described precisely how he had first seen her: 'Her voice gripped me deep down inside. She moved me. She threw me into confusion ...' Leplée knew just how to appeal to his audience. 'And now I want you to make the acquaintance of this child of Paris . . .'

When she came on stage there was silence, and silence again when she finished, which unnerved her. She had been told to make no gestures, in order to hide that missing sleeve, but as she came to the end, without thinking she threw up her arms. The hard-to-please audience clapped as though they were applauding her bare arm and her poverty as much as her voice. Maurice Chevalier, who had been born in Belleville too, was one of the first to congratulate her; he was soon joined by Jean Mermoz, the pioneer aviator, and years later, in 1962, this first evening was remembered emotionally by the novelist Joseph Kessel as he introduced a recital by Edith, broadcast from the Eiffel Tower.

There was an extraordinary dichotomy about Edith's life at this time. If she was prepared to work hard and sing every night she was not prepared to give up the life she had been living, and she must have already realized, half-consciously, that there was more to her style than the mere possession of a voice, and a theatrical presence which in its way was anti-theatre, anti-glamour. Her style was her own life. She was not twenty until mid-December 1935, and she was more sure of herself as a singer than as a woman. Nearly every song she sang presented a situation between a man and a woman, and the intense way she expressed deep personal feelings – not just women's feelings – was the secret of her appeal. But if she could already deal with an audience, she could not deal with men, for she was pursuing a teenager's dream, looking for an ideal man, a man she could not find, perhaps because he never existed.

When she lived with Louis Dupont, 'in a confused way I felt something was lacking in that life ... the thing I've looked for unremittingly in life: the protective strength of a man, a real man'. However, she had not escaped the men of the real world, even if her waif-like physique probably helped her to escape prostitution, for men preferred a more obviously feminine body. In Pigalle she had earned money from singing on the same basis as a prostitute earns it from sex: she met a successful *souteneur*, or pimp, who took his commission from her, and for a time the arrangement seems to have worked fairly well. But it was an uncertain, violent world and soon there was a problem, the kind of problem in which Edith was so often enmeshed: she fell in love with the *souteneur*.

'He was called Albert, he had a beautiful smile, black eyes and flared trousers ...' He dominated her to such a degree that she would have done anything for him, except become a prostitute. She had always been 'too much in love with love', she said, to reduce it to mere commerce. Albert hit her, she bit him and scratched his face, but he gave in: very well, she was spared *le trottoir*, she could go on singing but she must pay him a commission, like Rosita the street-walker.

There was a drawback. 'I clung to that man.' She saw nothing wrong with the financial arrangement, which at least kept her working. 'It was a kind of happiness. I lived for years like this in Pigalle, with my "man".' She also knew, when she was very young, that singing made her 'totally happy'. Later, she realized what this meant: she had a vocation.

Albert had a different vocation. He operated by mafia–type methods and allowed no complacency. Edith was given the thankless job of finding victims for him; she was told to go into the dance–halls and keep her eye on any well–dressed women who were wearing jewellery. She would report to Albert. 'He would note down all my information in a little notebook and then, on Saturday evenings, or Sundays, wearing his best suit', he would make advances to one of the women he had been told about. He was apparently so handsome, so confident, that he was always successful. He would offer to escort the woman home, take her to a dark deserted alleyway, the Impasse Lemercier, and rob her. He would then come back quickly to the well-known café La Nouvelle Athènes and, if there had been a good haul, he, Edith and their friends would drink champagne all night.

Edith might have drifted even more deeply into *le milieu* had it not been for Nadia. Nadia loved Albert's friend André, who was trying to turn her into a prostitute. André told the beautiful fair-haired girl that if she did not do as he wished he would destroy her looks for ever, using vitriol no doubt. Nadia confessed to Edith that she would rather die than lose André's love, but when she tried to pick up men she failed, and ran away. Edith had warned Nadia and told her to escape while she still had the chance. A few days later the river police found Nadia's body in the Seine.

Edith was so shocked by what happened that she spat in Albert's face and ran away. She said that she 'wanted to be like other women again', but she knew that *le milieu* did not let peo-ple escape so easily. If melodrama was to fill Edith's life, and most of her songs, it is because she acquired the habit early. Albert had her kidnapped by one of his *durs*, who left her in a locked room. When Albert came she said he could kill her if he wanted, she would never go back to him. Incredibly Albert broke down and wept. In La Nouvelle Athènes he told her that if she did not come back he would shoot her. Her reply was:

'"Shoot, if you're a man." I saw his expression harden. Then there was a shot. I felt a burning at my neck.'

Fortunately a man standing next to Albert had jogged his arm, presumably on purpose. Is it surprising that all her life Edith could not bear to be alone? She had been too badly frightened in her teens.

The song that Edith sang for the first time a few years later, *Elle fréquentait la rue Pigalle*, did not narrate what happened to her, only what might have happened. In the five-verse *poème réaliste* by Raymond Asso (of whom much more later) there was a story which might also have had a happy ending: the girl was pale but deep in her eyes was something miraculous ... She met a man who told her she was beautiful; they never say that sort of thing to the girls who do that job; she wanted to escape her past and asked him to take her to Montparnasse. But there things began to change. 'I thought you were prettier than that. The light here shows you up too well. Your vices are only too obvious, you'd better go back up there, and each of us take up our old life.' She went back to Pigalle and this time nobody came to rescue her. When she saw lovers walking along the street, tears came to her big blue eyes. It was truly *une chanson réaliste*.

As Edith moved into the world of the professional singer, she realized that there was even more competition among the singers trying to make a name for themselves in the clubs and cabarets than she had encountered as a street singer, especially now that the record industry was becoming big business and the radio stations were gaining more and more listeners.

When it came to finding songs Edith had her own aggressive policy, for her success had been so rapid after a very short time at Gerny's that she had to find new songs at all costs. She heard one of her potential rivals, Annette Lajon, rehearsing a song called *L'Etranger*, which impressed her. She asked her to sing it twice again, by which time of course she knew it. It was the custom for a singer to keep the exclusive rights on a song for six months or so, but Edith did not care about that: she wanted the song, took it, sang it successfully and recorded it in February 1936. Annette Lajon could have complained but the two women apparently congratulated each other on their differing versions, and in the same year Annette Lajon won the Disque d'Or with *her* recording, the first year that prize was awarded. The words for this song, a long one, had been written by Robert Malleron, and describe the lonely wandering sailor who could find contentment only on the high seas, a theme which would reappear often in Piaf songs. The music had been written by two people, a man called Robert Juel – inseparable from that comic song *Au Lycée Papillon* – and a woman who was to be one of Edith's closest musical associates almost until the end of her life, Marguerite Monnot. This song was Monnot's first success – a success she needed, for after being a child prodigy, admired by the composer Saint-Saëns, she had studied under Alfred Cortot and Nadia Boulanger and then had given up a career as a concert pianist in order to compose in a popular style.

No girl could have lived through a more exciting autumn than did Edith Gassion in 1936, when the discerning Jacques Canetti befriended her and did his best to help her with broadcasts from Radio Cité, and also with records. Her first broadcasts brought many telephone calls, rare at the time. Yet she apparently did not give up her old associates in Pigalle for she had not yet discovered any other means of having such a riotously good time. Her emotional life was an essential ingredient in her singing: she could not sing without it. After recounting her sordid relationship with Albert she admitted it was obvious that if she could learn a song after three hearings she still could not learn how to avoid the wrong man. 'All this should have made me disgusted with men, and in any case taught me to behave with caution. 'Far from it ...'

It was not, she said, that she had *le diable au corps*, it was not sex that she wanted, she had a desperate need to be loved, all the more so because she felt she was plain, despicable, unlovable. She had received so little love as a child that at this chaotic moment of her life, when she needed reliable support and people around her, she behaved as though she were almost unstable and became involved with three men all at once: Pierrot, a sailor, Léon, a spahi, and René, a former miner. 'I had met Pierrot at the bar of the Hôtel au Clair de Lune, where I was living, Léon in the street, and René in a cabaret.' She confessed that she lied to all three men, but at least she admitted to loving one of them, and it was Pierrot for whom she cared, but he was unfortunately broke. Anyone knowing how Edith behaved in later life can only be amused by her reasons for responding to him more than to the others: 'He was so gentle and patient. He put up with all my crazy ideas without too much protest.'

She was already generous, now that she was earning, for she met him during the early days at Gerny's. She wanted to buy him a pair of shoes, but he was only allowed to have a pair that was too small for him because, she thought, in common with her generation, that big feet were not *chic*. So he had to accept size 39, which is very small for a man, and they seem to have been the nearest thing to the winkle-pickers of the 1960s. When he was out with her he had to wear them and suffer. For other occasions he was allowed a pair of lined slippers.

It was a bad moment when the three men came to realize that Edith was being unfaithful to each of them with the other two. Léon disappeared, she was still in love with Pierrot, but René would not let her go. 'He spied on me. He was a big, tall man from Lille, he had a hard face. He was a man capable of killing …' Crisis came one night just before Edith was due to go to a singing engagement in the provinces. She succeeded in joining Pierrot in his ground-floor room in the rue des Abbesses in Montmartre. The room was in darkness but the headlights of a passing car threw a shadow on the ceiling, a shadow she recognized.

René was pacing up and down outside, his hand in the pocket where he kept his flick-knife. Pierrot wanted to go out and fight him, but Edith would not let him – she knew he would have no chance against the big northerner. René stayed outside until seven in the morning, then he gave up and left. Less than an hour later Edith, according to her own memories, was on the train for Troyes.

Of Pierrot, the man she loved, nothing more is heard, for she went on to love other men. Of René, who frightened her, much more was heard, for apart from three years he spent in prison for wounding a man in a café fight, he haunted her, threatening. He went back to Lille, and when she sang there he would follow her to restaurants after the show. This went on for twenty years. On his last appearance in 1956 he approached her. She was terrified. He produced, not a flick-knife, but something guaranteed to break her heart ... 'He held out to me a lock of fair hair and the only photo of my daughter Marcelle which he had stolen in 1936 in order to have a permanent means of blackmail, in order to make me go back to him. He knew now that he had lost me for good.'

All this formed a dark chapter, and how much Piaf and her journalist friends invented later in her life will never be known. If Piaf invented it all, then she had a novelist's imagination, but a novelist usually starts from fact somewhere. She probably allowed her 'ghosts' inventions, believing they explained to her something about her own past. She used to say that the words of a song were important to her because she always wanted a story, however small-scale or simple. The stories in *Ma vie* explain something of Piaf's nature, something of what can only be called her irresponsibility, her obsessions, her refusal to 'settle down', to compromise in any way, to follow any trend or to go far into the future. Her past constantly dragged her back, and her later efforts to talk it out, write it out or laugh it off were only partly successful.

Fortunately for her, if she tended to pick the wrong lovers at this stage of her life, the friends she made when she was twenty, as when she was thirty or forty, were good friends. She was, in fact, saved from what might have been personal disaster by several very different relationships. Louis Leplée, who loved men, not women, was genuinely fond of her; she was not just a discovery for his cabaret, he understood her background and her need not only for money, but for love. She called him 'Papa Leplée', and although she loved her own father until the end of his life, he could not have made her into a professional singer. Leplée did his best to remind her she was something more now than the little sparrow he had encountered on the pavement. When she told him one day that an all-night party had left her too tired to go to an early-morning recording session he simply said: 'Get there', and she did. She herself remembered one incident which makes both of them sound sentimental: they went together to the cemetery of Thiais to visit the graves of the two people who had mattered so much in their lives: Leplée's mother and Edith's little daughter. Leplée, she said, told her that 'They wanted us to meet so that we would no longer be alone'. For the rest of her life Edith was never afraid of beliefs like this, which took her sometimes to the fringes of the occult.

She also made another valuable, older friend, the minor writer Jacques Bourgeat, who was taken to Gerny's to hear her as her reputation spread. A rewarding relationship developed, for he took charge of her education. He saw her potential, the speed at which she could learn anything, and he became her friendly teacher, talking to her about the great French writers of the past and present, and about music, about philosophy. He wrote poetry, and very soon he had written the words of a new song for her, *'Chand (Marchand) d'habits*, probably the very first song composed specially for her. They remained good friends for a long time, he outlived her and bequeathed the many letters she wrote him to the Bibliothèque Nationale, where they will not be available to the public until the year 2004 has passed. He wanted them to be truly preserved and not, figuratively speaking, torn apart in order to discredit her.

Her closest friends were, of course, musicians and songwriters, including the accordionist-composer Juel, and Raymond Asso, a gifted librettist who was to become more than important in her life fairly soon. As early as November that autumn Edith was given an engagement at a cabaret called *Les Six Jours*, and early in the New Year she took part in a benefit gala (for the widow of a famous clown called Antonet) at the Cirque Medrano. By now she was seeing the names of well-established stars not far from her own on posters and programmes, and she began to study the performers and their interpretations, for she was keen to equal their success. Among the people she studied was 'Damia', who had been born Marie-Louise Damien in 1892, and was known in London when young for dancing the romantic *valse chaloupée*, initially performed by Mistinguett with Max Dearly. Later she had sung *L'Etranger*. She was highly successful on stage and screen, and was an innovator in a small but crucial way, for she liked to appear dressed in black – floor-length décolleté black – some time before Piaf performed in her short black dress and long before Juliette Gréco wore the black roll-neck sweater and dark trousers at Le Tabou which became the 'uniform' of Saint-Germain-des-Prés. More importantly perhaps, she was the first woman singer to use spotlights and projectors as an integral and creative part of her act, something she had learnt from the dancer Loïe Fuller. She was known as '*la tragédienne de la chanson*', sang until 1956, and lived another twenty-two years. (See Appendix 2 for more details.)

Edith certainly knew Damia, who appears to have been a hard-working and likable woman, and also Fréhel, who had sung on café tables at the age of five, had a highly melodramatic career, became famous and infamous, alcoholic and jealous. However, the singer who impressed her most was Marie Dubas, a star who was popular before the Second World War. Marie Dubas did not like making records and thought that only live theatre was genuinely alive: which is true, but then she was at her best before recording was fully developed, and Jacques Tati believed she was ten years ahead of her time. A very few records have preserved the highly individual art of the woman whose parents had come to Paris from Poland in 1886.

She had been trained for the stage, acted in drama, or rather melodrama, sang in operetta and came to *la chanson* in 1927 or so. She appeared at the Olympia, and the Casino de Paris, acting out parodies, interpreting poems – nothing was beyond her. In 1934 her long white dress was described as '*furieusement moderne*'. She was so successful that she needed a secretary, and it was Raymond Asso who worked for her, and also provided words for some of her songs. She created songs of her own and sang many others already known, until 1960, living on until 1971. Her range was unusually wide; she adapted folk-songs and poems and in fact seemed capable of handling any theme that was truly theatrical. She had learnt from Yvette Guilbert – queen of the *diseuses* – how to give the words of a song the attention they deserved, and if they did not deserve it they were no good. In fact, *la chanson* in France belies the so-called witticism that if a thing is too silly to say you can always sing it: this type of song is a French speciality, it rose above the average music-hall level and yet had no intention of going into the concert-hall: like the singers themselves each song had high individuality and needed to be 'produced'. From Esther Lekain and Yvette Guilbert to Edith Piaf this tradition established itself firmly, and of course there were other people, many women, for they seem to find it easier to keep their personal style, and of course some men. It was perhaps no coincidence that men singers were so often endowed with 'charm' and women with 'realism'. The writer Colette admired Marie Dubas so much that she made Camille, the heroine of her novel *La Chatte*, resemble her, while

Simone de Beauvoir noted with approval some songs which seemed to show criticism of the bourgeoisie, although Marie had no serious ambition to be a social critic. She had, however, an amazing gift for humorous, ironic interpretation.

Raymond Asso was much more than a secretary, and by the mid 1930s he had already lived several lives. Born in Nice in 1901 he had worked as a shepherd in Morocco, and joined a regiment of spahis when still a teenager, which took him to the Middle East. Later he ran a factory but preferred writing poems and hoped they could be set to music. Luckily for him he met Marguerite Monnot the composer, and together they produced three songs with a romantic, exotic, military background: *Mon amant de la Coloniale* and *Mon légionnaire* in 1936, then *Le Fanion de la Légion* in 1937. They were to last well.

Piaf maintained that she had inspired the first two by recounting her amorous adventures to Asso, but it was Marie Dubas who created the last two. Early in 1936 she sang *Mon légionnaire* in Marseilles. It would be easy two generations later to condemn the song as melodramatic, but that would be a pity, it was meant to stir the heart, and it did. The French public, short of work and short of money, looked constantly for some sort of glamour, French-style glamour, and they found it in a song like this:

Il était mince, il était beau,
Il sentait bon le sable chaud,
Mon légionnaire,
Y avait du soleil sur son front
Qui mettait dans ses cheveux blonds
De la lumière.

It was very different from the drama of Marlene Dietrich and Gary Cooper in the film *Morocco*. This public surely did not know much about the brutalities of the Foreign Legion and probably did not want to know. Neither were they influenced by the romances of 'Ouida' or P.C. Wren. But twenty years of fighting in Morocco were over in 1935, and according to Marie Dubas's son the lucky people who had won the first paid holidays out of the new Popular Front government went off to the seaside that summer whistling *Mon légionnaire*. Marie had enormous success with the song and told *Paris-Soir* in November 1936 that she had a talisman to help her sing it: a woman in Marseilles had heard the first performance and sent her money with which to perpetuate the memory of her son who had been killed with the Legion. So Marie wore a special scarf whenever she sang it, and she was constantly praised for the way in which she put aside her usual light-hearted approach, and moved her audience literally to tears. She recorded the song in 1936 for Columbia and the publicity material showed an inset photograph of her above the romantic silhouette of the légionnaire against *le sable chaud*. Edith of course could not sing the song for some time at least, and on this occasion did not attempt to steal it. In fact she apparently refused it, though in 1937 she recorded it for Polydor and the music publishers substituted her photograph for that of Marie Dubas. It was her second interpretation of 1938 that became a huge success; the sound of the distant bugle and the tears in the singer's voice can almost bring tears to our cynical eyes today, over sixty years later.

But this was not the end of the Legion. Marie Dubas had also recorded at the same time *Le Fanion de la Légion*, the other Asso-Monnot success, which could almost be a theme-song for the Legion, had they not already had their own, *Le Boudin*. That same year Edith had *Mon amant de la Coloniale* to herself and said she preferred it. In the meantime, when everything was going so well that it hardly seemed to be true, the curtain suddenly came down, and the house lights failed.

Louis Leplée spent every evening at his successful club and rarely left before all his artistes and clients had gone, which was in the early hours of the morning. But he had other interests: he had been overheard talking about a successful property deal that had brought him money, and the news was spread to someone who assumed that the cash must still be in his apartment. Just before 8 o'clock in the morning four young men rang the door bell; the housekeeper let them in, they immediately bound and gagged her and went in search of her employer. He was in bed. They asked for the money, there was some sort of scuffle, they gagged him and shot him just below the right eye. Maybe they did not mean to kill him, but they did. When Edith telephoned his apartment shortly afterwards a strange voice asked her to come at once. It was a police voice. The police were asking for everyone remotely connected with Gerny's club, and also attempting to reconstruct the crime. The late Henri Merlin, a publisher, who lived at the same house as the victim, 83 avenue de la Grande Armée, remembered clearly that this was his first glimpse of Edith Gassion, la Môme Piaf, the latest of Leplée's discoveries, the girl whom everyone had been talking about.

The news flew round Paris and was taken up by the sensationalist press: journalists wrote that Piaf was surely implicated, for she knew a fair number of sinister people. Leplée had met several of them at the club, and had looked enviously at several of the handsome young men. The police interrogated Edith for a long time but fortunately she had an alibi, while her friend who was most likely to be under suspicion, Henri Vallette, did not seem to have been involved: the housekeeper could not identify him as one of the four young men she had seen. In the end the case had to be closed, the police could prove nothing. Years later Edith remembered that Leplée had told her about a warning dream: his mother, he said, had appeared to him and told him that they would soon be reunited.

Edith felt abandoned. A surviving photograph of Leplée's funeral, that includes her all in black, with black stockings, supported by one of Leplée's associates, reveals her as a pitiful waif. Night-club owners and their eccentric entourage were fair game to journalists, and if this unsolved murder came nowhere near the recent sensational case of Violette Nozière who had poisoned her parents, the news spread all over France, and the person who suffered most, because she was the most vulnerable, was of course Edith. Her lightning start looked as though it might also be the end, for nobody wanted her. Fortunately, however, not everyone believed the gossip, and she had at least the support of a young journalist who wrote for the magazine *Le Détective*, Marcel Montarron, while his colleague Jean-Gabriel Séruzier took some remarkable photographs. Fortunately, too, various acquaintances found minor engagements for her, and Roméo Carlès, the *chansonnier*, befriended her and wrote a song for her, *La Petite Boutique*. It was not too difficult in the late 1930s for music-hall performers to find engagements in cinemas, where they came on stage between various parts of the film programme, but when Piaf appeared in this sort of show in the Paris suburbs she had to listen to cat-calls and hisses from scandal-mongers. However, when she went out to Brest, the naval town in Brittany, the cinema was naturally full of sailors and they, who did not care about the sinister rumours, gave her and her friend Momone such a cheerful, noisy reception that the regular customers were scared away.

After a short contract in Brussels Edith attempted a Paris comeback at a boîte called Chez Marius, and then O'Dett's Club in the Place Pigalle where the artistic director was Bruno Coquatrix, the man who was later to resurrect the big Paris music-hall, the Olympia. He wanted Edith to look well dressed and appear as a 'real' singer, not as a curiosity brought in from the streets; the club's couturière suggested a long red dress, but Coquatrix turned down the offer on Edith's behalf; she needed, he said, a little black dress with a pleated skirt, and it must have pockets, because she still did not know what to do with her hands. But the audience at O'Dett's did not find her appealing, and soon she was reduced to selling whatever good clothes she had acquired since her promotion from the streets.

The Leplée scandal was intense, but in the end Edith's luck held and now she found someone who believed in her just as much as, and more constructively so, than Papa Leplée had done, for he was even better placed professionally to help her. This was Raymond Asso whom, of course, she had met occasionally, for she had already sung *Mon amant de la Coloniale*. When they had first met, in a music publisher's office, Asso thought she looked like 'a Spanish beggar, proud and scornful at the same time, timid and frightened'. He was impressed by her singing but wondered if she was too unstable to become a star, for he had heard about some of her drunken escapades, and when not euphoric she appeared crushed. He found her a short contract in Nice, but the Leplée story had not yet grown cold: the cabaret where she was billed to appear was using it for publicity, telling people to come to *La Boîte à Vitesse* and decide for themselves: was La Môme Piaf a murderess?

For the time being however, La Môme had discovered how to make the best use of adverse publicity, and even if she chose to have a hectic time with the sailors from nearby Villefranche – she still could not resist them – even if she had never heard that famous English song, she stayed in Nice not one month but three.

When she came back to Paris there was only one person on whom she could rely, even if she had already let him down by her bad behaviour: Raymond Asso. He fell in love with her as he became her artistic director, impresario and father-figure. She moved into the Hôtel Piccadilly in Pigalle where Asso lived, and as he began to create the real Edith Piaf she began to love him, *à sa façon*. He parted from his own companion and firmly sent Momone away.

Asso was not just a song-writer or a stage-manager. He knew he had to create the whole woman. Edith's approach to work was not yet professional. 'I trained her', he said later. 'I taught her everything, gestures, inflection, how to dress. But she went on doing silly things and mixing with impossible people. I would lock her in. I would follow her about. I didn't want her to make mistakes. I only imposed one rule on her: hard work.'

Apparently he also had to teach her how to handle a knife and fork, how often to wash, how to spell and write, how and what to read. She never forgot one book he bought her before her train journey to Nice, *La Petite Fille comme ça* by the Honfleur novelist Lucie Delarue-Mardrus, and would mention it in interviews years later. It was, she said, almost her story, and indeed it was not far from it. The man who runs a touring theatrical company falls in love with one of his actresses. His wife tries to shoot him, so he and the other actress run away. The wife leaves their ten-year-old daughter in a *pension*, and the child feels abandoned. She had had no education but the girl is intelligent and learns fast – like Edith – while later in life their two destinies were to coincide again.

She was learning fast now. Asso was possibly more important to Edith than anyone else in her career. She called him '*mon poète*', and indeed all the poetry in him was called out into the songs he wrote for her. As the Leplée affair at last faded from the headlines, Edith could sing again without being booed. Marcel Achard, the poet and playwright, heard about her and arranged for her to sing at a private party in a smart house. When asked about her song-writer she confessed that her 'poet' had not been allowed in because he was wearing a pullover and not a dinner jacket. He was rescued, and Achard remained Edith's firm friend for years.

The year 1936, the historian Philip Guedalla decided, was one of transition when we moved from 'post-war to the present'. Since he completed his book, *The Hundredth Year 1936*, only in July 1939, he was not thinking about pre-war; some events in 1936 did point to a new kind of world, marked in Britain by the arrival (to prove temporary) of Edward VIII, after the long years of George V. It was the same year that saw the end of Italy's Abyssinian war, the start of the Spanish Civil war, and the arrival in France of the Popular Front led by the intelligent Léon Blum.

Asso, who had served in the army when very young, had already sensed that songs about the Legion and the Colonial Army would be successful, and he began to think of songs about sailors, especially for Edith, for she had been deeply impressed by *L'Etranger* two years earlier. Deserts and the high seas were vast open spaces, far removed from smoke-filled cabarets and music-halls, and he knew that Edith's voice, accompanied by Marguerite Monnot's evocative music, could transport audiences far away, and earn immense success for his singer and himself. At the same time he rehearsed her in what was now a wide repertoire, mainly because he had big plans.

Edith was ready for them, as ready as she could ever be. She admitted later that she needed the Asso years – there were three of them in the end – to emerge from her childhood and from Pigalle. She said that the 'ugliness' of her first songs had made her feel ugly herself, and destructive. By 'ugly' songs she no doubt meant songs that had been sung for too many years by too many other singers, songs that aimed for easy, cheap effects. Now she felt she could believe in love, happiness and luck. When she sang Asso's songs she felt she was becoming a star and no longer a 'phenomenon', which she had been in the brief days with Leplée.

Asso was the ideal song-writer because he did not write superficially. In his own memoirs he set out his method – he would write only when he had something to say, only of real life 'in the purest way possible', and he would write simply, so that everyone could understand him. And now of course he was writing specifically for Edith, especially after she had interpreted in her own way the two 'Legion' songs. *Paris-*

Méditerranée was based on one of Edith's many encounters with a man, this time on the train to Nice. They held hands, but as she awoke in a sunlit station, she saw him leave the train, and the police were waiting with handcuffs. *Browning*, the story of an American gangster, '*Le roi du revolver*', has often been quoted as an indirect memory of the death of Leplée, but in any case it was a dramatic story perfectly suited to Edith. Then there was *Elle fréquentait la rue Pigalle*, already described, and many others – *Le Grand Voyage du pauvre nègre*, or *J'entends la sirène* and *Le Mauvais Matelot*.

The year 1936 was one of extreme hard work for Edith, carefully watched over by Asso, who had become extremely ambitious for her. He had set his heart on a contract at the A.B.C., the cabaret in the boulevard Poissonnière, run by the Hungarian Mitty Goldin, for it was the mecca for the music-hall stars of the time. Goldin was difficult and did not want La Môme, but eventually Asso convinced him and she was booked for the first half of the programme in March 1937. Asso was tireless, and as he looked round for a suitable place for a practice session he found that the Popular Front had organized a gala at the vast stadium known as the Vel' d'Hiv (Vélodrome d'Hiver). Edith's name was added to the list of artistes. Halfway through her first song the microphone failed, but she did not. Her immense voice filled the stadium and Edith discovered powers she hardly knew she possessed, for she had come a long way from the days when she sang through a megaphone in the street. There was one more training session, a different one this time. Asso took Edith to the A.B.C. just before she was due to appear herself, to see Marie Dubas. She was overwhelmed, and ten years later she told the theatrical revue *Opéra* what she remembered, but found it difficult to express her excitement. She could not take her eyes from Marie's ever-changing face, and she knew her own eyes were filled with tears. She remembered Asso's question: 'Now have you understood what makes a real artist?' Something within herself had changed, she said, she was no longer the same person. Fourteen times in all she went back. 'I went in the afternoons and evenings to watch Marie Dubas: she inspired me, it was from her that I took all my courage, my happiness and also all my sadness.'

Even in 1961 she could still remember what she noticed in the theatre: 'Just before Marie came on', she said on Radio Europe I, 'there was an extraordinary atmosphere in the auditorium ... All these people, their faces full of expectation, formed one single heart together ... When Marie appeared there was such enthusiasm that I too wanted the public to love me like that ...'

Edith sang in the first half of the A.B.C. programme with such success that she was at once promoted to join Charles Trenet in the second half. She was also, at the suggestion of Madame Breton, known as 'La Marquise', the wife of Raoul Breton the music publisher, transformed from La Môme Piaf into Edith Piaf. She was a star, and Asso, who had told her to aim at big audiences, the real public, had achieved his ambition on her behalf.

It has been alleged, especially since Piaf's death, that the British intellectuals, who insist that her songs be kept in French, have tried to make her into a vaguely literary over-dramatic figure representing some mysterious chapter of European social history. It was in fact the French critics and writers who took notice of her very early, long before the British realized she was not just another singer. At the A.B.C. in 1937 she appeared in her usual little black dress, but wore a starched white crochet collar. In Paris this alone asked for one inevitable comparison. 'How much', wrote Maurice Verne in L'Intransigeant, 'she reminds us of the Claudine of 1900! Oh Colette! here is the miraculous resurrection of Claudine's short hair, her white collar and her cravat, her black dress resembling a schoolgirl's uniform.' The critic mused on the metallic element in her voice:

'La Môme Piaf is not yet literary – long may that last!' – but said she must have her own songs, reflecting in realistic fashion the working-class world of factory chimneys and the refrains of songs picked up from radio sets in the bistrot. In 1938 the poet Léon-Paul Fargue took her further along the literary road. 'She gazes into the distance at horizons full of miracles, imagined by desperate people at the very end of their stories of *ennui* … Her entire art consists in placing the development (she achieves) within the hand of emotion, and in becoming herself, gradually, the strongest and purest emotion of the melody. So when she is evoking for us the triumph of love, the harshness of destiny, the breathless anxiety of railway trains, the joy of light or the fatality of the heart, her voice rises to the last vibrant notes clear and pure, resembling those divine brush-strokes which appear in the dark subjects of Goya, Delacroix or Forain.'

This is the type of high-flying literary criticism which the French enjoy, where the criticism is more literary than what is criticized. In fact Edith now excelled in her own type of song, because she had been lucky enough to meet Raymond Asso and Marguerite Monnot; their creations remained simple in outline, allowing Piaf the maximum scope for intense development, and yet remaining memorable, which the mass of the public wanted. In the autumn of 1937 she sang at the A.B.C. again, and the next year gave a recital at the Bobino music-hall in which nearly all the songs were Asso creations.

She already showed clear signs of her later tyranny. In 1938 a private recording was made at Marie Dubas's home of Edith and a pianist in a rehearsal session. The song was *La Java en mineur* and one is reminded of that famous title *Don't Shoot the Pianist*, an easy death compared to the one Edith seems ready to inflict upon the poor man with her endless complaints and instructions. But all was well on this occasion, the whole performance was reported to be a joke. The fierce, demanding Piaf of the late 1950s already existed, she would accept nothing less than perfection and was always impatient with people who could not read her mind: and the comic actress existed too.

The year 1938, the Parisians thought, was starting well. They had sighed romantically over the abdication of Edward VIII, and now they welcomed George VI and Queen Elizabeth of Britain. The bourgeoisie saw very little wrong with Hitler and Mussolini, the right-wing newspapers saw a great deal wrong with the behaviour, indeed the very existence of the Jews, and everyone, nearly everyone, thought the Maginot Line was very comforting. Sartre, on the other hand, published *La Nausée*, and the world had changed.

It was also a good year for Piaf. Thanks to Asso, everyone wanted her. Thanks especially to Jacques Canetti and others, she recorded more and more songs, and her records were selling well. However, as the false security of Paris would soon dissolve into war, Asso saw with great sorrow, where Edith's success was taking her.

Back in 1936 she had already sung in her first film, and this was *La Garçonne*. The song was entitled *Quand même*, with music by Jean Wiener and words by Louis Poterat, a librettist who specialized in songs for films and was to write *Le Billard électrique* for Edith much later, in 1961. This forgotten film included a song by one of Edith's potential rivals, Suzy Solidor (see Appendix 2), and at least two famous actresses appeared in it – Marie Bell and Arletty. The film had been based on the novel by Victor Margueritte that had seemed so wicked in 1922 that its author was stripped of his Légion d'Honneur. Why was it wicked, and why did Pierre Flandin, Minister for Foreign Affairs, believe it would give foreigners a false idea of French morality? Because the heroine, finding that her fiancé is unfaithful, wanted to make a life of her own. Edith was beginning to have similar ideas, although Asso was the most faithful of lovers.

At thirty-eight Raymond Asso could hardly have been a total romantic, for there is realism and tragedy in his songs. However, he had not been able to create Edith Piaf without loving her. He had taken her to the Hôtel Alsina in the avenue Junot, installed a Chinese cook and a secretary, but surely he could hardly have thought, even in happy moments, that it would be *'l'amour tou-jours'. C'est lui que mon cœur a choisi*, he wrote for her in 1939, convincing himself, perhaps, that *lui* was himself. Edith had been with him for less than three years, but despite all she owed him she now began to bite the hand that fed her, looking with interest at other men and, worst infidelity of all, seeing more of Simone Berteaut than Asso wanted, for he regarded her as a seriously destructive influence. When Edith was singing in Le Night-Club, a smart bar in the rue Arsène Houssaye, she was attracted to a young man with charming manners and an air of distant, cold indifference. This was a challenge to her, for nobody had ever been indifferent to her. She was soon to meet him. He was Paul Meurisse, who was performing in, Amiral, a nearby cabaret. There were other men too, all of which led to rows in the Hôtel Alsina.

Events in the outside world clarified the situation, as they did for most people in Europe that year, in varying ways. 'It was the summer of 1939', wrote Maurice Chevalier, in *The Man in the Straw Hat*, 'and the Riviera was seething with crowds of bewildered people. They were all wondering if there really would be a war. I myself did not believe it. I was still sure that Hitler was bluffing.' The Duke of Windsor invited him to lunch, but during the meal 'we heard over the radio that the Germans had invaded Poland. We were all stunned. Of course that meant that England and France were in the war. Now golf was out of the question …'

In September the weather in Europe was beautiful and during the first few days Paris was flooded with a still and golden light. In the entertainment world there was a stunned silence, but not for long. 'In Paris', the Man in the Straw Hat went on, 'the atmosphere was a little better. In spite of everything you saw people smile and you heard them telling jokes.' And in London, the Café de Paris, closed like all theatres and cinemas by government decree, reopened on 12 September. Chevalier reported that 'the winter of 1939–40 slipped by, and Paris suffered very little from this "phoney war". At the Casino we played to a full house every night.' Noël Coward's apartment in the Place Vendôme was 'filled nearly every night from six to nine – the martinis so dry they were known as *dynamites* – and by 9 o'clock everyone was on the town … At L'Amiral, a boîte not far from the Arc de Triomphe everybody went night after night', wrote Cole Lesley, 'to see and hear a young singer called Edith Piaf, white faced in her black dress, passionately singing her passionate songs – *C'est lui que mon cœur a choisi* and *Je n'en connais pas la fin*, long before *La Vie en rose*.' Life went on. 'Of course', said Chevalier, 'we understood that terrible things were happening in Poland and Austria. But Parisians don't really care about anything but Paris.' Nobody would disagree with that. 'Those of us who aren't politicians pay very little attention to the rest of the world. And an entertainer's profession is his whole life. If we *have* to fight for France or die for her we are ready to do so. But the rest of the time we just want to be let alone. I guess we feel that we are doing our share by giving laughter and gaiety to the nation.'

Raymond Asso was one of those who had to fight, potentially at least, for France. He was called up into the army and had to go miles from Paris to Digne in the Alps of Haute Provence to join his unit. Edith had only to join her friends in the bar at L'Amiral, accept drinks from the young man, Paul Meurisse, and listen to his act. Meurisse came from northern France, and had been so badly stage-struck that he had escaped from his middle-class family – his father was a banker – and his legal work, won a song competition at the Alhambra music-hall, made his début in Marseilles, and was given minor engagements in the ubiquitous Paris bars and night clubs. When Edith met him he was singing at L'Amiral, and she thought nothing of his act, which seems to have consisted mainly of comic songs. On the other hand she thought everything of his smooth behaviour even if she found it odd, as she was soon to find out, that he washed and shaved not only once but twice a day.

Odd too to find a man who was prepared to tolerate her exaggerated, uncompromising behaviour – and give as good as he got, in his own way. They were soon living together, at 10 bis, rue Anatole-de-la-Forge where he had taken an apartment, and according to one of the more picturesque legends she always hoped he would beat her, an old Belleville-style treatment which she was said to enjoy. There was much breaking of crockery and if he did not beat her he was observed holding her down as she lay on the pavement. This was said to be a joke, but he had to do it as she might have run away while he was paying the driver of the *fiacre* which had brought them home. Although she was not necessarily drunk at the time, Meurisse, along with all her lovers over the years, tried to stop her drinking, if only for the sake of her general health, which was known to be fragile, and the quality of her performance. Their task was futile as many of Edith's friends believe she had a form of alcoholism probably inherited from both her parents.

She in her turn was quite ready to walk over Raymond Asso. She encouraged Meurisse to move into the Hôtel Alsina when Asso had gone to the war. One day the deserted man came back on leave and there was a worse, if briefer, war. Edith threw him out, it was all over: he was a song-writer, no longer a lover.

Years later she sincerely said she was sorry, and after the first bitterness she never lost touch with Asso for long, while she certainly could not have afforded to stop singing his songs. In 1940 he took his leave of her as a lover by writing one of the saddest songs in her repertoire, with a theme which recurs in many of them. This was *On danse sur ma chanson (They're dancing to my song)*:

> *J'ai voulu finir la chanson*
> *Qu'au printemps j'avais commencée*
> *Mais tu n'es plus à la maison*
> *Et les fleurs sont toutes fanées*
>
> *J'aurais dû chanter comme les poètes*
> *Avec de grands mots notre bel amour,*
> *Mais je n'ai pas su, ma chanson est faite*
> *De tout petits mots, ceux de tous les jours:*
> *Car sur les mots que tu disais*
> *Amour, serment, toujours, jamais*
> > *On danse …*

And at the end

> *Alors, j'ai voulu t'oublier,*
> *Quelqu'un m'a appris à danser*
> *Et maintenant sur le passé …*
> > *Je danse …*

[*And now I'm dancing on the past*]

Raymond Asso was left with his poems, which later he would recite in public. He followed Edith's career closely, not always with approval, and for many years worked as an administrator in the S.A.C.E.M., the Société d'Auteurs, Compositeurs et Editeurs de Musique, the equivalent of the British Performing Rights Society, and the American Society of Composers, Authors, and Publishers.

If Edith had deserted her first poet, she immediately found another one, and seemed to be moving even more deeply into the literary scene. Through Madame Breton, who appeared at crucial moments in her life – as she did in the lives of many singers – she met one of the most outstanding and controversial poets of the century: Jean Cocteau, who had been publishing poems, plays, novels and non-fiction on a vast range of themes ever since his youth. In 1938 he had had success after much controversy with his play *Les Parents terribles*, while his theatrical reminiscences, *Portraits-Souvenir*, serialized in *Le Figaro* a few years earlier, were full of nostalgia and sparkle. He was in his way a theatrical genius and always insisted that his work in all genres was *poésie*. Edith had been nervous about meeting him but was immediately charmed, as everyone who met Cocteau always was. When she asked Paul Meurisse to find one of Cocteau's books so that she could know more about him, Meurisse is said to have given her *Le Potomak*, Cocteau's first so-called novel of 1919, but in any case an almost unintelligible work. However, the book may have been *La Fin du Potomak*, which seemed to foreshadow the chaos of the Second World War, for it was published in 1939 and although listed in the *Poésie du Roman* nobody could really call it fiction, it was closer to philosophy. Cocteau himself was understanding, and recommended to Edith that she should read *Les Enfants terribles*, his most accessible novel, which was later filmed, and also translated by the British novelist Rosamond Lehmann. Cocteau went to see Edith's performance in cabaret and immediately was ready to classify her as one of the 'sacred monsters', the highly individual artists whose performances he enjoyed so much. That year, 1940 he published a collection of essays about them, and was writing a play called *Les Monstres sacrés* in which a few of them were virtually to play themselves.

Edith apparently confided in him that her ménage with Paul Meurisse was often difficult: why would he not join in a good soul-searing row? Cocteau listened sympathetically and wrote a one-act play, or rather monologue, entitled *Le Bel indifférent* (meaning literally 'the handsome indifferent man'), that Piaf was to perform. The protagonist Emile stubbornly refused to utter a word despite his partner's desperate pleas. It has always been assumed that the character was based on that of Meurisse, who always denied it. In the play Emile is described as 'a magnificent gigolo' who would not be one much longer, while the 'actress', who is nameless, refers to her *tour de chant*. Some people believed that Cocteau had originally sketched out the idea for the singer Suzy Solidor. Emile's rôle is to remain unresponsive, say nothing, read the paper and go out, leaving the desperate girl, who only wants a loving response of some sort, to throw herself out of the window. Cocteau enjoyed writing any piece that would allow an actor or actress to give a virtuoso-like performance as in *La Voix humaine* of 1930, performed by a variety of leading actresses, including Ingrid Bergman, on stage and screen with nothing but a telephone to move the action along. In *Le Bel indifférent* there was the telephone, the sound of elevator gates outside the apartment, a jazz record, knocking on the wall from a protesting neighbour, traffic noises through the window at the end; Emile himself was totally silent but on stage the entire time there was Piaf.

The play was put on at Les Bouffes Parisiens, where Offenbach's theatre had once stood, in May 1940. It followed *Les Monstres sacrés*, starring one of Cocteau's favourite actresses, Yvonne de Bray, transferred from the Théâtre Michel, with production by André Brulé and décor by Christian Bérard, whose work always pleased Cocteau. The description of the setting recalled any number of Piaf songs and could have served for the ballet that Cocteau was to devise later for Jean Babilée, *Le Jeune Homme et la mort*: 'A dingy hotel bedroom lit by illuminated signs in the street. Divan-bed, gramophone'. The stage directions identify the actress with Piaf: 'as the curtain rises the actress, wearing a little black dress, is alone. She watches from the window, and runs to the door to look at the elevator, then she goes to sit down by the telephone, then she puts on a record of herself singing, and takes it off. She goes back to the telephone and dials a number.' In this half-hour sketch Cocteau arranged a development and dénouement almost as if he were writing a song for his heroine. The one-sided telephone calls are closely reminiscent of *La Voix humaine*, and the wait for a call, if not looking back to the hero's long wait in *A la recherche du temps perdu*, foreshadows a song written for Piaf by Michel Vaucaire in 1961, *C'est peut-être ça*, about waiting for a telephone call that never comes:

> *C'est peut-être ça*
> *Qui fait battre le cœur,*
> *Qui pendant des heures*
> *Vous fera rester là,*
> *Devant un téléphone*
> *Pour entendre une voix,*
> *Devant un téléphone*
> *Qui ne sonnera pas …*
>
> *[Perhaps that's*
> *what makes the heart beat,*
> *it keeps you there for hours*
> *beside a telephone,*
> *waiting to hear a voice,*
> *beside a telephone*
> *that will not ring . . .]*

It is a play evoking total, almost masochistic devotion which fails to win over the actress's unfaithful, uncaring lover; it fails so badly that he will not even speak to her and reduces her to suicide because she thinks she is abandoned.

Edith had never appeared on the stage as a 'straight' actress, and suddenly, despite the presence of 'Emile', she was alone with words to be spoken, not sung. She had potential as an actress, through her speaking voice and her gestures, but she had been very nervous and was afraid of forgetting her words. However, the critical audience eventually accepted her and Cocteau made a vivid drawing of her, later produced with the text of the monologue in the *Théâtre de Poche* in 1949.

Since this was 1940 the production was not without problems. Paul Meurisse duly received his call-up papers and Edith had to write personally to the Minister of War before he could be given a reprieve for ten days. After that he was replaced by Jean Marconi. At the same time the cast of *Les Monstres sacrés* suffered casualties: Piaf had to read the part for one actress who fell ill while Cocteau himself had to replace André Brulé in the actor's temporary absence.

The most interesting description of the production came from Cocteau himself in the daily if undated letters he was writing at the time to his lover Jean Marais, the actor, who had been called up. The author recorded a great success for the actress Madeleine Robinson in *Les Monstres sacrés* but the reception for *Le Bel indifférent* was muted, although Cocteau himself thought the performance was 'sublime'. 'The public listened with respect and even applauded several times – but there was the unease caused by beautiful, enviable things – too beautiful. At the end I realized we hadn't won. Yet as people left there was only praise to be heard.' Marais had apparently advised Cocteau to open with the Piaf-Meurisse play, but now it was too late to make the change, it would look like defeat. Of Edith's performance one of Cocteau's women friends said 'Poor thing, they applauded out of pity.'

In his next letter Cocteau sent Marais a drawing of Piaf, similar to others he made at this period, while a few letters later he wrote that the situation was 'very strange. There's a kind of silent struggle between this play and the public – but it isn't a failure – far from it.' He then put it differently – the audience were astonished and they seemed to be running away 'after looking through a key-hole, trying to make as little sound as possible'. By the next letter Piaf was winning. Then she was in tears because Paul Meurisse had to go back finally to the army. However, she herself added a few lines to Cocteau's letter, thanking Marais for the one he had written to her: 'I received it just before going onstage. It was kind of you ... and my fondest wish is to act in one of Jean's plays with you.' That never happened. When Jean Marconi replaced Meurisse in *Le Bel indifférent* the public was not aware of the change but box office receipts improved slightly.

Cocteau also made a special adaptation for Piaf of his haunting story *Le Fantôme de Marseille*, in which an old gentleman falls in love with a 'girl' who is in fact a disguised boy and on the run. After a horrible accident the old gentleman discovers the truth. In the monologue the boy's girlfriend addresses the magistrate in court, explaining why she shot the hopeful old man: '*Monsieur le juge d'instruction, moi aussi j'ai de l'instruction ...*' Edith's steel-edged voice would have interpreted very well the despair of the ending, but in fact she does not seem to have performed this macabre little work.

In *Le Bel indifférent* Paul Meurisse had had a great success, and much later he got his own back following Edith's remarks about his singing; she could play this part, he said, without being an actress, just as General de Gaulle could sing *La Marseillaise* very well without being a singer. Edith kindly said that if Meurisse couldn't sing he could at least act, even if he had not a word to say. The name of Meurisse, little known outside France to later generations, is at least remembered for his appearances with Simone Signoret in *Les Diaboliques* of 1954.

Les Bouffes Parisiens closed in the early summer as the audiences took fright. Cocteau went temporarily to live in the south, now officially the unoccupied zone or *la zone libre*, staying with a Doctor Nicoleau in Perpignan, having been driven there by the music publisher Raoul Breton who was on his way further south still. For Edith cabaret work at L'Aiglon was over and after singing at the Bobino music-hall in a gala for the Red Cross she was left without engagements. However, Paul Meurisse suffered so badly from bronchitis that he was not much use to the army and he was sent to Toulouse, expecting demobilization. Edith rapidly joined him there just before the armistice was signed, a week after the Germans had reached the capital. Edith and Meurisse were lucky, for among the many show-business people who had fled south from Paris was Jacques Canetti, one of Edith's early supporters at Radio-Cité in 1936. He had continued his activities in the unoccupied zone and thanks to him Edith and her partner were able to appear onstage in Toulouse, later in Nîmes, Béziers, Narbonne and several other venues. But summer came to an end, there were no more engagements and the couple took the risk of returning to the capital, not knowing what they would find there.

4

Making the best of things

In some ways Paris might have become a different place, but over the centuries the city had learnt how to deal with life under foreign occupation. On 14 June 1940, at 5.30 a.m. the Germans entered Paris, and four hours later the swastika was flying over the Arc de Triomphe. The Pigalle cinema opened the next afternoon, others soon followed and by the autumn many theatres, including the Comédie-Française, were busy. Its last production before the Occupation had been, ironically enough, *On ne saurait penser à tout*, by Alfred de Musset. The Opéra had opened at the end of August with a fascinating choice, *The Damnation of Faust* by Berlioz. Hervé le Boterf, in his two volumes describing *La Vie Parisienne pendant l'Occupation*, remarks that 'even during the most disturbed periods of its history the French capital never renounced its pleasures and diversions. People danced during the Terror (of 1792) and theatres continued to give performances while the enemies of the Empire were encamped in the Champs-Elysées in 1815. In the same way the Comédie-Française played without interruption during the siege of Paris and throughout the duration of the Commune'. (This was in 1870.)

Although various well-known theatrical personalities fled to the south in 1940, they soon came back. For entertainers who were Jewish life was of course far from easy, not to say dangerous, and the unfortunate Marie Dubas, who had sailed to South America in 1939, returning to Portugal only two years later, was absent from the Paris theatre for several years. Michel Emer, the gifted young man who wrote both words and music for his songs, was also forced to hide in the unoccupied zone. Piaf had discovered him early in the war, on the very day he was due to join his army unit in 1939. On that day he played to her *L'Accordéoniste*, one of the songs closely associated with her for nearly twenty years. Sadly he died at the end of 1984.

Edith did her best to protect him, and she also helped another Jewish friend, the brilliant Polish-born pianist and composer Norbert Glanzberg, who became her lover for a time.

The French population, during these uneasy months, needed distraction and entertainment, needed it so desperately that the personalities of the show-business world felt it was their duty to supply it. Mistinguett was soon seen cycling about Paris, and men carrying sandwich-boards advertised the new activity at the Concert Mayol:

Kabarett Mayol
Immer Paris
Gross Revue.

This big music-hall, and the Casino de Paris, were probably regarded by the Nazis as symbols of non-Aryan Western decadence, but the directors opened with any French artists available in a desperate bid to keep away German directors and stars. Maurice Chevalier helped, and was glad to use this engagement as a reason for refusing any more tours of German prison camps. He had already agreed to one on the understanding that prisoners from his native Ménilmontant and Belleville would be returned to France.

That other native of Belleville, Edith Piaf, like all French entertainers, had to appear before the German Propaganda-staffel and submit the texts of her songs to them, or there would be no permission to work. She was in fact very busy, for with the help of Asso she had a good varied repertoire which the public liked, she could not be accused of any political or anti-Nazi activity, and of course her name was already known in Germany. She sang at a Red Cross gala at Bobino and also at the A.B.C. in company with Paul Meurisse. She had perfected several new songs, varying from the usual tense situations between lovers – *Simple comme bonjour*, a tragic rivalry between a blonde and a brunette, or *Y en a un de trop* in which the singer cannot make up her mind between two men, to the setting of a poem by Jacques Prévert on one of his favourite themes, the plight of children uncared for in a poor district: *Embrasse-moi*. Edith made several recordings during 1940 and the next year even recorded a song which had already caused her some trouble with the occupying authorities. It is particularly interesting because it is one of the very first for which she wrote the words herself: *Où sont-ils mes petits copains?* about her friends who had gone off to the war, singing. They, and those left behind, would somehow get used to the idea. At one performance she transformed the song into a daring patriotic statement: 'When she called out "There they are!!!" ' wrote Joëlle Monserrat, 'a tiny spot of light appeared at the back of the stage, grew larger and gradually took over the whole stage, so that in the end Edith was draped in the French flag'. Many people in the audience had been weeping, now everyone stood up and sang with her. This is the sort of protest that occurred frequently in the French theatres during the occupation, and even Mistinguett had added telling little asides to songs like *Mon homme* at the Casino de Paris. On this occasion Edith had trouble with the censorship but survived.

Another incident might have given her worse trouble. This involved Pierre Hiégel, well-known in the recording business and a successful radio presenter. He was later suspected of collaboration with the occupying power, but it was probably not understood that he had been lucky in one way, for the German officer with whom he worked happened to be a man of culture who left him a free hand and Hiégel said that this gave him an impression of perfect freedom. He had known Piaf since she was very young and enjoyed playing her records during his radio programmes. One day by some ghastly mistake the wrong side of a record was placed on the turntable. Although it was an old song and hardly typical Piaf, dating from 1936, *Il n'est pas distingué*, it contained by chance a statement that was now *verboten*:

> *Moi Hitler j'l'ai dans l'blair*
> *Et je peux pas l'renifler*
> *Les nazis ont l'air d'oublier*
> *Qu'c'est nous dans la bagarre qu'on les a zigouillés …*

meaning, 'I can't stand Hitler, the Nazis seem to forget that we were the people who slammed them in the war …' The First World War, of course.

When Hiégel realized his mistake, he immediately signalled to the sound engineer who silenced the record, but it was almost too late. Hiégel was cautioned, but he had been indirectly lucky in one detail: Marc Hély, the lyric writer, may have laughed at Hitler in 1936 but a few years later the occupying powers in Paris apparently did not regard him as sinister in any way. He escaped trouble and so did Edith.

If there had not been a war it is unlikely that Piaf's career as a singer would have been very different, for she was continually successful and still acquired new songs, even if she did not record many during 1941. More and more she came to realize that she needed songs created specially to serve her individual voice with its narrow, rather low range and her talent for the dramatic, unhappy ending. Good song-writers were now rare. Asso had been rusticated, Michel Emer was still half in hiding, so were many others if they were not on active service. So gradually she began to write more lyrics herself and *C'était un jour de fête* with music by Marguerite Monnot was a great success, telling the story of a broken love affair for, after all, especially in wartime, that was a common experience.

Without the war and the occupation however, Edith might not have been given a part in a film made in 1941 by Georges Lacombe, *Montmartre-sur-Seine*. Paul Meurisse was included in the cast though he had just run into trouble. He had been forced to appear in a German-directed film, because if he had refused to do so he would not have been allowed to sing in cabaret. If Meurisse had decided that Edith could not act, she and others had decided he could, although of course she still insisted that he could not sing.

Many people now might say that she could not yet write songs, for of the four that she contributed to this film, all with music by Marguerite Monnot, none are of great interest. *J'ai dansé avec l'amour* has been described as a kind of musical pastiche of Count Basie or Duke Ellington', a concession perhaps to the nostalgic taste of the time. In the film Edith was accompanied by Le Jazz de Paris, an experiment for her but one which proved her amazing, adept ability. The rather sentimental song, *Tu es partout*, about the departed but ever-present lover, was later used in Steven Spielberg film *Saving Private Ryan*.

Montmartre-sur-Seine told a kind of Piaf story – how a little flower-seller achieved her ambition of becoming a singer after, naturally, various amorous imbroglios. There were two minor points of historical interest – Jean-Louis Barrault appeared in the film as Edith's great admirer, and Kiffer, the celebrated poster artist, made an early striking drawing of her for the film's publicity.

It was this publicity which led to a new and highly creative period in Edith's life as a singer, for in charge of publicizing the film was a man named Henri Contet, who had left the engineering profession for a career in journalism and had even made a short film. He liked Edith, and noted with amusement that her ménage with Paul Meurisse was hardly a happy one at this time. In some ways Meurisse was more of a *bel indifférent* than ever, except that *he* noted Edith's obvious interest in Henri Vidal the actor, who was also in the film. When Henri Contet became a close, admiring friend, soon a lover, Paul Meurisse retired with dignity from Edith's life and soon married the actress Michèle Alfa.

Since Henri Contet, in addition to his journalism, was also a poet, naturally Edith pressed him into service and during the next few years it was Contet who produced the words for some of her most successful songs. The best known were to come later, but for the immediate future there were the five songs that Edith was to sing in the film: *C'était une histoire d'amour, Adieu mon coeur, C'est merveilleux, Le Chant du Pirate* and *Mariage*.

However, the film was not released until the spring of 1946 and a good deal was to happen now in Edith's life during the last years of the war, which in France came to an end in 1944.

The winters in Paris were arctic, any form of heating could only be obtained through heavy bribery, and even popular theatrical stars received no favours in this respect. However, through a friend, not apparently Henri Contet, as some have thought, she was lucky anough to find a privileged place that was always warm, understandably so, since it was a high-class *maison close* or house of assignation, popular with French and German officers and many high-ranking people from the diplomatic corps.

It was in the rue de Villejust, now the rue Paul Valéry, well placed between the avenue Kléber and the avenue Victor Hugo. Number 44 had sheltered Colette when she had left her husband for the Marquise de Belbœuf in 1906. The poet Valéry had lived at number 40 and after his death in 1945 the street was renamed in his honour.

If many cinemas and theatres in Paris opened again fairly soon after the arrival of the occupants, most brothels took a little longer, for they had to wait for their girls to come back from their hiding-places. Like other members of the entertainment profession, however, they did not stay away from the capital for too long, especially when the news spread that the freelance operators who had stayed there had trebled their charges and still had to turn clients away. One well-known superior establishment, however, Le Chabanais, opened during the afternoon of 14 June 1940. 'Horizontal collaboration', wrote Hervé le Boterf, 'needed only one morning of reflection.' The Germans organized this aspect of social life with speedy efficiency: some forty of the *maisons closes* were for the army of occupation, some sixty for the French, and bilingual notices on the doors made the situation perfectly clear. Naturally there was strict medical supervision.

Number 4 rue de Villejust was far from being a mere brothel and its owner, Madame Billy, was no ordinary 'Madame'. Born in an obscure wine-growing Burgundy village in 1901, she escaped as soon as possible via Dijon into the world where 'love' is equated with money, and her life during the 1920s and 1930s makes most fiction seem weary, stale, flat and unprofitable. She later married a music-hall artist but earlier on had begun a successful business career in the rue de Cardinet. She moved into the rue de Villejust in 1941, bricked out the rats and decorated the whole house. Her bar, restaurant and later her girls, were appreciated by members of *le gratin*: senators, serving officers, writers, journalists and entertainers. She was obviously a genius at organizing a particular type of life and was seriously conscious of carrying out a public duty; she was businesslike yet generous and took a personal interest in everyone who came to the house. It was of course well heated. Edith and Simone Berteaut – she was always present when there was no resident lover – moved into two rooms on the top floor which were not used by clients, and a third was available for any visiting musicians or for the storage of music and equipment.

Edith could at least eat well in this house, and although clients were not encouraged to pay in kind they would often make useful donations, such as a whole tunny fish or a vast Cantal cheese. There was a Chinese cook, but Edith's favourite food at the time was simple, as it usually was, grilled steak smothered in pounded raw garlic, and her drink tended to be mint syrup. Having discovered a grand piano in the *grand salon* she asked permission to rehearse with a pianist, guitarist or accordionist.

Madame Billy had not realized that rehearsals or singing sessions of any sort usually took place at three in the morning. Result: despite closed shutters and heavy curtains the entire neighbourhood in the narrow steep street was awakened, and everyone rushed to the telephone to complain. Even the German police turned up, for their local headquarters was very near, but once informed that Madame Piaf was rehearsing they took no further action, beyond lingering outside to listen, for the Germans admired her as much as the French did, and Edith did not care whether they came in or not. Madame Billy did care, however, for she received and helped many people in serious difficulties, from persecuted Jews to members of the Resistance and possible spies.

Edith, despite her chaotic nocturnal timetable, brought happiness to the house. Her landlady is worth quoting on the subject: 'What wonderful evenings we spent with her! She gave everything she had in her heart. Her happiness lay in giving pleasure. Edith, who was not loved enough, loved to please others. She needed to charm them. Not only through singing. She had learnt many poems by heart and was capable of reciting them all night long'. Understandably Madame Billy observed how her desire to please affected her conduct towards men. 'When she had set her cap at some handsome young man, he had to give in. There was no escape.' Edith put everything into her attempts at conquest. 'Charm, poetry, consideration, tenderness. And it is true that she was seductive. She was the only one to doubt it.'

She was apparently still unsure of herself, and gratefully accepted Madame Billy's advice that her secretary, Andrée

Bigard, should move into the remaining room on the top floor. Andrée Bigard was no mere answerer of letters, for she helped Edith with her constant attempts at self-education and at the same time worked skilfully and secretly for the Resistance movement.

Edith, as Billy knew, 'suffered from her origins'. Of course she loved her father, who had been forced to give up work in 1937 and had registered as unemployed. He came to the house once a week or so and was made very welcome by his daughter and her landlady but felt out of his element. He would accept Edith's money and Billy's black-market food parcels but could not bring himself to sit down for a meal. Billy remembered how closely Edith resembled him: they walked in the same way, tended to stand as though they were round-shouldered and held their heads the same way. (Edith's cousin, Marcelle Lallier, also a Gassion, had the same physique.) Edith's father was not the only relative to come to the house. Her pathetic mother, Line Marsa, found her way there too, and was discovered one day sitting at the piano, poorly dressed, and attempting to play one of Edith's most successful songs, *De l'autre côté de la rue*. Madame Billy had already given her food on past visits, for Edith usually refused to see her: she had never forgiven her mother for abandoning her as a small child. The unfortunate woman had been in prison for drug abuse and alcoholism; now she was free, but she was broke and wanted Edith to give her some songs. After keeping her waiting for hours Edith consented to see her in the end, and after an obvious row behind closed doors Line Marsa left, carrying what was clearly a parcel of songs. If Edith had given her money she would no doubt have spent it on more drugs. She did not come to the house again.

It is untrue to say that Edith and her mother were never on good terms, for Denise Gassion remembered one particular family reunion at her father's apartment, when Line Marsa was present. An unexpected visitor arrived on this occasion: a young man, in military uniform, who embraced both Line and Edith. He was none other than Edith's own brother, Herbert Gassion. When Line Marsa had left her husband and daughter some twenty years earlier she had been pregnant and did not know it. Her baby was duly born but of course she could not take care of him. Her son Herbert had been brought up by the Assistance Publique and now his father met him for the first time.

Madame Billy, who seemed to understand how everybody felt in all situations – this was her form of *déformation professionnelle*, no doubt – was probably the best mother Edith ever had. She valued Edith for herself, forgave her everything, tantrums, rows and scenes, but insisted on her near-genius and total honesty, for even if she lived extravagantly on credit she always paid all bills in the end. Billy was also one of the few people to record in detail the intriguing details of the relationship between Piaf and the man who had realized her potential as an actress – Jean Cocteau.

The poet would dine at number 4 rue de Villejust two or three times a week, often in company with some of the best-known stage personalities of the day, such as Marie Bell, Michèle Morgan, Madeleine Robinson and Michel Simon, that most loved of ugly actors who had been brought up in a brothel himself and never failed to say what good mothers the girls made. But apparently, despite the number of dinner guests, 'Edith and Jean were alone'. Their particular intimacy isolated them from the others, and who could resist their hostess's recollection:

'Jean Cocteau had eyes for (Edith) alone. Edith saw only him. She had become a little girl again, well behaved, eager to learn and understand. They were united by the same love of poetry. Jean would often recite his own texts. When Edith did not understand she would ask him to explain, without any false shame. He would do so patiently, translating the ideas concealed behind the words, indicating the meaning of the images.'

No wonder, on evenings when Cocteau was there, that Madame Billy would leave the hard work to her domestic staff, for she could not bear to miss one moment of the interplay between the two *monstres sacrés*. 'When Edith was feeling in good form she would sometimes act parts of *Le Bel indifférent*. It was her way of saying thank you to her poet. One evening, in order to give him a surprise, she recited to him *L'Endroit et l'envers*, a poem Cocteau had written in the 1920s. It began like this:

Je vois la mort en bas, du haut de ce bel âge
Où je me trouve, hélas! au milieu du voyage ...

Death was in fact alive and made up the texture of our fabric. 'Edith could not know, as she spoke these lines, that she was making a premonitory gesture and that death would carry them away, twenty years later, within a few hours of each other. Together.'

This was far from being a one-sided relationship. Both Cocteau and Piaf possessed extraordinary powers of seduction and in this case Cocteau's mysterious and irresistible charm had encountered someone who wanted to be charmed. 'In the poet's hands she was like a plaything, an amorous plaything. When he was there, she was no longer with us. She was a violin vibrating beneath a magic bow. They were in communion. She would have gone without everything in order to hear him talk.'

His presence transformed her as nothing else did, except the stage. 'In Cocteau's presence she was as beautiful as when she sang. She was no longer the same woman. A mysterious radiance emanated from her. It gave you gooseflesh.' Cocteau was not merely the admired poet, the sublimated lover, he was Edith's teacher and adviser. As Madame Billy said: 'I think he was the only man who came so close to her, so close to her sensibility.'

Late in 1943 Edith told her landlady that she would be leaving. The house was busier than ever and Edith's professional visitors might not have understood what all the business was about. Billy missed her and was distressed some time later when visiting her former protégée in a rented house in Boulogne.

Edith had installed a camp-bed in the kitchen and surrounded it with bottles of wine, maintaining that life was easier that way. She had forgotten her promise to Henri Contet that she would drink only mineral water: all her close friends or lovers had the same experience. The other rooms in the house were empty, while the salon contained a piano, three chairs and a deck-chair.

Yet life was far from empty for Edith. She went to sing to French prisoners of war in Germany, accompanied by her secretary Andrée Bigard who, under cover of Edith's popularity, was carrying out a remarkable clandestine operation. She arranged for Edith to be photographed with the 120 prisoners for whom she was officially 'god-mother' and then, with the help of a skilful photographer in Paris, prepared false identity papers for each man in the group. On the next trip the prisoners were given the papers, and all they had to do was to escape, which many of them did. A little later the camp was bombed, and something had to be done to help the families of the victims. Edith succeeded in persuading Sacha Guitry, the doyen of French actors, to conduct an auction at a benefit gala. The results were stupendous, all due to Edith's power of persuasion and her great popularity.

On a later occasion Edith did not wait for any official invitation to Germany, she decided to go again and sing for French prisoners, a visit notable for the way she dealt with the German officers and the so-called hospitality her group received. She refused the German invitations or blandishments and complained about the conditions in which she and her small troup were expected to stay. Such was her power that she won all the concessions she asked for.

Her personal life was, as usual, complex. Henri Contet was officially her lover, but he infuriated her by failing to leave his wife, Charlotte Dauvia, who was also a singer. She had found out what was happening and, at her own request, met Edith. Nobody left anybody, and Edith, with cynical and catty politeness, would sometimes ask Henti, as he was leaving her, to pass on her greetings to Charlotte. Henri continued to love Edith and to write songs for her.

In 1944 and 1945 when she herself was twenty-nine, and then nearly thirty, Edith now lost her two very different parents.

On 3 March 1944, that *enfant de la balle*, Louis-Alphonse Gassion, died at his home in the rue Rébeval in Belleville. He was sixty-two. Edith, not knowing how best to help him, had insisted that he should have a manservant, whom she paid, but it is not clear whether Gassion père knew how to employ him. He had received the last rites and was subsequently given a very proper funeral in the local church of Saint-Jean-Baptiste in Belleville. The choir stalls were draped in regulation black, there was a black carpet and the whole family attended. Denise Gassion remembered the day well, for it was her thirteenth birthday. Tante Zaza and Tante Mathilde came from Normandy and the funeral cards were sent out with many names on them, starting of course with those of the three Gassion children, Edith, Denise and Herbert. Later, Edith would go regularly to the grave and leave bunches of violets there. On the evening of the funeral she sang as usual, her audiences expected her to do so, and in one sense this was the best way in which Edith could honour her father's memory.

The following year, on 6 February, Edith's mother Line Marsa, who was barely fifty died, hardly *une mort très douce*, and one which Edith succeeded in ignoring. The newspaper report makes macabre reading. The concierge at 25 rue Elysée-des-Beaux-Arts saw one of her tenants, André Comès, a forty-four-year-old *artiste lyrique*, carrying downstairs a vast bundle 'which had a human shape'. He placed it in a ground floor bedroom and disappeared. The concierge investigated. The bundle contained the body of 'Madame Anetta Maillard, aged fifty of Italian origin, mother of the singer Edith Piaf'. She had apparently died in André Comès's apartment after a drug overdose. The body was later found in the street outside and taken to the morgue.

Edith had never lost touch with her father, she had helped him, she loved him. She had not loved the unstable woman who had deserted her husband and baby daughter and then spent years drifting about the streets of Paris and elsewhere attempting to earn some sort of living by singing. Anything she earned was spent on drink and drugs. She was said to have visited Turkey, as Fréhel had done, for Westerners were welcome there and drugs were unfortunately available. She had had some minor success, and when Edith was looking for work she had seen her photograph displayed in small clubs and been told to come back when she could sing as well as Line had done.

Unfortunately the unhappy woman became so destitute that the Paris police classed her as a vagrant and during the Occupation she found herself in and out of prison. There she met someone even more famous than her daughter, the film star Arletty, detained because she had fraternized too openly with admiring German officers. Arletty apparently believed Line Marsa's stories but they were not true. Through her secretary Andrée Bigard Edith regularly sent her all the things she so desperately needed: money, food, soap and other basic necessities. Line Marsa, signing herself Jacqueline Maillard, wrote endless begging letters, which Edith eventually gave to her trusted friend and helper Danielle Vignault, a former classical dancer who married Edith's accordionist Marc Bonel. In 1993 Danielle decided to publish some of them in the book she wrote with her husband, so that 'readers could make up their own minds' about the wretched existence of Line Marsa and Edith's attitude towards her. When not in detention the failed singer would occasionally try to approach her daughter outside various theatres or music halls but she received no reaction from Edith and no support from the public.

Predictably, Edith was in no mood to take any responsibility in this situation and it was left to Henri Contet to make the funeral arrangements. Line Marsa was buried at the paupers' cemetery of Thiais and according to Edith in her autobiography, *Au bal de la chance*, she joined her own little daughter Marcelle. So ended the *chanteuse réaliste* who is known to us merely through a few publicity photographs, in which she nearly always looks very cheerful, a few music covers, and the titles of her songs, some with evocative titles: *Pour que ça vous attache, La dernière cigarette, Filles de joie, Mon tour de Java, Tu as besoin de moi, Valse en mineur*. If Edith had not been able to love her mother, she at least included, or allowed her collaborators to include in her early autobiography, *Au bal de la chance*, a kind of obituary. Her mother, she said 'had show business in her blood; her parents had roamed Algeria with their small travelling circus. My mother had come to Paris hoping to make her name as a singer but she never progressed beyond singing in cafés. I have always believed that she failed not through any lack of talent, but because luck was not on her side, and that Fate, in atonement, led me to the career of which she had dreamed.' Line Marsa may not have loved her daughter but she had left her a legacy beyond price – a voice that was, and remains, individual, inimitable. Denise Gassion has said that when Edith had begun to be successful she had seen her mother from time to time, and that Piaf money had helped the morale of both of them. But the period of tolerance appears to have been short, and her mother's name was not added to the family tomb in the cemetery of Père Lachaise.

The military map of Europe had changed, there was tense hope in the corners of the Resistance movement and French culture and theatrical life had somehow survived. The German writer Ernst Jünger has told, in his *Journal Parisien*, some strange stories of literary life in its most lofty reaches while some writers even of international stature were attacked as collaborators, and 1944 produced some outstanding and very different literary events, such as the production of Sartre's *Huis clos* and Jean Genet's *Notre Dame des Fleurs*. In 1945 Edith herself succeeded in recording only half a dozen songs but she was constantly busy and had even given the first ever concert of *la chanson populaire* at the Salle Pleyel, usually associated only with classical music. She could almost have said, as the Liberation and the end of hostilities approached, 'Oh what a lovely war', for she had become gradually better known, she had found first-rate composers and lyric-writers, and very few rivals, even if Léo Marjane had sometimes been mentioned as a rising star. Marjane's behaviour during the Occupation had however done her harm in the end.

Edith had kept the continuity of her songs and her stage personality with great care, and such was her own nature and style that she could hardly have changed in any case. Damia had given up her black dress and suddenly appeared wearing white, but not so Edith, even if her black dresses were now as well cut as war conditions allowed. She was so successful that she was said to earn as much in one evening as an average office-worker earned in a whole year, a fact which led to her being denounced by some as a symbol of decadence, an accusation which she answered in her usual unprintable terms.

But the atmosphere of 1944–5, chaotic as it was, probably suited Edith for that very reason. It produced at least one unexpected musical success for her. A singer named Roland Gerbeau, who was already quite well known in France, had the good luck to meet her one day in the Champs-Elysées. She told him she had a marvellous song for him, and if he wanted to sing it she would give it to him. She herself had written the words, and also the music, or at least the melody, but vis-à-vis the S.A.C.E.M. she did not yet have the right to call herself a composer and so could not sign the music as her own. At first the musicians she approached, including Marguerite Monnot, had not cared for her musical idea. In the end it was 'Louiguy', an old associate of Spanish origin, who agreed to lend his name as the composer of the song. Roland Gerbeau sang it, so did Marianne Michel, and *La Vie en rose* was such a success that Edith eventually sang it herself. She had not cared too much for her own idea because the song did not tell a story, and of course it was sentimental. The public certainly cared, and the song obviously appeared at the right moment, although Edith did not record it until 1946 and then its success was sensational, so much so that it remains one of the few Piaf songs well known outside the French-speaking world.

She qualified in her second attempt to be a member of the S.A.C.E.M.; in her case it meant composing a song on the title 'Rue de la Gare', recalling the address of a well-known recording studio in the boulevard of the same name. At the same time a young man called Louis Barrier, who had some experience with an agency that ran the shows at the Alhambra, asked if he could be her exclusive agent. She liked him, and was amused that he had forgotten to remove his trouser-clips, having left his bicycle outside. He was to be her agent and friend the rest of her life.

The end of the war and its immediate aftermath brought other important new developments into Edith's life, for she met the only one of her show-business lovers destined to acquire an international reputation as a singer and a screen actor. This was a young man who had already chosen a stage-name for himself, Yves Montand, six years younger than herself. His family, named Livi, had left Italy for Marseilles before the war to escape Mussolini's anti-semitic policy. He had supported himself with a variety of jobs from metallurgy to hairdressing but it was his admiration for Fred Astaire that had led him to the music-hall. In Marseilles audiences had liked his American-style songs for as Europe waited desperately for a second front, America and all that it stood for was immensely fashionable. He had begun to appear in Paris, and Edith at least knew of him, even if she had not been interested enough to hear him sing.

In the late summer of 1944 however, she was in need of a presentable singer who had to be available at short notice. She had been engaged to occupy the second half of a programme at the

Moulin Rouge in the Place Blanche but a few days before the show was due to open the singer who had been booked as *vedette américaine*, i.e. appearing just before the interval, had unaccountably vanished, and unless he was replaced the whole show would probably be cancelled. Various candidates were offered by agents but most of them did not appeal to Edith, so she reluctantly agreed to give Montand an audition. It was decided that they would both come to the Moulin Rouge one morning and would both sing. He was fascinated by the woman and her singing, he remembered that Edith was wearing a summer dress with a pattern of blue flowers. And while he was fascinated, she was impressed, to her own surprise, and included her memories in *Au Bal de la chance*. She found him a 'terrific personality', she noted 'an impression of power and strength, hands that were eloquent, powerful, admirable, a handsome, tormented face'. She described, memorably, how, after four of his songs, she left her seat and went, forward to the edge of the stage. 'He came up to the footlights.' She remembered vividly the contrast between them: she was tiny, he was tall, she looked up at him, her face 'more or less level with his ankles. I told him he was *formidable* and that it could certainly be predicted that he would have a magnificent career.'

Within a week they were lovers, but there was one problem: she did not like his songs, she saw no point in a singer pretending to be a cowboy and dreaming of the Far West. Edith was nearly thirty now, she could no longer leave singers to do what they liked; if they worked close to her, they must do what *she* liked, a pattern she would now follow for the rest of her life. So Montand must change, throw away those pseudo-Stetsons and checked shirts, and sing something worthwhile in his own style. She was determined to help him find what that style was, and from now on she developed her own style as a Pygmalion. She had had some practice when she was staying with Madame Billy in trying to make Yvon Jean-Claude into a singer, but her success had been limited. Montand was obviously good material, and she made him work as no hopeful singer had ever worked before, changing his pronunciation, his gestures, his clothes, everything. After being made to talk with a pencil in his mouth he lost his Marseilles accent. And what about some goods songs? She wrote four for him herself, including *Sophie* and *Le Balayeur*. After all, there was a librettist near to hand, Heni Contet, still her 'official' lover. If Henri suspected she was being unfaithful to him, he would still do anything to please her, and he wrote for her 'discovery' *Gilet rayé, Ma gosse, ma petite môme*, which latter had been intended for Maurice Chevalier. But Henri did as Edith wanted, and Montand got the song.

She took her successful trainee on tour with her, and Contet came too. Apparently he would share the bedroom with her while Montand shared the stage. Edith met Montand's family and his sister Lydia asked him directly if he was thinking of marrying her. She was told to mind her own business. Contet, who was of course still married, did not leave the scene, continued to suspect what went on between Edith and Yves but did not ask direct questions. Eventually Montand admitted what was happening. Gradually, too, Edith had realized that she could teach her young admirer no more, but she was reluctant to dismiss him. They were both successful at L'Etoile, but she behaved mysteriously for a time and eventually it was all over, she moved on. Montand had learnt all she could teach him but he still loved her and wanted to stay close to her.

In the meantime Edith insisted that Montand should be given a part in the film in which she was taking part in 1945, *Etoile sans lumière*, which Marcel Blistène was making. She always said this was her favourite film out of the handful she made, and its subject was historically interesting even then: when the 'talkies' arrive in 1930, a star of the silent screen has to have a 'double' with a voice, for hers does not pass the test. The double, played by Edith, is not satisfied to remain a 'star without light', she branches out, deserts her fiancé in the hopes of impressing someone more glamorous. Eventually she is disillusioned and returns to the man she had first chosen as her fiancé: played by Montand. This surely forgotten film was a great success both in Europe and the US and was eventually made into a video-cassette. Edith referred to it later as her favourite among the few in which she both sang and acted. Montand's future career in film was in fact due to Edith, even though he realized he was losing her. Everyone in Paris knew the current gossip about Jean Gabin and Marlene Dietrich: they imagined themselves deeply in love, so much so that they felt they could not appear in Marcel Carné's new film, *Les Portes de la nuit*. Edith saw a chance for Montand, she persuaded Carné to give him a film test and in the end he won the part intended for Gabin. Unfortunately the film was poorly received by the critics, but Montand the screen actor never looked back.

Years later Simone Signoret, Yves Montand's wife since 1951, wrote that he was deeply hurt when Edith left him, for they had enjoyed good times together. She had not taught him everything, for 'one already has within oneself the things that no one can teach anyone'. The pattern of Piaf's behaviour was set in love as with everything else: 'And then, as soon as he began to fly with his own wings and choose his own songs, or not to want to sing those that Edith wanted him to sing, she left him. Since he loved her, and since he also liked to laugh with her – because you laugh a lot with Edith and you laugh well – he had been very unhappy for a long time'.

What happened to Henri Contet, one of the most understanding and perceptive people in Edith's life? He was never far away, and if Edith had now dismissed Montand, having taken a fancy to someone else, she still needed Henri for the supply of words, meaningful words, for her songs, and he continued to write them for her for the rest of her life. 1951 brought *Padam ... padam ...* and *Opinion publique*, one of her more sophisticated creations, won the Grand Prix de l'Académie du Disque in 1952. *Bravo pour le clown*, created in the following year, became one of the most successful items in Edith's repertoire, while Contet was still so devoted to her that in 1959 he collaborated with her one-time lover Moustaki to write *T'es beau, tu sais*. The last song he wrote for her seems to have been *Le vieux piano*, which she attempted to record in 1960 but her health was not good enough at the time.

Henri understood a great deal about Edith, and why she behaved as she did. She was unfaithful to her lovers with her songs, he said. Songs mattered to her more than anything or anyone else, because they created her, just as much as she created them.

No Sagittarian, say the astrologers and Edith certainly believed it, could lead a quiet life, there must always be something happening. The disappearance of Montand the lover was taking place while Edith was making new discoveries among music and men. She encountered the group of eight, very soon increased to nine young men who were suddenly very popular in France and in Europe generally: Les Compagnons de la Chanson. They had first called themselves Les Compagnons de la Musique and during service with the army they had sung mainly songs from French folklore, carefully harmonized for their three tenor, three baritone and three bass voices. They apparently met Edith during their first gala performance in Paris which was interrupted by an air-raid alert. Their first successes were at the A.B.C. and they were soon so much in demand that they are said to have given no fewer than twenty-two shows in four days, although not, obviously, at large music-halls.

Edith wanted them to appear in the same programme as herself at L'Etoile and as usual could not refrain from 'improving' their presentation in some way, telling them that folklore would never earn them big money. However, she had been impressed by a song she had heard in Switzerland, *Les trois cloches*, and

83

wanted them to sing it. They were not too keen on it, but then Jean Cocteau was asked to listen and give his opinion. He compared the men's voices to the sound of a bell cast in bronze and gold with Edith's voice running through it like a vein of agate. So they had to sing it. Edith then made them a rare offer: she would sing it with them, and so of course they then became enthusiastic. The group had once taken on two girl singers and soon sacked them on the advice of the critics, but nobody could resist Piaf, whose name on a programme always boosted audiences. She appeared in a full-length pale blue dress while the men wore their usual white shirts and blue trousers.

The song, though always successful, nowadays seems unoriginal and sentimental, merely telling the story of Jean-François Nicot (Jimmy Brown in the translation), how he was born, married and died in his valley. However, Edith presumably liked this minimal story and its air of religiosity, preferring it to many of the more folksy items in which Les Compagnons specialized. In 1946 she recorded it and a few other songs she sang with the group while she also took the group's leader, Jean-Louis Jaubert, as her lover. The following year she toured with the group and made a film with them, *Neuf garçons, un coeur*, in which impoverished singers long for their dreams to come true; they do so, of course. Everyone sang. Edith sang several of her own songs, including *Sophie, Un refrain courait dans la rue*, and *La Vie en rose*. She joined them in *Les trois cloches* and in the Contet-Monnot song *C'est pour ça* in which love reconciles two lovers.

Just before Louis Barrier became her exclusive agent Edith had been represented briefly by a group called the Organisation Sportive et Artistique which also handled arrangements for sporting personalities. It was run through Le Club des Cinq, which had grown out of wartime friendships in North Africa and later transferred itself to Paris where it took over a large basement room in the faubourg Montmartre and turned itself into a high-class night club. It controlled the rights of such different people or groups as Les Compagnons de la Chanson, Aimé Barelli's orchestra, Edith Piaf and the Algerian-born boxer Marcel Cerdan. Michel Emer, who had already composed several successful songs for Edith, conducted an enthusiastic swing band which always brought everyone on to the dance floor very quickly, especially as Emer's favourite number at the time was *In the Mood*. The club had its own song, '*Ils étaient cinq, cinq, cinq, Comme les cinq doigts de la main*': of no distinction whatsoever, but the place was soon a great success, with well-known stars, including Edith, appearing in the cabaret every evening.

'In Paris', wrote Irwin Shaw in 1976, 'everything begins and ends at a café table'. Almost everything, perhaps. The relationship between Piaf and the boxer Marcel Cerdan, which over fifty years later still preoccupies writers, journalists and film directors, certainly began at a table in the Club des Cinq, but it did not blossom suddenly against the background of Michel Emer's band, it began more dangerously in a low key, liable to make it last longer. They were not immediately starry-eyed about each other. Cerdan admired the singer and Piaf found him pleasant and good-mannered, even if he was not tall or especially handsome and had a surprisingly high-pitched voice.

From Sidi-bel-Abbès in Algeria, home of the Foreign Legion, the journey to Paris is fairly long, but Cerdan, who had been born there in 1916, first travelled to Paris when he was twenty-one. His father was a Spaniard who had a French wife, five children, no money and a variety of jobs. At one time he drove tourists about in a fiacre but in 1922 he moved to Casablanca in Morocco to work as a butcher. All his sons were interested in boxing, but the eldest, Vincent, gave it up for a business career in Argentina and the youngest, Armand, apparently the most promising boxer of all four brothers, had to give up the sport following a football accident.

Football was Marcel's favourite game too, but as his friend and sparring partner Maurice Rouff remembered, that did not bring any money into the family of seven. Fortunately Marcel showed so much aptitude as a boxer from the age of eight that his father soon had ideas about how the boy could help to support the family. By good luck Cerdan senior met a Parisian, Lucien Roupp, who had opened a gymnasium above his garage. Marcel became one of his recruits and very soon began to win any amateur fight that came along. His father acted as his manager for some time until Roupp himself took over and between 1933 and the autumn of 1937 he won every contest arranged for him in any North African country. He then began to fight in the European capitals and the only time he lost was in January 1939 when he fought Harry Craster in London and was disqualified for allegedly hitting below the belt.

Cerdan had known fame early because in 1939 he became European middleweight champion in Milan. He was so popular at the time that his fans blocked the streets of the town for half the night and tore his pale blue dressing-gown into shreds for souvenirs. He was not led astray by this hero-worship, but unfortunately the period of his greatest potential skill coincided with the Second World War, when he was in the French Navy for a time. There was no chance for him to meet a worthwhile opponent until the US forces landed in North Africa. His stays in Paris after the war brought him to the Club des Cinq, which he enjoyed, especially because he was an expert ballroom dancer and had even won prizes for his performances. Then came his chance to go to New York. In December 1946 he fought Georgie Abrams at Madison Square Garden and won on points after ten rounds. The many celebrities at the ringside included Frank Sinatra and the French singer Jean Sablon. This seems to have been a tough fight, for the photographs of the two bleeding, bleary-eyed protagonists afterwards could be described as supplying effective propaganda for the suppression of boxing.

However, back in Paris the members of the Club des Cinq crowded round the radio with champagne at the ready, and among the many telegrams received by Cerdan in New York was one which read simply: 'Bravo, Marcel, I knew it all along. Edith.'

5

New life, new love

As soon as the war ended all successful entertainment stars in Europe hoped for engagements in the US and Louis Barrier began to arrange them for Edith as soon as he could. There were to be various appearance in the French provinces first and then, in the summer of 1946, a visit to Athens, to coincide with the premiere of the film *Etoile sans lumière*. The venue, where the show never began before midnight, was a glamorous cabaret, the Miami, where the stage was in the open air, with tables arranged by the surrounding hedges. Edith was not too successful, for Greece was in the midst of political upheavals and nobody had told her that audiences in Athens were accustomed to seeing star performers at the start of the show and not at the end, as in France.

But in Athens she lived through a romantic drama of her own. An unknown admirer was leaving flowers for her every night, but he never appeared. Then, as she remembered or perhaps half-invented, in *Ma Vie*, 'one night he came', and Takis Menelas, who was an actor, was well cast. 'Tall, with dark curly hair, proud and romantic ... He took me to the foot of the Acropolis ... The moonlight, the sound of singing that rose from the town and the voice of Takis beside me, a warm, vibrant voice ... I felt like a young girl hearing a declaration of love for the first time'. He begged her to stay in Athens, he would get a divorce, they would be married. 'But I didn't believe him. I'd thrown away love so often myself that I didn't believe in anything any more, except perhaps in pleasure'. She realized later that she had 'passed happiness by'. It was her own fault, she lacked confidence, she said. Takis Menelas never forgot her.

One can imagine Edith taking a deep breath, embarking on a tour of the provinces, appearing at the Théâtre de l'Etoile, then Switzerland, Brussels, next, accompanied by the Compagnons de la Chanson, a tour of Scandinavia, three weeks in Norway, then Stockholm and Göteborg in Sweden. Edith and her party reached Norway by ice-breaker, a memorable trip, and if she was successful, despite the fact that no one in the audience understood French, and were dependent on commentaries and translations, she hated the food. There was no bread and the group had to rely on smoked fish and the cans of vegetables which Danielle heated up on a paraffin stove in the hotel bedrooms or bathrooms.

Then, at last, the *Queen Mary* took the party to New York, after they had first journeyed to London and Southampton via Le Havre.

She made her New York début on 30 October at the Playhouse, the big Broadway music hall, with the Compagnons at the close of the first part. They were well received, but she remained a disappointing mystery to this first American audience. They had assumed that any woman singer from Paris would be glamorous, singing romantic songs about love and gaiety, songs with sentimental or sexy themes. This small woman in her plain black dress did not entertain them at all. It took a forthright article by Virgil Thomson in the *New York Times* to put them right. He understood Edith and her background very well: 'Miss Piaf presents the art of the chansonnière at its most classical. The vocalism is styled and powerful. Her diction is clarity itself.' There followed a picture of Edith as vivid as any photograph: 'She stands in the middle of the stage in the classical black dress of medium length ...' The journalist placed Piaf in context:

she followed Yvette Guilbert, Polaire and Damia. 'She is not tense, but intense. In no way spontaneous, just thoroughly concentrated and impersonal'. He referred to her sparing use of gestures and found that 'Her power of dramatic projection' was 'tremendous'. 'She is a great artiste because she gives you a clear vision of the scene or subject she is depicting, with a minimum injection of personality'.

This knowledgeable, understanding piece was helpful to Edith, although she was disappointed by her reception. She envied the success of the Compagnons, whose folklore style was more understandable to the Americans, but after six weeks at the Playhouse she found herself in a much more congenial atmosphere: the Versailles (also in Broadway), a restaurant-cabaret where many French singers had already appeared. It was not a suitable venue for the Compagnons, who set out on a tour across the country. For Edith, whose name was known to the francophile guests for they had seen her in the film *Etoile sans lumière*, it was ideal. She was encouraged to prepare some songs in English, which she did, accepting various adaptations by American librettists, and she spent a good deal of time studying English. The Versailles management also helped her by having a special platform built on the stage, which meant that she could be seen more clearly by more people in the audience, and she could see them.

Seeing people, more especially meeting and talking to them, transformed Edith's visits to the States and South America, and made them into something more important to her than a repetition of her provincial tours in France and the neighbouring European countries. She made friends early with Marlene Dietrich who became more than a friend, a kind of mother-figure for her. Later, Dietrich's younger daughter, Maria Riva, suggested in a book about her mother that the two women had a lesbian relationship. Danielle Bonel and others in Paris were stunned by the revelation. 'Of course', wrote the daughter, 'my

mother succumbed to Piaf's charm and as always happened
when she was in love, she took her under her wing, overwhelmed her with gifts, gave her advice and found the drugs
that her new flame needed'. Danielle quoted these remarks
and readers will wonder how far Dietrich's 'love' was maternal.
In a sense it was, but it can never be proved that Dietrich found
'drugs' for her new friend. She may have done so, or she may
simply have supplied 'drugs' in the form of medicine, but it
has to be admitted that when Edith died Marlene felt guilty
about neglecting her in her later struggles with alcoholism
and the hard 'drugs' that were enhanced pain-killers. Whatever
the relationship between the two women it seems to bear out
in an odd way the judgement once pronounced by Kenneth
Tynan: 'Dietrich's masculinity appealed to women and her
sexuality to men'.

Edith's friendships with American stars, some close, some
fleeting, have been publicized by many cheerful photographs
showing her with a whole gallery of successful people, women
and men, including, as the 1950s passed, Lena Horne, Leslie
Caron, Danny Kaye, Rock Hudson, Claudette Colbert, and
one star whose friendly charm impressed her in particular:
Charlie Chaplin. He said he would a write a song for her, she
was convinced he would, one day.

Edith was fascinated by success and popularity, she felt proud
of her own achievements, proud to be accepted by these people
who had all worked hard to achieve their names in permanent
lights. Some had known harsh backgrounds, but none, perhaps,
as harsh as her own. She realized that she could only achieve a
reputation in the US and in other countries where French
remained an unknown language, if she learnt to sing in good
English. She worked hard at the language, learning it quickly
and, as far as singing was concerned, giving the words all the
clarity they deserved, as she did with any libretto in French. She
could not resist teaching scraps of French to her English teacher,

concentrating on bad jokes and obscene words, something which appealed to her love of practical jokes, popular at the time and never out of fashion in France.

When she was in North America Edith did not spend her entire free time in the company of show-business friends or with her English teacher. Seeing the sights, or visiting art galleries or museums did not interest her at all, although she was not averse to shopping, especially when accompanied by her young friend Ginette Richer. When her engagements took her to Canada she visited her half-sister Denise, now married with a young family. She also went to see someone whose work in France had impressed her, the Abbé Pierre, who had helped thousands of unemployed and homeless people to experience something of a near-normal life, She never forgot her own teenage years, even, if her own way of helping the under-privileged was always spontaneous and in no way organized. Danielle, her long-time companion and helper, was to say later, after accompanying Edith on many American tours, that she always seemed more relaxed when a long way from Paris: she was more sure of herself and not distracted by the hangers-on who amused her but drained her energy.

At the same time various situations, and various men, did distract her. If Jean-Louis Jaubert was still her lover he was often away on tour with Les Compagnons, who were popular wherever they went. It was only to be expected that Edith, the star singer from Paris, would be attractive to many Americans. One of them, the actor John Garfield, was indeed attracted to her, and she might have been ready to respond, but he got his act wrong. Garfield is best remembered now for his screen perfor-mance in *The Postman Always Rings Twice* but Edith had been impressed when she saw him in the theatre playing Hamlet. Later he was invited to a supper party she gave in her hotel for a number of show-business people. In *Ma Vie* she described what happened after she had accompanied her guests to the door at the end of the evening: 'when I came back to the drawing-room John had disappeared. I looked for him everywhere and finally I found him, very sure of himself, lying on my bed, smoking a cigarette and completely naked'. Edith was shocked and disgusted. She always wanted some signs of love, not just a crude display of sexual attributes. 'I threw his clothes in his face and chucked him out, then I flung myself on my bed in tears and swore I'd turn over a new leaf.'

That leaf was turned during the last years of the 1940s.

Edith had not forgotten Marcel Cerdan, the gentle, well-mannered boxer, who was often in the US and gaining popularity all the time. Their engagements had kept them apart for a long time, but now, in New York, they finally came together, and it looked as though La Vie en rose was really happening, and the faithful husband Marcel temporarily forgot his faithful wife Marinette who hated boxing. The press were quietly bribed to keep this entanglement out of the newspapers, in case the public were shocked. The men who managed Cerdan thought nothing of the relationship, for they knew their man was not particularly strong-minded and his motivation to fight was not as firm as they wanted it to be: had he not once 'forgotten' a fight in Europe and gone off on a lion-hunt in the Atlas mountains? They had to watch him, but they obviously could not prevent the crowd at an amusement park from recognizing the lovers one day. Edith was asked to sing, and Cerdan marvelled at the degree of pleasure she gave to her audience, even in the open air. However, he too became popular enough, especially after defeating the Estonian Anton Raadik in Chicago on points, after ten tough rounds. He did not have an easy time when he met the Texan, Lavern Roach, in New York, the following year, 1948. Everyone thought the fight was over in the second round when Roach seemed incapable of getting up after one of Cerdan's formidable left hooks. The French managerial camp had been fairly sure that the American referee would favour Roach and apparently the latter was inexplicably allowed twenty seconds before getting up. The fight went on until the seventh round, after which nobody could maintain any longer that Cerdan was not the winner. The combat was officially listed as 'abandoned' and both the American and the French boxing press made outspoken comments about the long count, which established an unfortunate record.

Luckily Edith's audiences never tired of her old songs, for Edith, her success constantly growing worldwide, was too busy travelling and too occupied emotionally to take on many new numbers. Her life did not, could not consist entirely of meetings with Cerdan in New York or in the house she had bought in Boulogne, Paris. In 1948 she was invited to the Carrère nightclub to sing before the then Princess Elizabeth of England and her husband, who were visiting the capital. If we can know nothing of the present Queen Elizabeth's reaction there is no shortage of amusing detail in the account that Edith gave to her friend Marcel Blistène. The princess was much more photogenic than she appeared in the news films. 'Frankly, if she had a film make-up man she could be an amazing star.' As for Prince Philip, Gary Cooper and Clark Gable were nothing in comparison. He was charming, distinguished, unaffected. The future Queen of England was lucky in her destiny and in her husband. The thing that impressed Edith most was the fact that King George VI wanted to own her records. Lord Bessborough, who had been asked by Sir Oliver Harvey, the British Ambassador, to be host, remembers that the then princess enjoyed herself very much that evening. Edith maintained later that she was not really at her best that evening for she had already sung at a matinée plus one later performance and kept on telling the princess so, although the latter assured the singer how much she had enjoyed the performance.

The audience in these elegant surroundings probably heard three new songs: *Les Amants de Paris*, *Il pleut* and *Monsieur*

Lenoble, the last two being far from cheerful. Monsieur Lenoble had come to a sad end for he had accepted too much for granted and not taken the trouble to make his wife happy.

Despite their attempts at discreet behaviour, Marcel's visits to his family in Casablanca and Edith's remarks that they were just good friends, their infatuation with each other was only too well known to journalists in France and anecdotes began to circulate, as in fact they are still doing nearly forty years later. Sometimes Edith appeared more ready for action than her lover did. Once, when they returned from the US to Orly airport on the same plane they left by different exits, but when Edith found herself pursued by a hopeful photographer she called out to Marcel to smash his face in. However, the boxer avoided any such confrontation. On a later occasion, though, according to Dominique Grimault and Patrick Mahé, Cerdan, angered by the gossip, summoned a journalist to the house they had bought together and asked him if he had given Edith's private telephone number to the newspaper *France-Dimanche*. The journalist admitted he had. With lightning speed Cerdan administered the 'punishment' he thought fitting. The journalist remained on his feet, but fled. He said later that the interview had lasted exactly fifteen seconds.

In May 1948 Cerdan lost his title as European middleweight champion, on points, to the Belgian Cyrille Delannoit in Brussels, and shortly afterwards *France-Dimanche* launched the rumour that Piaf brought Cerdan bad luck. However, two months later Cerdan had beaten Delannoit and won the title back again. Edith had arranged to sing in Brussels at the time of the fight but to the relief of the boxer's entourage she did not go to watch it. Edith's friends had never seen her so happy, but Yves Montand had already warned Cerdan's manager about the danger of a takeover bid by Edith – she simply could not help it, for with her, love inevitably led to attempted domination. For the time being she restrained herself, merely taking Cerdan to

pray to Saint Thérèse at Lisieux; the lovers, suitably chaper-
oned and accompanied by the training staff, spent a few happy
days at Oullins, very near Anet in the Eure-et-Loir.

Edith however was immensely happy, as photographs of the
period show, trying to educate the long-suffering Cerdan whenever she had a chance, giving him the regulation suits and gold
jewellery, knitting pullovers in hideous colours which found
their way into his suitcases but not on to his person for she
hardly ever finished them. On the whole he did not think much
of the clothes she wore off the stage but presumably he had to
accept the celluloid ducks she bought him for his bath.

Perhaps neither of them remembered, or ever knew, that Jack
Doyle, the Irish heavyweight boxer of the 1930s, suddenly
decided at one point that he would burst into song. However,
this did not do him much good, and the poet Vernon Scannell,
a sports writer at the time, has quoted what was said of him: 'he
sang like Dempsey and boxed like Caruso'. Fortunately even
Edith did not consider making her boxing champion into a
singer – her ambitious Pygmalionism did not extend so far –
and in any case Cerdan, however much he might have been in
love, would never have given her the chance.

She did try to educate him, giving him the 'right' books to
read. André Gide puzzled him; was he not 'un peu pédé?' And
she begged him to get rid of his gold teeth, fashionable at the
time. She preferred them to be white.

The biggest of his big fights was in September 1948 when he
met Tony Zale at the Roosevelt Stadium in Jersey City. His
manager insisted on a serious training programme out of town,
at Loch Sheldrake in the Catskill mountains, and did not want
Edith to be too close. Her friend Simone Berteaut had arrived,
and such was Edith's persuasive power that the two women
were smuggled into one of the cottages near Marcel's. They
were allowed to meet, but the management made everything
quite plain: no sex, please, we're boxers. Edith obeyed the rules

because she wanted Marcel to be world middleweight champion just as much as she wanted her protégé singers to be top of the bill. Cerdan won, Zale was knocked out after twelve rounds, after which a passionate good time was had by Edith and her lover. She had ordered five hundred red roses for his hotel suite, for she had refused to believe that he could lose. By a cunning move in the inner circles of boxing he was not to receive his prize-money until after a return fight with Zale. Reluctantly he left Edith and went back to Paris, where he was driven round the city through endlessly cheering crowds and later received at the Elysée Palace by President Auriol.

Edith could not give up all her engagements although, she wanted to spend as much time as possible with Marcel. Early in 1949 she sang in Cairo and Alexandria and was photographed riding on a camel. It had been named after Mistinguett, now it was to be called Edith Piaf. Her next appearance was at the Kit-Kat in Beïrut in the Lebanon and she came back to France via Cairo. Unfortunately the Middle Eastern climate had affected her voice badly and she had to cancel some appearances in France, where she should have sung in Rouen and later in Paris, at the A.B.C. She was replaced there by Yves Montand, the singer whom she had done so much to create. When she had recovered sufficiently to sing again in various Provençal venues, Cerdan, who was free of boxing engagements at the time, went with her and watched her performances from the wings.

In his own sphere he continued to be successful. He visited London in March 1949 to meet Dick Turpin at the Empress Hall in Earl's Court and defeated him after seven rounds. Edith is supposed to have come in secret with Cerdan, on one of her very rare visits to England, and stayed with him at the Mayfair Hotel, but no details are known about this trip.

Edith could not care for a man without attempting to organize him in some way. She could not herself make this one into a better boxer but she seemed to think there were ways of arranging better fights and better terms for him. Edith is supposed to have acted behind the scenes in the mafia-like politics behind the disappearance of the faithful Lucien Roupp, and the takeover by the enigmatic Jo Longman. There were even rumours that she was interested in a break-up of the Cerdan ménage in Casablanca, and it was too much to hope that Marinette Cerdan had heard nothing whatever of the whole liaison. Marcel had been asked to take part in a film, *L'Homme aux mains d'argile*, and Edith at first opposed the idea, saying the film would be no good, that the director was not good enough, etc, etc. In the end the film, supposedly based on Marcel's life, was made, and Edith even contributed a song, entitled simply *Paris*. He later made another film in Italy: *Al diavolo la celebrità*. According to his son Marcel, who saw the failure later, they were both bad.

There was an extraordinary incident in New York which might have belonged in some ways to Edith's life in the mid-thirties, the pre-Piaf days, as it were. It was all due to Momone (Simone Berteaut), whom Edith seemed to tolerate because they had lived through such hard times together when they were very young. Momone saw another chance to bite the hand that continually fed her. Since that same hand had written letters to Cerdan and received replies, Momone thought that she might somehow get hold of the letters, which she did, and offer them, for sale of course, to the unfortunate Marinette Cerdan. She also threatened to tell the American press about the Piaf-Cerdan romance, magnifying any sensational aspects she could think of. She then alleged that Cerdan knocked her out and later forced her on to a plane for France. Back in Paris Momone took Cerdan and Piaf to court on the subject. Edith admitted that *she* hit her, and Cerdan pointed out what might have happened if he had administered his left hook. In court Momone finally withdrew her allegations and left with Edith in a taxi, all smiles. One explanation of the story is that Momone was so jealous of Edith that she had to have her own form of revenge. In her later book about Edith she wrote, for good measure, that she herself had met Cerdan long before Edith ever did, on a beach in North Africa.

In mid-June 1949 the unthinkable happened: Cerdan lost his title to Jake La Motta in Detroit, the match being abandoned in the tenth round. Everybody, even the boxer's supporters, were ready to blame Edith for wasting Cerdan's time and generally bringing him bad luck. The two men were due to fight again at the end of the month but the contest was postponed when La Motta complained of a painful shoulder. Edith, back in New York, still wanted Cerdan with her as soon as possible.

The story has been told and contested a dozen times, how she probably telephoned him in France: come back quickly, take a plane, I must see you. He took a plane which never arrived, an Air-France Constellation, due to reach New York in the small hours of 28 October. It crashed against the peak Rodonta on the island of São Miguel in the Azores, the first ever crash on this route for Air France. Nobody survived.

Edith's way of dealing with the tragedy was not to pass the next few days in hysterical weeping. Nobody thought she would go to the Versailles, where she was due to sing, but she did, and announced that she would sing that evening for Marcel Cerdan alone. There have been conflicting accounts of the few songs she sang before collaping on stage: probably *L'Hymne à l'amour*, possibly that evocative song of 1938, *Escale*. The singer meets a sailor on the quayside, they fall in love, but his ship is lost:

Un navire qui s'est perdu
Quant aux marins nul n'en peut plus
Rien dire ...

It ends, as did several of her songs, with a few spoken words:

Le ciel est bas,
La mer est grise.
Ferme la fenêtre à la brise ...

Cerdan, the most popular boxer in France since Georges Carpentier, was given a splendid funeral in Casablanca and the posthumous award of the Legion of Honour. Later a mass held at the Cathedral of Notre-Dame de-Lourdes in Casablanca was attended by 70,000 people.

In the year 2000 Cerdan was remembered by the French postal service in one of a set of stamps recalling famous sports personalities of the previous century. As far as Edith was concerned, the Cerdan story was not yet over. Later French boxing experts, however, hinted that he would probably have lost any return match with La Motta. One dare not speculate on how that might have affected the love-affair which in Edith's memory remained ideal.

Cerdan had been wearing a watch given to him by Edith. It had come from Cartier, the prestigious Paris jeweller and since it was engraved with the initials M.C. it had confirmed the identification of the body. Many watches were stolen from the victims' bodies but this one was given to the Cerdan family and Marcel Cerdan jr. wore it for years, until, he said, he had 'stupidly' lost it. It had stopped at 9 o.clock. 'Morning or evening?' asked a French journalist writing in *L'Equipe*. 'We shall never know.'

Edith soon drew nearer to the Cerdan family, the widow and her three sons. Marcel Junior was to become a young friend and reappears in the story later.

Fifty years after his father's death Marcel, who had by then given up his own boxing career, went to the Azores and climbed up the steep slopes of Mount Rodonta on the island of São Miguel where a cross of volcanic rock, surmounting a simple stele, commemorated the fatal crash. Thirty-seven passengers

and eleven crew members had died after the pilot had presumably mistaken the lights of Provação, a small seaside town, for
those of the airport.

Part Two

Tempo di Valse Moderato

6

The show must go on

Edith did not give up her contract, as some performers might have done, she did not return to Paris, but instead she immediately had something of Paris brought to her. Jacques Bourgeat, the teacher of her younger years, and no longer young himself, was summoned to New York by cable and stayed close to her for two months, during which time, he claimed, he never saw daylight, for he was obliged to live with Edith's timetable, which meant late nights prolonged into early mornings, and late mornings which were already early evenings.

When she did return to Paris early in 1950, Edith not surprisingly went through one of her much publicized black periods, her worst. If she had been accused of bringing Cerdan bad luck in June 1949, she was obviously made to feel deeply guilty now. She survived, supported by her public, living for them and through them more closely than ever, for they did not see her as sinister, as did those in boxing circles. The music-hall public, deeply moved by Edith's tragedy and dimly aware perhaps that many of her songs anticipated this, for nature inevitably imitates art, felt closer to their suffering idol than ever before. They had always realized how deeply her songs and her style expressed the sufferings of her early life, and there was now no escape; she was doomed to suffer, she invited suffering. It was surely the intensity of her personal loss that led to two new songs, with music by Marguerite Monnot: first, *La Chanson bleue*, which was the lamentable product of the new element in Edith's life, her attempt to make contact with the spirit of Marcel Cerdan, on 'the other side'.

She had always been the kind of would-be Catholic who did not attend Mass – she did not like being recognized she said – but faithfully said her prayers every night, with earnest naïveté lit candles to Saint Thérèse who was supposed to have cured her of blindness, and regularly gave medallions of the same saint to her lovers. As soon as she could afford it the medallions were of gold. Saint Thérèse had let her down but her faith was not shaken. However, something more than prayer was needed now, and several people were ready to advise her on how it could be found. Marcel Blistène even said that she had considered taking the veil.

When someone who is dearly loved dies most people eventually accept their disappearance as final. They accept that they must live with memory, and as Benedetto Croce said, memory is immortality. But that was not enough for Edith, she needed Marcel too much, and never before had any lover disappeared from her life until she had ordered him out of it. She had always been the one in charge of any sexual situation and on this occasion she was simply not ready to find herself abandoned, as it were. Obviously she loved Marcel Cerdan *à sa façon*, meaning that the love was far from immortal, for there was very little chance at the age of thirty-five that her long-established emotional pattern would suddenly be transformed. But she could not live without drama, and now there would be a new act in the drama, a new verse to the song.

One of her later lovers believes that she never loved Cerdan so much as she did after his death. Somehow she had to make amends for what looked like her first inefficient piece of stage management, quite apart from the macabre proof of the earlier rumours about bad luck. Since she needed to conclude this relationship on her own terms before moving on to the next one, she needed contact of some sort with the dead man, and several people now explained to her how to establish it.

Ginette Neveu, the outstanding French violinist, had been on that fated plane, with her brother, and suddenly her mother told Edith that she had been in communication with her dead daughter, using the time-worn method of table-rapping. Edith, whose religious belief clearly contained a large measure of superstition, and who had already, it is reported, been influenced by Marlene Dietrich's talk about Allan Kardec and the spirit world, was ready to try anything and immediately bought a suitable table, *un guéridon*, with three legs, and learnt how to use it.

Eventually messages arrived from Cerdan, but it never occurred to Edith that the table did not talk without some help. This was supplied by the person who was always by her side in moments of crisis, Momone, of course, again the apparently faithful but never-to-be-trusted dark angel. How strange that the messages received from the spirit world so often involved money, some to be paid to Momone for the support of her daughter Marcelle, for whom Edith and Marcel had been god-parents. Other beneficiaries included the new presence in Edith's life, Marinette Cerdan, whom she had visited in Casablanca after her first overtures had been refused. The widow's brother-in-law interceded on Edith's behalf; Marinette, receiving her at four o'clock in the morning, had eventually admitted 'a favourable impression'.

Edith seems to have believed, at least for a time, that she was genuinely in touch with her lover, but he did not seem to be much of a song-writer, for *La Chanson bleue*, alleged to have been composed by the 'dead' man, and transmitted through the *guéridon*, has never been highly rated by those who evaluate the Piaf repertoire. This song was not recorded until 1951, for the latter part of 1949 was too occupied with love, travel, boxing and mourning to allow time for any recording sessions. Edith was not to know that Momone would later make no secret about her part in the table-rapping.

Only work and the ready adoration of her public could bring Edith back to life, for despite the affectionate presence of her close friends, her agent, her musicians and domestic staff, she was for a time as 'dead' as the man she had loved so deeply. However, life was not the unending desert waste it had seemed during the previous autumn in New York. New singers and musicians appeared, the young Charles Aznavour became part of her life and was to stay close to her for a long time. As early as April 1950 she was singing at the A.B.C., applauded by her faithful public who soon welcomed her old songs, a few new ones and a changed silhouette, for Edith had decided to adopt a new short hair style. Soon after Cerdan's death she had cut her hair short, saying this would show that she was no longer the same person as she had been before.

The most important of the new songs recorded in 1950 was *L'Hymne à l'amour*, music by Marguerite Monnot and the words by Edith: one verse of eight lines, two of six lines, and a final one of eight again. Piaf was fond of saying about herself *Je suis entière* – total, incapable of compromise – and this is a song of total commitment. There is no precise record that she had written it for Cerdan, as has been assumed, but of course it could be for him or for any of her lovers, and for any listener who feels he or she is totally in love and will stay in love for ever, even if the loved one dies. There is literally hope in heaven:

> *Car moi, je mourrais aussi.*
> *Nous aurons pour nous l'éternité*
> *Dans le bleu de toute l'immensité.*

1950 developed other friendships. During that year Charles Aznavour, whose name, fifty years later, is internationally known, was struggling to become known to more than a handful

of people. He has described amusingly how he first met Edith.
Along with Pierre Roche, a talented pianist from an affluent
upper-crust family, he had been slowly building up a double act.
The partnership had begun during the German occupation and
lasted a long time; but Aznavour could not find enough suitable
songs, and Roche was too lazy to look. So Aznavour began to
write them himself, first the words, then the melody, to which
Roche added the harmony. The song *J'ai bu* was offered to Piaf.
'Too masculine', she said. She was right: how could she have
sung a drunken man's song especially as she was not supposed to
drink herself? It was hard work selling a song to a well-known
artist when you yourself were unheard of. Mistinguett might
have sung the Aznavour-Roche number *Le Bal du faubourg* but
the old style singer insisted that they would have to transpose it
into a major key: she even showed them how her face sagged
when she sang in the minor.

The young men admired Mistinguett but she was too old.
They wanted Piaf, the singer whom Mistinguett pretended to
dislike. Aznavour wanted that voice and suddenly won a belly-
laugh from its owner when he and Roche opened a live broadcast
from the Salle Washington. When they went to see her
Aznavour was soon telling her the story of his life, and there was
a joke about wearing black clothes to disguise a dirty shirt. Then
the two of them went back in imagination to the sound of a *valse
musette*, played by Roche, to the Paris streets where they had
both lived and worked. And now they danced, the *java*, a paso
doble and a tango. Aznavour and Roche eventually made the
grade in a discussion with Piaf the next day while she was
having breakfast in bed. Even then there was an explosion
because Aznavour foolishly asked what she would pay them
while on tour. They did join Piaf and Les Compagnons de la
Chanson, but started the tour badly by missing the train from
Paris, though they found a convenient goods train and arrived
at their destination, Roubaix, in the north of France, before the

rest of the party. Even Edith, who was furious with them, had to laugh.

When she parted from the Aznavour-Roche duo on her way to Sweden in 1958 they helped her by smuggling forbidden bottles of beer into the pockets of her fur coat and under the mattress in her wagon-lit. She did not want to sing *J'ai bu* but she and Aznavour understood each other. She did not, however, kill him with kindness, and refused to take him with her to New York. He could find his own way there, she said, she 'couldn't afford his passage'. He had to learn the hard way.

He and Roche *did* find their own way there, but as they had done nothing about visas they found themselves, not surprisingly, on Ellis Island. Edith fortunately came back from a tour in Canada and generously arranged matters for them. These were the days of Cerdan, however, and the two young men realized they were in the way. They liked Cerdan, as everyone had done. They had their little pretend sparring match with him, as Maurice Chevalier had done, but Edith wanted to be alone with her boxer and quickly packed them off to an engagement in Montreal. They were a great success, all the more satisfying since they had been laughed at in New York, when the audience at the Society Room thought they were trying to imitate French singers. Piaf was not the only French star to find the USA difficult at first.

The Aznavour-Roche duo split up. Roche decided to marry a Canadian girl who later became known as the singer Agläé, and Aznavour, back in Paris, realized his own first marriage was over. He moved into Piaf's home, not as her lover, but as her secretary, companion and, unfortunately, dog's-body. This close association taught Aznavour the value of professionalism, and among all the people who have written and spoken about Piaf in the last forty years nobody has shown more understanding, appreciation, admiration and love.

If he learnt from her the dedicated art of singing to a mass audience he paid for it in suffering, even if he was rewarded by true friendship. She laughed at his not too handsome nose but paid for the plastic surgery to improve its shape. She called him her *petit génie con*, but she treated him badly when it suited her. I have already mentioned how she woke him up twice during one night in a New York skyscraper hotel because she thought his tiny room would be more comfortable than her large suite – but it was not, and in both places she complained that the building was swaying.

In fact she was swaying in one sense, for she was drinking too much, having not yet found a lover who could replace the emotional satisfaction she had lost. But it was Aznavour who helped her constantly. He was there, and came when she called him. Surely, he thought, she will sing one of my songs, and he offered her *Je hais les dimanches*, 'I Hate Sundays'. 'Idiot', she said, 'you can't destroy Sundays for the people who haven't any other day's holiday'. So Aznavour took the song to Juliette Gréco, a rising star, who made a great success of it. Edith did condescend to sing *Je hais les dimanches*, however, and record it, because she thought Gréco should be shown the right way to sing it. A similar story is told of other songs which rivals performed before she did. Piaf and Gréco belonged to different generations, different styles of singing, and did not understand or appreciate each other at the time. Later, Gréco came to admire Piaf and cried when she heard her sing later in her career. It should be added that Edith always 'forgot' that a song made successful by another singer had been offered to her first, and she had refused it.

Piaf had to be busy, it was her only chance of recovery. We know from an earlier letter to Raymond Asso that she even prayed for death. The year 1950 saw no fewer than eighteen recordings, including five in English, which she produced especially with her American friends in mind. She had worked hard at her English, and in fact was once photographed leaving her plane with a well-known course book *L'Anglais sans peine*, clearly visible in her hand. There were never enough new songs for her so the old ones sometimes had to be revamped. *La Vie en rose*, one of her best known, was turned unfortunately into something totally alien from its original self by an accompaniment which included a good deal of rhythmic drumming. It had originally been rather sentimental and old-fashioned, which no doubt explains its success. Surely it would have been better to leave it alone.

However, the new songs in 1950 included a dramatic work by Michel Emer, *La Fête continue*, totally suited to Piaf and inevitably a success. Emer had built into it all the sounds of the fairground and enough human drama for half a dozen songs: hunger, suicide, unhappy love, it is all there, and Piaf's voice welds the words and music together in a kind of counterpoint inseparable from the fairground noise and music.

Piaf needed desperately to communicate now, and so she accepted the bonus of the vast English-speaking public. Naturally she met hopeful translators, whose work was difficult and in almost all cases a total failure. In 1950 the American actor Eddie Constantine thought he would attempt some translations for her. He had already met Aznavour in New York and now met him again in Paris where he was entertaining the guests at Carrère as a crooner.

Aznavour has recounted in *Yesterday When I Was Young* how Edith and Eddie first met. Edith, still in her post-Cerdan gloom, had at first refused to see him but relented at the mention of songs. Aznavour instructed Constantine how to behave and told him 'smile as you smiled at me on the night we met'. Edith again did not want to see him even when he arrived at her home, so Aznavour had to improvise a little stage-management. There was a large mirror in the room, and in the mirror she could see the waiting Constantine. 'Hi,' he said, turning towards her, 'and that was the second death of Cerdan'.

The Piaf-Constantine relationship would last about two years, and all the usual procedures were followed, starting with the gold cufflinks and the blue suits. The other more important aspect was, of course, the man's career, for he had to be more than Piaf's escort. He had to be somebody. Eddie Constantine was already a minor singer of sorts, but that was not good enough. He moved into the house at Boulogne where she set to work on his American-style French and his whole style of singing.

Constantine had left his dancer-wife and his daughter behind in the United States, and Edith seemed to think he was divorced, which he wasn't. However, they both found each other irresistible. 'One look from her', Constantine said many years later, 'could pull down a ten-storey building'. Edith thought him physically so magnificent that on one occasion, according to Charles Aznavour, she demonstrated his nudity to a young Breton maid, throwing back the bed-clothes and saying, 'Did you ever see anything like that?' The poor little maid, who had brought in the breakfast, was deeply shocked.

Eddie was strong enough physically to live at the Piaf pace for two years or so, snatching a little sleep whenever he had the chance – at the cinema perhaps, where he often sat behind Edith and her gang for this very purpose. Good years on the whole, for he was a useful escort and even a promising student; the constant pressure to study and improve was, after all, the cost of a relationship with Piaf.

He had surely not seen himself on the musical comedy stage, but that is where Constantine appeared on 3 March 1951. The first night of Marcel Achard's entertaining and essentially Parisian composition *La P'tite Lili* at the A.B.C. was the climax of two or more long, complicated, hair-tearing years for many people.

This operetta is unknown to later generations, a mere title to anyone who is not concerned with the details of the Piaf progress. She had indeed progressed a long way from her first contacts, during the far-off Raymond Asso period when that sophisticated, delightful playwright Achard, who had always believed in her talent, invited her to sing in his house. Before leaving for an American tour in the early summer of 1950 she had given him an idea – during her absence she hoped he would write a play or *opérette* in which she could both sing and act. She was aiming at the A.B.C., for the hard-to-please Mitty Goldin had now been impressed by her achievements since the time he had first heard, met, and disliked her.

Achard soon developed the most Piaf-orientated idea that anyone, even she, could have hoped for. His play, with a fair number of lyrics, would be about a young heroine, Lili, who works for a *grand couturier*. She is in love with Mario, the porter, but he cannot supply the romance she feels she must have. Unfortunately she is soon sacked for singing in the workroom. She meets Spencer, an American gangster involved in a murder, thinks she loves him and goes to live with him briefly. When he deserts her she decides to kill herself, but an understanding pharmacist sells her imitation poison; she survives and she and Mario live, of course, happily ever after. Marcel Achard had first thought of Edith in the part of a maid, *une petite bonne*, but soon abandoned this unglamorous idea, and cast her as Lili, *une petite main*, an apprentice seamstress. He had seen her in the film *Etoile sans lumière* and believed that her acting showed an unsuspected talent for comedy, something that should be developed. His plan was that she would say amusing things and sing sad ones. His mix, he planned, would be three-quarters *drôle* and one-quarter *émouvant*.

The writing took a long time and was not even complete when rehearsals began. The cast had no chance to read the whole play and would crowd round Achard whenever he appeared, carrying sheaves of paper, and demand to know what would be happening to them in the next scene. The actors had not been chosen easily: Edith was living with Constantine and so she insisted that he should play the part of Spencer, and the popular entertainer Robert Lamoureux should have the other main rôle, that of

Mario. The producer was the prestigious Raymond Rouleau, and Marguerite Monnot the ideal composer. Lamoureux was accepted quickly by Mitty Goldin because he seemed 'right', and was clearly destined for success. But Constantine had a hard time of it because his acting was 'wooden' and his French was too American. The scenes between the organizers were much more dramatic than anything in the play, although nobody was actually shot. In the end, everyone having refused to work with everyone else, everyone *did* work with everyone else, but Raymond Rouleau cut out most of Spencer's part and Goldin refused to pay him more than the minimum salary. But Edith outwitted Goldin by saying that she would pay the extra money herself.

When the curtain finally rose on the first night at the A.B.C. the audience saw the stage divided into three – the clever décors were by that enchanting designer Lila de Nobili – and the beautiful blonde Praline, the renowned former mannequin, playing the gangster's girlfriend, was being pinned into a long gown by Lili herself. Very soon Lili is singing

> *Avant l'heure, c'est pas l'heure*
> *Après l'heure, c'est plus l'heure*

a song about the importance of falling in love at precisely the right moment. The lyric, and also that for the equally charming

> *Mademoiselle,*
> *Mon amour*
> *Est aussi sage*
> *Que le jour*
> *De ma première communion*

plus Lili's song about her ideal man – *L'Homme que j'aimerai* – were written by Achard, while Aznavour contributed *Rien de rien*, which proved that Piaf could easily sing an ironic comic

115

song if she wanted to. She also wrote the words of three songs herself: *Du matin jusqu' au soir, C'est toi que je chante dans mes chansons*, both suitable for operetta, but the most moving, to use Achard's word, was the lyric she wrote for Spencer to sing when he left her: *Petite si jolie* he sings, 'Don't ever believe in me, I'm too selfish. I'll never do or become anything interesting'.

> *Si j'ai le cœur artiste*
> *Je n'ai aucune valeur.*

Despite the hostility towards Constantine from the management the records of the *P'tite Lili* songs that he made with Edith, including *Si, Si, Si, Si*, which had been written for Robert Lamoureux as Mario, have an old-fashioned gentle charm, due of course mainly to the composer and Edith herself. It is obvious that she had made him work hard, as she had done and was to do with the lovers whom she destined to be singers. Yves Montand, the first victim, had probably suffered the most, but he was also the most successful. One of the most appreciative things that Constantine ever said about Edith later in life, was to acknowledge how she built up his confidence, and always told him that he had been singing better than she had. 'In the end', he added, 'you came to believe it'.

Back in March 1951 it was almost all right on the night. At one point Constantine forgot his words, but Edith apologized for him so prettily that the audience applauded, just as they observed with amazement the effortless way in which the music-hall Piaf, whom they had only seen centre-stage behind a microphone, wearing her regulation black dress, now appeared as an actress, charming if lightweight, as the rôle demanded, and moved from speech to song and back again with graceful ease. How had she learnt? Had she known all the time? Probably, for her theatrical instinct, partly inherited and now enriched by fifteen years' experience, never let her down. Even if the audience still wanted the Piaf they had always known, and demanded encores from her own repertoire, she told them that any 'extras' could only come from the show itself. The critics enjoyed themselves, talking about delicate, naïve poetry, a 14 July atmosphere, accordion music, or 'a tender story in pink and grey with sweet, sparkling touches of mauve'. One reviewer thought the piece would have such a long run that Mitty Goldin could carve his posters on marble, and the cast were thinking of looking for apartments in the area.

It was not quite so simple as that, for just as Lili and Spencer did not stay together for very long, neither did Edith and Eddie. At one point the newspapers hinted that they were going to be married, but Constantine had not in fact divorced his dancer-wife; he brought her over to Paris, and Edith, seeing her *en civil*, found her unglamorous. It was, of course, Lili and not Spencer who was incapable of remaining a partner for very long, at least from the emotional point of view. Spencer–Eddie had to admit that he could not stand the pace, as he told a journalist from *France-Soir* in 1969, long after Edith's death: 'Life with Edith was terrible . . . she was not attracted by physical love. Men had done her so much harm when she was young. I think she was taking her revenge by seducing all possible men ... the best-looking and the most important ... for her this compensated for all her sufferings.'

He gave the same message to other interviewers over the years, and never forgot to add that the sexual side of love did not really interest her. He believed that she was an 'unhappy woman, only happy for two weeks or more when she had seduced a handsome man'. And he was also convinced that nobody could resist her.

Lili and Spencer continued their touching love-duets on stage for no less than seven months, then Spencer–Eddie went back to his wife but it was a new lover of Edith's who unwit-tingly brought the show to an end. Lili–Edith went on tour and soon acquired a new lover, *un bel homme* and some thirty years later he still was. If in 1984 you were prepared to drive through what looks like a film set near the rue Balard in the 15th arrondissement somewhere between the old Citroën works and a dépôt for ownerless cars, then you could find his small chic restaurant, popular with show-biz people, the discreet décor including a very early Mistinguett poster and photographs of *le bel homme* himself, André Pousse, in many of his very successful and always expert manifestations.

By the end of the 1940s he had been a professional cyclist for ten years or so with several championships behind him. He then thought he might make a fortune as a swimmer, but didn't, yet life changed when he met one of his former cyclist fans in New York. This was Louis Barrier, Piaf's agent, and Pousse enjoyed going to hear all the French entertainers at the Versailles where he had once called out in French to Piaf to sing *L'Accordéoniste*. He met her of course, but distantly, for in those days she still thought only of Cerdan. Louis Barrier however was not an impresario for nothing, he needed an assistant and he needed presentable men in the Piaf entourage. Back in Paris André Pousse received some brisk training and took up a new career in theatrical management, later becoming a successful actor and film star himself.

He moved into the house at Boulogne, thus limiting Edith's relationship with Eddie Constantine to the stage at the A.B.C. It was the turn of Pousse now to receive the regulation treatment, including the gold cufflinks and cigarette-lighter, and the attempted stage management of his own life. But a former cycling champion who enjoyed driving racing cars was not going to be managed. He was not going to be a singer, he was not even going to appear in a revival of *Le Bel indifférent*, as Edith hoped. She liked her escorts to be at least as famous as herself, and tried to make him return to the cycle-track, no doubt dreaming of sensational international triumphs, but he refused.

She even offered to sell the country house she had bought at Le Hallier, near Dreux, and buy him a racing car. He refused that too. In fact she had met her match, for *he* made a serious attempt to manage *her*. He hoped to stop her drinking by making her swear solemnly, at her father's grave, that she would give it up. For a time she did so. Pousse also hoped that he might control the speed and irrationality with which she gave away or spent money, but neither he nor Louis Barrier had any success there. In fact her 'generosity', which might well have reflected a deep-seated lack of confidence and a refusal to accept adult responsible life, led her into accepting far too much work in order to maintain her spending. She accepted gala performances anywhere in France whenever *La P'tite Lili* was not playing. This meant long drives, and once when Aznavour was at the wheel, there had been an accident, fortunately slight. One day in September 1951 Pousse crashed her car near Tarascon, which resulted in a broken arm and ribs for Edith.

The surgeons at the local hospital dared not operate on anyone so famous. Instead they patched her up but left her in pain. She insisted that the show must go on and for a time she even played Lili with her arm in a sling, but she could not tolerate the pain she was suffering, and was given injections of morphine. Unfortunately she became addicted, and this was the start of her dependence on opiates, which hardly ever left her. An understudy took her part for a time, but the show crumbled, for Constantine and Robert Lamoureux regularly received offers for other and better parts.

No messages had been received through the still existent table, warning of danger. Neither was Saint Thérèse watching over this show as closely as she could have done, and Marcel Achard was very superstitious. He had been upset when the beautiful Praline had appeared in the theatre wearing a bright green coat, for the colour brought him bad luck. It was in fact Praline who suffered – she was killed in a car accident. Now, with the principals out of the show, it was all over, despite the success, and apparently Achard and his wife were angry.

Edith's own personal show had to go on, of course. In addition to the performances at the A.B.C and the personal appearances in the provinces, she had recorded all the songs from *La P'tite Lili*. She even found the time to perform and record other numbers, including the enormously popular *Padam ... padam* which Henri Contet, who wrote the lyrics, remembers as possibly the most successful of the many he devised for her. Norbert Glanzberg had composed the music earlier but no librettist had been able to produce the right, and singable words to go with it. Aznavour had made a special arrangement for her of *Jézébel*, amazing for the power in her voice and the hard-to-describe oriental quality. Among the lesser known titles is *La Chanson de Catherine*, with a story which seems only too right for Piaf: the young girl marries without love, the man she really cared for kills himself and she then drowns herself, all of which sounds like the worst sort of melodrama ever made into a song. But the music is half-reminiscent of folk-song, and this is one of the few songs which one imagines to be set in the countryside and not in Paris itself. There was also Michel Emer's *Télégramme*, not perhaps his greatest, and again a melodramatic piece. A woman receives a telegram from the lover she has not seen for twenty years: when she goes to meet him at the airport he fails to recognize her, for he is looking for the elegant girl he had first known.

The value of the song is, of course, that such things do happen, and surely this is one of the things that women dread: that their former lovers of years back will not recognize them because they still think of them being as young and attractive as in the days when they first met. But, to quote from that even more famous song, *tout passe, tout casse, tout lasse*.

Perhaps other singers could convince their listeners that these things happen without putting their hearts into the songs.

Piaf, of course, put her entire life into them. If she had not already lived through these events when the songs were offered to her, she still seemed to have experienced every word of the story by the time she reached the recording studio. André Pousse was sharing her life still in the autumn of 1951, and showed no signs of dwindling into Monsieur Piaf, the rôle that she expected her lovers to assume. When Edith behaved like a child, or when she lost all common sense, he punished her. Suddenly he decided that he had had enough of that tedious small table which travelled everywhere with them in its specially made black velvet case, waiting for messages. He had had enough too, of telephone calls from people who had become only too accustomed to receiving money because the table had said they must have it. The table had also, through the trickery of Simone Berteaut, allowed Edith to drink beer. So one day Pousse broke it up with his own hands and threw it away.

The spirit world did not take its revenge just yet, but scenes between the lovers began to be even more dramatic than the current type of Piaf song. In 1983, twenty years later, André Pousse suspected that Edith was in love with him but he could not respond; he was sorry about it, but that was the way it was. One night, during one of the great rows, Pousse threw his gold cufflinks out of the window. Edith was so hurt and hysterical that Pousse said they would go out and look for them in the shrubbery below. He found one, she found the other. It was symbolic, she said. They had become two separate people. So they parted. André Pousse left the house in the rue Gambetta with its empty rooms and superb pink marble bathroom, and nearly thirty years later, after a successful and many-sided career, this immensely likable man spoke of Piaf with great affection and still, no doubt, received the protection of Saint Thérèse for he continued to wear the gold medallion and chain that Piaf gave him as part of the regulation issue.

Pousse was also the first to recount how his place was taken by another cyclist, 'Toto' (Louis) Gérardin, who had been a winner of the Six Jours cycle race and trained the French international cycling team. If Edith had probably loved Pousse after her fashion, Gérardin possibly loved Edith. When he moved into her house he either seemed to think of staying there for ever or else he had no time to buy her presents: he brought things from his own home, having forgotten no doubt that some of them belonged to his wife and others were jointly owned by the two of them. Edith often 'forgot' the existence of wives but they, including Alice Gérardin, did not forget her. She employed a private detective and took legal action for the restitution of her goods, which included some of her own jewellery, a mink coat, a porcelain vase and eighteen kilos of gold bars. Her husband's silver trophies had also gone with him. It took a police visit to get them back and of course the story got into the newspapers. Gérardin may have been much in love but finally decided that he had better return home. Edith happened to be on tour in the north of France when Toto concluded he must tell her his decision at once. So he took her car, which had remained in Paris, and drove to Lille, where she was appearing that night. When he broke the news she, who had sung in New York on the night that Cerdan died, even cancelled her next appearances at Roubaix and Tourcoing and made him drive her back to Paris. Surprisingly there were no accidents on the way. It seems a pity that Gérardin did not write songs – somewhere there was a good one in this drama. But Gérardin will not be forgotten: 'Forty-eight hours with Piaf', he said, 'are more tiring than a lap in the Tour de France'.

One of the last songs Edith recorded in 1951 was *A l'enseigne de la fille sans cœur*, which tells of a girl in a waterfront bar who at last met a man she cared for. They left together and the bar became a tax office: an amusing final touch. It had been a chaotic year of mixed fortunes. The musical comedy might have given Edith a new direction for a short time, but nothing could really change her. It looked as though a replacement for Cerdan could never be found, and in a sense she knew that very well, while André Pousse and others have always said that she loved him more after his death than during his life. The tragedy had become part of her act, the proof that destiny denied her the ideal love for which she genuinely thought she was searching.

Marcel Cerdan, as we know from Charles Aznavour, died a second time when Eddie Constantine appeared, but he was never quite dead. Edith had continued to light candles for Cerdan, going to the church of Saint Vincent de Paul when she was in New York, and to the nearest church in Boulogne when in Paris, accompanied usually by her secretary and sometimes by Constantine.

In an attempt to save money and forget the past Piaf sold her house in the rue Gambetta in 1951 – she usually made a loss when selling property – and on this occasion merely salvaged a little ready cash. For a time she rented an apartment in the boulevard Péreire from the retired actor Constant Rémy, who suffered terribly from the noise, not so much her singing as the record player and the comings and goings of the entourage, the hangers-on Edith could not manage without.

Constantine, Pousse and Gérardin had occupied her time and to some extent her emotions, but drama had often degener-ated into farce, and there was still a gap in her life especially after Gérardin, like Constantine, had gone back to his wife. Wife: a rôle Edith had not yet played even at the age of thirty-seven as she was in 1952, after being some man's woman ever since she was seventeen. She might have looked too old to play Lili, who was *une petite main*, and had not even acted the part of a wife in the few films she had made so far. But, suddenly, there was a possibility of taking on the rôle of wife in reality.

The man concerned was almost as well known as she was, even if his international reputation was limited to singing and not 'colourful' behaviour. Born Jacques Ducos in 1910 in Tulle, he was no *enfant de la balle* and had even begun medical training.

He gave up a possible professional career to become one of those tall handsome young men who supported Mistinguett at the Casino de Paris. But he wanted to sing. He took the name of Jacques Pills – 'Peals' in the US, for obvious reasons – and found a partner, Georges Tabet. The singing duo lasted well and everyone who knew France in the 1930s also knew that immensely successful song:

> *Couchés dans le foin,*
> *Avec le soleil pour témoin.*

It was composed by Jean Nohain and Mireille back in 1928, won the Grand Prix du Disque in 1932, and years later was successfully recorded in the United States by the Andrews Sisters. Pills had been married to the singer Lucienne Boyer for a time (*her* big success was *Parlez-moi d'amour*) and had become known as 'Monsieur Charme'. He had the kind of face that can hardly be imagined without a smile. He began to write songs and suitably enough it was a song that introduced him to Edith. He wrote the words, and his pianist at the time, François Silly (soon to take the name of Gilbert Bécaud), wrote the music. The story goes that the American agent, Clifford Fischer, heard Pills humming a certain song when they were returning to France aboard the *Ile de France*. He liked the sound of it:

> *Je t'ai dans la peau*
> *Y a rien à faire*
> *Obstinément tu es là …*

and asked what they were going to do with it. Soon enough the song brought Jacques Pills to Edith's drawing-room. She loved the song which, in fact, sounded as though it had been written expressly for her, and gradually, not instantly, she loved Jacques Pills.

7

Marriage and more

There has always been a rumour that Jacques Pills did not dare ask Edith to marry him, and that *she* asked him. She was, of course, so experienced in trying to run men's lives for them that the rumour could possibly be true, but she herself in a recorded interview put it quite differently. He said he was ready to get married but she must ask herself if *she* was ready. 'Nobody', she remembered, 'had ever spoken to me like that'.

Piaf and Pills had first thought of being married on board ship, for they were both due to go to the US shortly, but gave up the idea as impractical.

In June 1952 they were married at the Mairie of the 16th arrondissement and moved into the large ground-floor apartment 67, boulevard Lannes, on the outskirts of Auteuil. A month earlier Edith had recorded the song that had brought Pills to her, *Je t'ai dans la peau*, the most sexy of her numbers with its slow fox-trot rhythm and the feeling, due to the obsessive intimacy of her interpretation, that it is being sung by someone dancing cheek to cheek who wants to be, intends to be, even more intimate still with her partner. It has none of the drama so characteristic of the best Piaf songs, and it is even possible to find an echo of the 1930s which, after all, was the time of Jacques Pills' early successes. Taking at least one-third of the credit was of course the pianist composer Gilbert Bécaud, once described as 'the spiritual nephew of Charles Trenet'. Bécaud

125

also set for her another song to her own words, *Elle a dit*, about the break-up of two lovers, a theme so frequent in her repertoire and her own life.

Edith's own attitude to marriage was simple – she had always found it inconvenient of most of her lovers to have wives, but she does not seem to have contemplated their removal. With very few exceptions she did not like women, she tended to ignore them, use them, or be jealous of them. No fewer than eight of her songs include the phrase *les amants* in the title alone. *La Chanson de Catherine* is about a girl who married without love and *Mariage* from the film *Etoile sans lumière* is unfortunately about a woman who kills her husband.

The year of Piaf's own marriage also produced *Monsieur et Madame*, Michel Emer's evocation of a couple who have been married for twenty years and only survive together because they can each close their eyes and think of their ideal but often absent partner. If Edith had always looked for love she could hardly have seen it against a background of domestic bliss. For a time, however, Monsieur and Madame Ducos showed every sign of being a happily married couple. They rented a large apartment at 67 boulevard Lannes, bordering on the Auteuil racecourse, and despite their busy life in the theatre they had a kind of home. There have been many references to the empty rooms full of unopened suitcases, but there are photographs of the Piaf-Pills salon with armchairs, and on the walls paintings by Pills himself. Piaf even sat in an armchair and continued her fidgety, neurotic knitting. Her husband said, many years later, that he never actually wore one of these hand-knitted pullovers because, of course, not a single one was ever finished. Years later too, Henri Contet remembered how cheerful Edith was at the time, and much given to *fou-rire*, wild laughter. If nobody seriously expected the couple to live happily ever after, they made the best of things at least for a time.

Was there a danger of her 'settling down', which everyone had assumed to be impossible? Edith looked happy, less emaciated and better dressed. Unfortunately, her husband soon realized that she could not break the habit of comforting herself and appeasing her rheumatism and post-accident problems with pain-killing drugs. Strong measures would be necessary, he realized, to deal with this situation, but they must wait, for the couple had to take up engagements in New York, and there was one more important event in front of them. Edith had been legally married but she did not feel *really* married, for as a naïve would-be Roman Catholic she yearned for a church wedding. She always regretted that she had never had the chance to take her First Communion, and many of her songs, not the most successful it must be said, contain vague aspirations towards heaven, usually accompanied by would-be celestial choirs.

Jacques Pills, still charmed and charming, was ready to comply. Once in the States the couple first went through a brief civil ceremony at the New York Town Hall and five days later, on 20 September 1952, there followed the religious ceremony at the church of Saint Vincent de Paul in the Chelsea area of New York where some traces of old French influence still lingered. Edith already knew one of the priests, Father Salvatore Piccirillo, who had helped her recover after the death of Cerdan, but there was a problem. Edith was a spinster but Pills had been divorced, something which the Catholic Church disliked. However, he had previously married a divorced woman (Lucienne Boyer), therefore the Church did not accept his earlier union as valid. Since no further objections were raised, the marriage was solemnized by a French priest and Father Piccirillo signed the register. The show was a success, mainly because it had been stage-managed by Marlene Dietrich, who had helped Edith to choose her outfit at Saks in Fifth Avenue and told the many reporters and photographers in the congregation how to behave. Marlene was Edith's witness and since she was not a

Catholic the bride had to obtain a special dispensation for her. In the autobiography published in France in 1984 Marlene remembered the occasion with emotion, realizing how much Edith was in need of motherly help especially on the morning of the wedding. 'She returned to the land of her memories and childish superstitions ... As I entered her bedroom I saw her seated on her bed, naked, in accordance with custom.' The 'custom' was an old one: if the bride began her day like this the couple would always be happy. Edith seemed small and solitary in the hotel bedroom, as she wore the cross set with emeralds that Marlene had given her, said to have been given to her by Jean Gabin.

The show was indeed a success. Edith's dress was in pale blue silk jersey, and the finely pleated skirt floated prettily as she walked. Since she had been to a beauty salon the previous day, she wore a pretty, conventional face, not a theatrical face, not a cheerful un-made-up everyday face. It was rumoured that she coped with the ceremony because she was high on drugs, and it was in this same church that she had lit so many candles in memory of Marcel Cerdan. But as Lili had sung so recently:

Demain, il fera jour
C'est quand tout est perdu que tout commence,

and Edith had the conventional wedding she wanted, clad in the colour, as Marlene noted in her *A.B.C. Meines Lebens*, that is the only one to promise pure love, 'the colour that governs our most secret dreams'. Edith was photographed kneeling at the altar, two French singers performed Schubert's *Ave Maria* and Mendelssohn's wedding march was played. There was no honeymoon, for both bride and groom were engaged to sing that evening, she at the Versailles and her husband at La Vie en Rose. However, three receptions followed the ceremony, and Edith was also photographed cutting a splendid wedding cake. That

Edith Gassion's mother, Line Marsa, who sang on the streets of Paris. Edith never forgave her for abandoning her as a baby.

A modern photograph of the house in Bernay in Normandy where Edith lived with her grandmother, the owner of the local *maison close*.

DÉTECTIVE

Les Quatre Tueurs

RENIÉ PAR SES COMPAGNONS DE VICE, LOUIS
LEPLÉE N'EUT QUE DES FEMMES, LA MOME PIAF
ET LAURE JARNY, POUR PLEURER A SES OBSÈQUES.

Pages 2 et 3, les révélations de Marcel MONTARRON.

A magazine cover showing Edith being comforted at the funeral of Louis Leplée, the club owner who first discovered her when she was singing in the streets. Leplée's murderers were never found, but the allegations that ensued could have wrecked Edith's career.

An early rare photograph of La Môme Piaf in the pre-war days when she first began to make records. The white hand-knitted collar was very much part of her stage costume.

Jean Cocteau, one of the first people
to appreciate Piaf's qualities as an
actress.
He wrote *Le Bel indifférent* for her.
Below is Cocteau's marvellous
drawing of Piaf in the play.

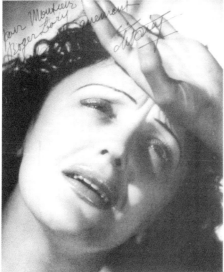

Edith's glamorous and
tragic faces in early
signed photographs.

Above: A still from Marcel Blistène's film, *Etoile sans lumière*, showing Piaf with her current lover, Yves Montand.
It was a short affair that caused him distress but did much for his career.

Right: Marcel Cerdan, European middleweight boxing champion with the smiling, happy Edith characteristic of their time together. Cerdan not only fought in the ring but also found time to appear in two films. Here he is a boxer in the Italian film, *Al diavolo la celebrità*.

20 September 1952 at the Catholic Church of Saint Vincent de Paul in New York where Edith married Jacques Pills for the second time (there had been an earlier civil ceremony in Paris). Marlene Dietrich was a witness and organized the wedding, even choosing the bridal outfit. In the background to the right of Piaf is another of her devoted friends – Ginette Richer.

Edith photographed in 1959 with Douglas Davis, a young American artist who not only became one of her lovers but also painted some striking and disturbing portraits of her. Although in her mid-forties Piaf shows a 'little-girl' quality characteristic of many of her relationships.

Piaf's height in daily record sales.

Right: Piaf in the 1953 film, *Si Versailles m'était conté* in which she sang the revolutionary song *Ça ira*.
Below: Piaf, the singer, taking her encore, surrounded by a sea of photographers, at the Olympia Music Hall.

The drama, the tragedy and the essence of the Piaf performance are captured here.

Above, with Bruno
Coquatrix, director of the
Paris Olympia and below
with Charles Dumont
who composed *Non, je ne
regrette rien*.

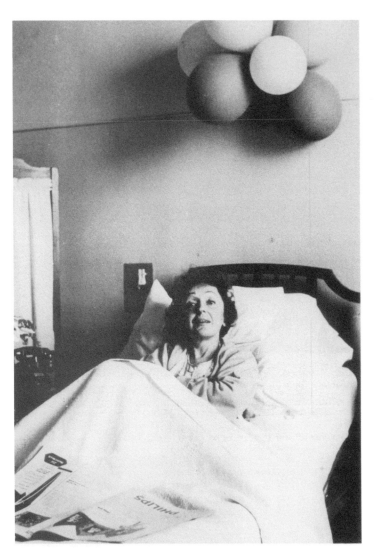

One of the many photographs of Piaf in a hospital bed. Marcel Blistène has told a story about the balloons – Piaf woke up in the American hospital in Paris one day and was so delighted to see coloured balloons on her ceiling that she said they made her feel alive.

Le Droit d'aimer. Piaf in the arms of her young Greek husband, Théo Sarapo.

Piaf at the Olympia in 1961.
Although frail and sick, her
need to communicate with her
adoring public kept her alive

was not yet the end, for a week later the married couple and their witnesses went to the French Consulate to register their marriage which could then be considered legal in France.

When Edith was first married she could hardly bear to be separated from Jacques Pills, even though they could hardly hope for continual engagements in the same city or even country. As time passed she enjoyed opportunities to escape, although not necessarily in search of amorous adventures, even if her young companion Ginette Richer lived through a romantic episode with Humphrey Bogart. She was not interested in going out 'on the town' and when in New York she preferred to employ a Martiniquaise cook because she had decided American food was disgusting. Sightseeing for her was always a waste of time. When taken unwillingly to see the Niagara Falls she remarked in jaded fashion that it was just a lot of water. She still preferred city streets to any other landscape.

The personalities and singing styles of Edith and her husband were totally different, hers was highly individual even if within the tradition of *la chanson*, whereas Jacques Pills' contribution was less unusual, if still personal, in a more conventional way. For a brief period they married their talents, just as it had all begun with a song. Edith did not always wait for other people to give them ideas: she devised, with the help of the composer Louiguy, an amusing sketch to be sung with her husband, *Pour qu'elle soit jolie ma chanson*, which included the themes of old and new songs. This, along with *Je t'ai dans la peau*, was included in the film *Boum sur Paris* (1952), a thin story (indirectly reminiscent of *The Lavender Hill Mob*) which allowed a whole galaxy of singing stars to demonstrate their brilliance.

Before the film was released, however, Edith was again trying to manage a theatrical event, just as she had persuaded Marcel Achard to devise *La P'tite Lili*. She remembered her success in *Le Bel indifférent* thirteen years earlier, and having failed to persuade André Pousse to join her she now found a willing partner in her husband. At her own expense she then took the Marigny Theatre for a new production.

The first part of the evening would consist of songs by Pills, followed by the play, and the second half would bring the two performers together in duets. There was only one problem: Pills was a singer but no actor, and that silent, unresponsive rôle of the indifferent lover demanded at least a stage presence. Paul Meurisse had possessed it, Pills did not. Edith inevitably lost money for it was hard to fill 1,000 seats every night, but several decades later we have the Pathé-Marconi record of her performance and its intensity, along with the discreet accompaniment of sound effects, never fails to produce a *frisson*. The music at the end was, appropriately, *Je t'ai dans la peau*.

Neither Edith nor Jacques was indifferent to each other, but of course they suffered from the malady so much described by Cocteau, existent in all countries but most of all perhaps in France, which gave it a name, *déformation professionelle*. If the theatre had brought them together it also separated them, for the spotlights shone brighter than the home fires, there were not too many joint appearances and soon, very few shared international trips. The couple accepted some unusual engagements and in 1955 even travelled in a caravan with the Supercircus where the first half was *un spectacle de cirque 100% nouveau*. Edith was billed as '*la plus célèbre chanteuse du monde*' and her husband's name was added in much smaller letters. The whole situation was summed up in a song that Edith and Gilbert Bécaud wrote for Pills to sing in 1952, *Ça gueule ça, Madame*, the untranslatable portrait of a partnership, which must have been highly entertaining in performance; the tiny little martinet wife creates scenes which fill the house, the husband thinks he can calm her by taking her in his arms, she is almost ready to say she is sorry:

C'est tout d'même un' satisfaction
D'lui fair' admettre qu'elle a tort—
Et que j'suis l'plus fort—

But there was no hope, really: 'The singer looks at his watch and goes off in a panic, saying, "Good God I'm late. *Ça va gueuler ça, Madame.*" ' He was not *le plus fort*, the stronger one.

There do not seem to have been painful rows but the marriage drifted to an end, they divorced in 1957, and years later Pills would describe how he could not eternally submit to Edith's system of 'educating' men, and he could not become 'Monsieur Piaf'. She had tried swimming because he enjoyed it, they had even cycled about on a tandem, she had even briefly stayed at his country property in the Landes. He liked to go to bed early, she did not. She had agreed to undertake a cure for drug addiction, as he had insisted, she was in fact cured for a time, but lapsed. He said years later that he had been proud to be her husband. She is said to have wept during an attempted reconciliation. The marriage, the cynics said, and might still say, could not have been a success. The stars were literally against it. The marriage did not end with the tragedy of the song *Mariage*, and the nature of Jacques Pills was to defuse drama rather than generate it. However, he knew by now that his wife felt restricted by her married state, and he realized that she would never win the battle against drugs because she probably did not want to win it hard enough. Fortunately the marriage was over without great pain and without shock, which meant that there was no repeat of the post-Cerdan situation.

What matters is the maturity which Edith reached as an artist during the few relatively happy years when she had a semblance of home life and not merely the support of her staff, who acted like an expensive and not too professional back-up group. She could never be totally mature as an individual, but the loss to the person meant a gain to the performer – a situation common enough in the theatre. In the case of Piaf the gap between the two aspects of existence was both narrow and wide at the same time, which sounds paradoxical, but if her audience today regrets the chaos of her life we know very well that she was not seriously interested in resolving it – she concentrated totally on the concept and presentation of her songs. The form of the songs gave shape to her existence. What else mattered?

The years of married life had also been years of travel. Piaf's audiences in the US had soon become enthusiastic, she earned magnificent money, spending a great deal of it on her astronomical telephone bills – she had a compulsive need to keep in close touch with her Paris friends.

It would be unfair to say that Edith only sang in the US for the dollars she earned but her whole nature and way of life were so distant from what one cautiously describes as the American character, the American way of entertainment life, that it is amazing she went there so often. Two of the songs that she recorded with success were American in origin, *L'Homme à la moto* and *Allentown Jail*, by Irving Gordon, adapted as *Les Prisons du Roy*, by Michel Rivgauche, telling a simple, sentimental, all-or-nothing story: the man was in prison for stealing diamonds for her, he would be there for ever, so she would join him; yes, she had stolen too, she had stolen his heart. And with American listeners in mind Edith recorded in English, the famous song by Prévert and Kosma, *Les Feuilles mortes*, translated as *Autumn Leaves*. Admittedly in France it had always been closely associated with Yves Montand.

The American nation, despite what Edith had said about their food, fared better than the British. According to 'Bunny' Lewis, the English music-hall agent, she did not come to Britain, despite good offers, because she was convinced the British would neither understand nor appreciate her. In the last year of her life she was to say the British did not understand love, but was never persuaded to develop this theme. Not long before she died, however, she said that she and Théo Sarapo had again been invited to London.

The many travels in the US had of course meant that recording sessions in Paris were sometimes limited, yet this same period produced some of Edith's most striking and memorable songs in all genres, some of them so outstanding that it would have been asking the impossible to expect more. In particular 1953 brought one of the great theatrical moments, *Bravo pour le clown*, much more than a song, a highly dramatic portrait, the evocation of a middle-aged clown who has to amuse the crowd while suffering from a particularly grim life of his own: his wife is unfaithful to him and his son is stealing his money. But of course the show must go on. Henri Contet, the librettist, says he was indeed thinking partly of that near-circus figure Louis Gassion and perhaps Edith's instinctive understanding of any solitary performer – for even a group of clowns keep their separate entities in the ring – combined with her love for her father, caused her to sing it with such amazing conviction, such shattering cries of *Bravo! Bravo!* Henri Contet remembers in particular how, even while she was still learning the song, she raised her arms with the hands turned inwards, a typical clown gesture.

Louiguy's music complemented the words with typical circus music, and if it is all a far cry from *Vesti la giubba*, the song and Edith's interpretation of it show both her own actual powers, the further potential of which she was probably capable and the talent she possessed for persuading writers and composers to produce songs for her, songs which surely could never be convincingly sung, or rather, performed by anyone else. Whenever this happens the immediate reaction is a comparison with Edith's own performance.

Another dramatic song, again almost more drama than song, was *N'y vas pas, Manuel*, recorded the same year. It was written and composed by that master of mini-drama, Michel Emer, about a young man who had been nagged, more or less, by his mother and later by his wife, in their attempts to keep him away from trouble and crime. He comes to grief because, of course, he does not listen to his parents or his conscience, even when its voice through Edith seems so compelling and irresistible. The words she speaks have as much authority as those she sings.

Jacques Pills obviously understood Edith well he had brought out the best in her, forgave her a good deal and had been the first to insist that she should undergo treatment for drug addiction. However, when they were both touring in the US their engagements often separated them. She had been faithful to him longer than with any of her earlier partners but after two or three years of marriage she was at least taking an interest in other men. On one occasion, when he was about to leave on a tour she reminded him, half-seriously perhaps, that it was 'dangerous' to leave her on her own. One man in particular was beginning to intrigue her, and as so often in her life it had all begun with a song. The man in question was Jean Dréjac, and the song was *Le Chemin des forains*. The music had been composed by Henri Sauguet for the very first ballet choreographed by Roland Petit back in 1945 when he was only twenty-one. Once seen, this haunting work with décor and costumes by Christian Bérard, cannot be forgotten. Cyril Beaumont wrote of Sauguet's score that 'Not only does it include a key melody which has the captivating bittersweet quality of one of Satie's *Gymnopédies*, and suggests both the drudgery and the glamour of stage life, but in its colourful orchestration, its gay, lilting, brassy accents, its booming big drum and the cracks of the ringmaster's whip create to perfection the atmosphere of the circus ring'. Edith presumably saw the ballet or at least heard the music, for it haunted her and she was convinced it could be transformed into a song for her. But it needed a lyric, and the words could not be ordinary or sentimental, the music needed a poet.

In her professional world, in Paris, she had already encountered Jean Dréjac. He was nine years younger than she was, had been a singer himself from the age of seventeen but had had more success, while still young, with two songs for which he had written the words. In 1945, the year of Liberation, everyone was singing *Ah! le petit vin blanc*, a song for festive occasions, and it seemed exactly right, as Ralph Harvey has written, for the *guinguettes* and the cheerful scenes on the river boats, like those once painted by the Impressionists. The wine-growers of the Marne valley, who produced the 'little white wine', were happy. Although Edith surely appreciated the atmosphere of this song, it was not one which she might have sung, but she did sing and record the other best known Dréjac success, the popular *Sous le ciel de Paris*, so evocative of the city that Julien Duvivier used it as the title for one of his films. Edith's recording is unfortunately not helped by the addition of choirs, introduced perhaps to make it 'different' from versions by other people, because it had been performed also by several French and international stars. Edith now asked Dréjac to add a libretto to Henri Sauguet's music and make it into a song for her. It was no easy task but finally he wrote a short evocative poem which recaptured the atmosphere of the music.

Ils ont troué la nuit d'un éclair de paillettes d'argent
Ils vont tuer l'ennui pour un soir dans la tête des gens

(Their golden sequins shone through the might
For a single evening they've made all darkness light)

and the song, complementing the ballet or the memory of it, makes everyone who hears it wish that Piaf had sung more work of such high musical and literary calibre, for it was no problem to her and she does full justice to the composer and the librettist, every word can be heard clearly and every word is given its full value.

And did she ever hear or know about that mysterious *Imprompta No 15* for piano composed by Francis Poulenc in 1959: *Hommage à Edith Piaf?* Mysterious because even those close to Poulenc's work know nothing about this evocative piece.

Edith liked the song and recorded it when she was back in Paris in 1955. In the meantime Jean Dréjac became her companion and soon her lover in the US, travelling with her, even when Jacques Pills was there too. The situation had to be managed in some way; everyone knew that Edith was respectably married and so it was decided that the young man who was always with her should acquire an alias and a supposed profession: he became 'le Docteur Denis', which made his continued presence acceptable. Whenever Jacques Pills and Edith were singing in different places, sometimes far apart, rumours about possible divorce began to circulate but whenever they appeared in the same programme the rumours stopped. But Jean Dréjac was close to Edith for two years, always in the US, far from family in France. At one point, when Edith was a grass widow and without urgent engagements, she rented a house for a short time at Malibu, when she and Dréjac, with Marc and Danielle Bonel in attendance as helpful chaperones, passed a happy carefree time. Danielle has told an amusing story about Dréjac's eccentric methods of cooking: for example, if you need to test whether pasta is ready, throw a few pieces up to the ceiling, and if they stick, it's ready. Dréjac was apparently a cheerful and discreet partner, loving Edith for herself and not because he hoped to further his own career. Perhaps the most enduring success he brought her was the libretto he wrote her *L'Homme à la moto*, a striking melodramatic song which was recorded in 1956. 'Fast, driving tempo' can be read at the start of the piece, which had once been called *Black Denim Trousers and Motor-Cycle Boots*. A strange song for Edith, perhaps, but of course here was a story and, as she had once agreed with Charles Aznavour perhaps more seriously than she had realized, she was always looking for

stories with 'a new way of dying'; and here she found it. The
demon motor-cyclist with the eagle on his black jacket was dec-
imated by a locomotive at a level crossing, having ignored his
girlfriend's pleas: it was a love story, for according to Jean Dréjac who wrote the French words, the young man loved his bitch
of a motor-cycle more than anyone, including his mother.
Edith's interpretation, backed up by an explosive alarming
accompaniment, has not dated even if it is fifty years old: it
brings Hell's Angels only too close and yet still remains a Piaf
song. When she first sang it the theme had a newspaper head-
line relevance, more fitting for a rock group perhaps, and Edith
did not usually like songs which had been written for, or sung
by, others, but she liked this one enough to make her audiences
love it. No wonder that she, briefly at least, loved Jean Dréjac.

This story came to an end when he made a return trip to
France and then rejoined Edith, who was in Havana, without
letting her know in advance. In the meantime she had found
another partner.

Edith was used to appearing on stage as a small solitary figure,
although the orchestra, and/or her accordionist or her guitarist
were sometimes not far away. But there had to be someone close
to her, at least off the stage. She never lost her fear of abandonment that had haunted her childhood. In Dréjac's absence it was
the guitarist who, surely with some encouragement, came closer.
This was Jacques Liébrard who had been with her musicians
since 1953, and Louis Barrier did not discourage the romance
that was now developing, for he and everyone else knew how
tiresome Edith could be if she had no admirer/escort/lover at
hand. Back in Paris Edith was heard to say that she had 'found
the man of her life' and seemed particularly pleased that he
never left her. He seems to have left his former partner for her,
at least temporarily and apparently the abandoned girl made a
scene outside the casino in Saint Raphael hoping perhaps for
some public support. But she received none, while Edith and her

lover remained unmoved. Marinette Cerdan, who was travelling with Edith, was upset by this scene. But the situation could not last, Edith had to move on.

Dréjac accepted his dismissal philosophically and returned later to his own singing career while still writing songs for Yves Montand and Juliette Gréco among others. For a time he was president of the S.A.C.E.M. In 1984 he wrote that he treasured the letters that Edith had written to him. She had kept those he had written to her, and he was grateful that Danielle Bonel returned them to him after Edith's death. One day, he said, he might consider writing something about the two years he had spent close to Edith.

There were two other dramatic songs from these years in which the treatment is much more lyrical, and the story, if handled by any other singer, could have been condemned as sentimental. *Les Amants de Venise* of 1953 is not about Venice, but about poor Italians living in Paris who are remembering their own country, especially as they see the plaque on the wall: Porte d'Italie. The music is not distinguished but the song deserves to be better known.

One that is understandably well known is of course *Les Amants d'un jour* from 1956, which could be short-listed as one of the most typical Piaf songs; it gives the full flavour of her work with its bitter-sweet note and captures that feeling of totality expressed so well by John Dryden in his eighteenth-century version of *Antony and Cleopatra*: he called it *All for Love* or *The World Well Lost*. Marguerite Monnot composed the music, Delécluse and Senlis the words. The song in its recorded version of three minutes and thirteen seconds, moving between the major and minor, tells a story that could be a novel. The girl who washes the glasses in a little hotel remembers how she showed two lovers to their room, with its yellowing wallpaper. Next day they are found dead, hand in hand. Something of their love remains:

Mais ils m'ont donné
Le goût du bonheur
Et j'ai leur soleil
Tout au fond du cœur
Qui me fait si mal,
Qui me fait si mal.

Nothing changes, the girl is still unhappily washing her glasses, the room is let again and, as the music ends with the sound of a glass breaking on the floor, you might condemn it as kitsch. But not if you listen to the crack in Piaf's voice as she envies those two who loved each other so much, and not if you remember those little hotels which used to exist in Paris. And inevitably, too, the classic films of Marcel Carné, made in the late 1930s, come to mind again.

Edith would drop the glass on to the stage at the end of the song. It had to be real crystal, she believed, the sound of the break was more convincing. When she sang this song at the Versailles in New York she would personally take a glass from the theatre bar – until the directors realized why all the bar glasses were disappearing. Later they made Edith a present: a large glass made of plastic – their idea of a joke presumably, not hers.

If some people see Piaf's life as a series of chapters with a man's name in the title, then that is a pity, for if this was an unexciting period from the biographical point of view with no 'official' lover, it was amazingly rich in songs. The title *La Goualante du pauvre Jean* may not be very clear to many non-French people, for this and many words in the song belong to argot, the Parisian slang which in its upper reaches is a different language. '*La Goualante*' means literally a popular song, and Jean was poor because he was rich, unloving and unloved. Another song, so right for Edith, for how could she fail:

139

Rien ne vaut une bell'fille
Qui partag' notre ragoût.
Sans amour, on n'est rien du tout.

This last line, 'without love you're nothing at all', is repeated at the end of the five seven-line stanzas, and the last shorter one ends with the sound advice: *Aimez-vous*, love each other. This song has had deserved success in the Winifred Atwell version, complete with mechanical piano, entitled 'The Poor People of Paris'.

A different piano, out of tune, gives a special flavour to the song *L'Homme au piano* (1954), and it echoes the thoughts of a man who hopes, if he plays it hard enough, he can forget his lost love and his unhappiness. The repeated phrase *au piano, au piano*, one of the many short, obsessive themes to be found in typical Piaf songs, is hard to forget. The out-of-tune piano can be heard again two years later in *Marie la Française*, that brief biography of a French girl who is a successful prostitute in Australia. She longs to see 'Paname' (Paris) again, but since her mother has been given to understand she has married a rich man, her return seems unlikely.

But Piaf's songs did not deal exclusively with these solitary unhappy people, many of them rejected, usually by themselves. She was inevitably not much concerned with happy families and children, for they did not often come her way; but sometimes she would accept songs dealing with a crowd. When she sang the famous revolutionary song *Ça ira* in the film *Si Versailles m'était conté*, she seemed to be singing for the whole Paris mob. In this vast film of 165 minutes made by Sacha Guitry in 1953 not long before he died, her performance is one of the few memorable ones, and her rôle is listed as *une fille du peuple*, a 'girl of the people'. She and Louiguy had together made a special arrangement of the song.

French Can-can, as the French always call this world-famous dance, apparently preferring the adjective to be in English, was the first film that the great French director Jean Renoir had made in his own country (1954) for fifteen years. It was a Franco-Italian production and was made in the Studio Francœur, the oldest studio in Paris which happened to be about a hundred yards from the site of the old Moulin Rouge itself, so famous in the history of both the music hall and modern painting. Many artists took part and in much of the publicity it was Piaf's name which headed the list of singers and other performers after those of the three principal actors, Jean Gabin, Françoise Arnoul and Maria Félix.

Edith portrayed Eugénie Buffet, the enormously popular singer who lived from 1866 to 1934 and, like Edith, had found her way up from the streets. Edith looked somewhat strange in the long skirt and bonnet she had to wear, and her singing suffered from the way the film was produced – the performers acted and sang in silence, the music and voices were recorded separately and later mixed in with the sound of the dancers' feet. But few people would question the success of the film.

A few months before she died Piaf suddenly developed a passion for reading the history of France, but in 1957 she illuminated those legendary figures from the Napoleonic wars, *Les Grognards*, the Emperor's Old Guard, who accepted terrible hardship for him and remained faithful to the end. The song opens with a spoken passage then, to the sound of an inevitable march, lists all the battles and all the sufferings. The Old Guard haunt Paris as they haunt history, for they have never had the chance to see the capital in reality. Even for listeners unmoved by any military nostalgia this song, which was incidentally a great success in New York, inevitably produces a *frisson*, for Edith seems to have understood with intensity the depth of feeling in those men, known to us through historical paintings, but never so convincingly as in this music, composed by Hubert Giraud to words by Pierre Delanoë. *Les Grognards* has no ambitions to be great music but it is more effective than many an *alla marcia* movement from symphonic works.

Edith, so closely associated with the individual, could still sing for the group, even for the mass, and the song *La Foule* is particularly effective because it tells of individuals, lovers, who are alternately thrown together and separated by the crowd. The music, marked *Tempo di Valse péruvienne*, was composed by Angel Cabral and brought back from South America by Edith who had heard it on one of her tours. She asked Michel Rivgauche to write words for it, which he did magnificently in two days. She always cared deeply about the words of her songs, for she wanted them to convey a story, or at least a mood. '*On peut toujours arranger la musique*', she said, and she was not referring to orchestral arrangements. The music must obey the words and obey her too.

Several years later, in 1960, Henri Crolla set for her a poem by Jacques Prévert, *Cri du coeur*, in which the singer is aware of all the other voices also singing, through her, so to speak:

> *C'est pas seul'ment ma voix qui chante,*
> *C'est d'autres voix, une foule de voix,*
> *Voix d'aujourd'hui ou d'autrefois …*

There is too much suffering, it must be overcome, and we must think beyond the individual:

> *Si on tirait l'signal d'alarme*
> *Pour des chagrins particuliers,*
> *Jamais les trains n'pourraient rouler …*

A typical Prévert attitude. But one day love will appear, 'As soon as I see his face I shall recognize him'.

Edith and Jean Dréjac had admired each other vastly, but strangely she had less success with one of his most famous songs, *Sous le ciel de Paris*. The recording includes a choir, and as nearly always happened when other voices were added, the resulting effect is weak.

The mid 1950s, coinciding with Edith's own early forties, produced songs of greater variety than those of any other time. Far too many people believe that Piaf never sang a cheerful song and Bruno Coquatrix thought, for one, that this side of her repertoire was too easily forgotten. 1954 produced *Enfin le printemps*, after René Rouzaud, one fine spring morning, had noticed a slogan over a famous big store in Paris saying exactly that. Henri Contet remembers that during the early years of her marriage Edith laughed easily whenever she had a chance, and she enjoyed a cheerful song. This libretto, full of argot and imagery which links the spring with *la java* and the sound of the accordion creates the ideal light-hearted song, its music by Marguerite Monnot far from great but still in tune with a little-known aspect of Piaf's talent. Another cheerful song, much better known, was *Mon manège à moi* from 1958.

During the previous year Edith had recorded one of her most ingenious interpretations, a song by Contet and Monnot who formed a brilliant team. This was *Opinion publique*, far too little known because it has no easy refrain and literally no love interest. Its inevitable affinity with the famous aria in Act I of Rossini's *Barber of Seville* sung by Don Basilio, *La Callunia*, has been noted by critics. Between the words as they stand

On dit qu'il a . . . on dit qu'il est . . .
On dit qu'il a fait . . .
A fait ceci . . . a fait cela . . .
Non, il a dit ça?
Oui, il a dit ça . . .

and Edith's half-sung, half-spoken rendering is a whole universe, and any singer or actress would do well to study this miniature masterpiece.

143

Maybe other people have interpreted *Opinion publique* but it is hard to imagine anyone more sensational than Edith. The sensation is one of subtlety rather than deep emotion, and particularly in the way that carefully managed inflections of the voice convey a whole dialogue, or series of dialogues between two or even more people, particularly since every word can be heard with total clarity.

Edith's professional life was brilliant, her personal life was not, consisting as it did of a series of men's names and short-lived presences, interspersed with periods of illness that began to occur far too often. The brighter intervals were due to worthwhile songs, sometimes to the appearance of new creative people.

8

More new worlds

Although Jacques Pills had left the domestic scene a different kind of intermittent family life developed later in the boulevard Lannes apartment, depending on Edith's own stays in Paris. As soon as she had made contact with the Cerdan family in Casablanca she had invited them to stay with her. At first Marinette had come on her own, then she brought her three young sons, and they all benefited from Edith's generosity. The sons were given splendid outfits from Ted Lapidus and plenty of toys well suited to their ages. Marcel, the eldest, closely resembled his father and as he became adolescent Edith grew particularly fond of him, almost as though he were the son she and Cerdan might have had, a fact she more or less admitted. As the boys grew up they were sent to school in Paris, and the boulevard Lannes apartment was a kind of home from home for them. Marcel's father had wanted his eldest son to study well and enter one of the professions, law for example. But the young man decided he would after all take up boxing and win the world title that his father – hopefully – would have won back if he had not met his death in 1949.

The boy became a lodger and lived in Edith's apartment for eight years. She told him he must train hard, and in her sentimental way tried to help him as she had tried to help his father, praying for divine protection and sewing medallions of Saint Thérése into his boxing shorts. She also attempted to educate him, as she had done in the case of his father, but Cerdan junior did not appreciate all the books she pressed into his hands. Cronin's novel *The Keys of the Kingdom* was not for him. But Edith loved him as a son: they went to Bernay together, looked at the school where Edith had been a pupil so long before and visited the church, where they lit candles and prayed for the young man's father. The latter was truly venerated by Edith, for in a small locked bedroom she had stored all the clothes and other items which Cerdan senior had left behind. Later, some were stolen while others were found in sale rooms, but fortunately some were sold and bought honestly.

The young Marcel saw Edith in relaxed mood, as few people had the chance to do, and he remembered seeing her jump into a pool of rainwater, just for fun, which she said she had done as a girl in Belleville. She did not even bother to take her shoes off and would go back to her chauffeur-driven car dripping wet and happy. Edith would remind Marcel that they were bound to get on well – they had both been born under the sign of Sagittarius.

At least once there was a cheerful Christmas party at the boulevard Lannes apartment, when the Cerdan children were joined by Jacqueline Boyer, Jacques Pills' daughter by his first wife Lucienne Boyer. Even as he grew up young Marcel Cerdan did not often become involved in Edith's hectic late-night parties, she would remind him that he must get up early and go out on his training runs before any studying that he had to do. If by chance Edith was 'resting' at home and somehow went to bed early, she would leave her bedroom door open if Marcel was out. When he came in, she would call out to him and say goodnight. She was a good 'mother' to him.

It would be all but impossible, and not very helpful, to attempt a list in strict chronological order, of all the places she visited in the US and other American countries in her many tours over there. Some incidents stand out, all the same, notably the amazing success at Carnegie Hall in January 1956. She was already tired when she came to New York to prepare for this recital, for she had been on tour in the mid-west and in the south of the country. As the day of her opening appearance approached she was suffering from bronchitis and conjunctivitis and realized she would have to blackmail the doctors or cancel the show. No doctor ever seems to have resisted her appeals for very long, she received the injections she knew to be essential for her, and she appeared on stage determined to be a success. Her success in fact was phenomenal. She sang no fewer than twenty-two songs, many of them in English, the performance was recorded by an amateur and has always been considered one of her greatest triumphs. Some performers, after such a success, might have been tempted to stay in New York and enjoy even more glamorous social life, but even if Edith had wanted that Louis Barrier had lined up contracts for her in places far away from the capital, starting with Havana, Cuba. There she met again Jean Dréjac who had returned from a few months' absence in France without letting her know in advance. She did not welcome him, for by now she had set her mind on someone else. Dréjac had stayed away too long, and now he went back to Paris, there was nothing else he could do. Jacques Pills too was back in France, but Jacques Liébrard, Edith's guitarist, was close.

Louis Barrier and Edith's entourage wanted her to be always in love, for it meant that she was enjoying life, she was happy and confident, although everyone knew when a change of key was imminent, they merely hoped the accidentals and the modulation would not be too painful for anyone. She was not short of new adventures in her professional life, with visits to Central and South America. Mexico was the next stop, she had three separate engagements there and enjoyed meeting local singers and musicians. She sang with them a Spanish song which announced that life was worth nothing – *La vida no vale nada*, but took care to sing also *La Vie en rose*, with some of the words in Spanish.

A TV appearance in New York, a further visit to Mexico and then a successful appearance in Rio de Janeiro, where, to her own surprise and that of everyone else Edith enjoyed herself hugely. In an interview published later in France Edith announced that Brazil was 'a wonderful country. For the first time I said to myself "*Tiens*. I could live here." ' On a gala evening there the stage around her was covered in flowers, thrown on to it by the audience, and she sang part of *La Vie en rose* in Portuguese, just as she had sung in Spanish for Mexico and also for Argentina. She enjoyed singing together with local folklore performers, Brazil enchanted her, but she knew she must return to Paris, her fans wanted her.

She rested for a time at Louis Barrier's country house, not far from the former farmhouse she had bought for herself at Condé-sur-Vesgre, to the southwest of the capital. But like Jean-Paul Sartre, she did not like the sight of green grass: country life was not for her.

Outside France the name of Félix Marten is known only to specialists and in fact he could be described as one of Edith's rare failures, in the sense that he soon chose to disobey her orders and that obviously meant disaster. Marten was four years younger than Edith, had a Dutch father, and had been born in Germany. He had first trained as an actor with the famous Charles Dullin. He later appeared at Bobino and the Alhambra and made one successful record, *La Marie-Vison*. It was decided late in 1957 that he would fit neatly into the next programme at the Olympia, which was to include Edith.

Marten was drawn closely into the Piaf ambiance, for any singer associated with her was usually destined for success. Like Aznavour he loved Piaf, but Piaf the star, not the woman. She wanted to make him the sort of star she liked best, the closest in style to her own, assuming he maintained a *macho* image, and there was every likelihood of that. She probably did not love him either, but she loved, or at least fancied, the potential star, essentially the star she would make. He has gone down in history as the 'cynical' singer, for he liked songs that had a causal, throwaway theme and that did not tell the story of some lost or longed-for love: *A Cannes au Carlton*, or *Fais-moi un chèque*. Edith had other plans, but all she won in the end were small concessions, no victory. She wanted him to sing love songs for that, she believed, was what the public really wanted and cared about. He didn't agree, he wanted to stick to the line he was beginning to make his own. In the end, during their brief association, he consented to sing two, *Je t'aime mon amour* and *Je me souviens d'une chanson*. The latter, with his words and music by Jean-Pierre Moulin, was in the tradition: 'I remember a song when we were in love, that song spoke words of love, it used to make me cry when we loved each other ...'

> *Une guitare a réveillé*
> *Une chanson presqu'endormie,*
> *Tu reviens, tu me fais rêver,*
> *Chanson d'amour en Italie ...*
> *Douce guitare, tendre mémoire,*
> *Racontez-moi la vieille histoire ...*

The phrase *les mots d'amour*, the words of love, occurred often in Piaf songs and later it was to be the title of a song all to itself. And while mentioning the 'cynical' singer it is worth remembering what another slightly less cynical friend said of her: she certainly sang more words of love than she spoke. The composer's direction is typical of this period of Edith's life, expressed in musical terms: *Tempo di Valse Moderato*.

The audience at the Olympia, appreciative but seriously critical at the same time, patiently sat through the first half of the programme, which included the singer Germaine Ricord, a team of performing dogs, a Brazilian dancer whom Edith had discovered, a juggler, a ventriloquist, a lively group of acrobats and then the *vedette américaine* Félix Marten, who, after intensive training by Edith, sang nine songs. Following all that excitement, finally Edith herself, who had not appeared at the Olympia for a long time and now sang fourteen songs, including eight which had not been heard in Paris before. She had planned to finish with the ecstatic, heaven-looking *Hymne à l'amour*, but the audience demanded *L'Accordéoniste*, and they got it. Edith was then engaged to appear for six more weeks and Félix Marten was to continue as *vedette américaine*. He did so, until he was so exhausted by the demanding Edith that he left the show. She had hoped to transform him into 'a French Cary Grant', but in that she failed. He too failed to keep her undivided attention as a lover, but since he had told her he didn't know what love was, she was ready to accept someone who did.

Just occasionally a non-singer appeared in Piaf's life. There was, according to Ginette Richer and Auguste Le Breton, a secret short-lived romance with a well-known figure in the art world: André Schoeller, director of a gallery in the rue de Miromesnil, an attractive man of twenty-nine, 'the perfect example of the intelligent *bourgeois*; elegant, cultivated and level-headed'. Everything was on his side, he had not needed too much effort to make his way for his father was one of the leading art experts in Paris. Admittedly he had a wife, but he enjoyed Piaf's company because he found her desperately attractive, someone from another world who not only sang brilliantly but also had a more than lively, even coarse sense of humour. His humour was of the dead-pan variety. His world was so different from hers in fact that when she went to his gallery she would dress with as much care as if she were going to an official reception.

Schoeller seems to have loved Edith, and never forgot her, but it suited him to keep the liaison secret, although this did not stop him from going to the boulevard Lannes. He acquired that special status granted only to a select few; he was allowed to telephone her at ten in the morning, whereas the unprivileged had to wait until at least early afternoon.

He took great risks in visiting Edith when Félix Marten was still abroad. On one occasion the latter came back unexpectedly and Schoeller had to hide in a wardrobe. Edith is said to have cared for him a great deal, so much so that she even – apparently – asked his mother if she could possibly have him all to herself, and also offered to bring up the child his wife was expecting. It does not matter if the stories are true or not, they fit neatly into the Piaf apocrypha, which is bound to go on lengthening for many years yet. It was at André Schoeller's gallery that Piaf bought one of the few paintings she ever possessed, an abstract by the Russian-born painter André Lanskoy. He had tried to give it to her, but she insisted on paying for it. She hung it in her bedroom, over the television, and it remained there for the rest of her life.

At this point readers of the Piaf story are tempted to look at the end, as though they have reached a comparatively dull chapter in an emotional, theatrical thriller. All the time the battle against drugs and drink went on. She had tried *désintoxication* in an attempt to lose the drug habit, as Cocteau had tried it during the 1920s, but he claimed that opium – his problem at the time – was not always willing to let people go. However, she did not receive even a little help from her friends, who went on smuggling into her apartment all the bottles, suppositories, ampoules, syringes and other equipment that were needed. Eventually friends reported that her body was covered with scars, the injections had become so frequent. It was also said that a glass of beer would make her drunk for a day, and the mere sight of a bottle of wine was almost as effective. Edith had not escaped this artificial paradise because her entire life had become artificial. Since she could not live without her audiences she had to go on stage however ill she was, and she would go to any lengths whatever in order to take those few steps from the wings to hear the applause and start to sing at the right bar. She loved her audiences, she needed their love, or preferably adoration, in return. Men were needed too, the individual man as a single unit of that vast audience, visible in the music-hall or theatre, invisible beyond the recording studio or the radio microphone. The response and support of one man was her other related source of strength which kept her on stage. He could be replaced to some extent by a pseudo-protective group of hangers-on, but the group was not entirely satisfactory. One man had to be there all the time, one who would take punishment without complaint, sitting through the same film or record a dozen times because she said he must; he must not show alarming individualism, if *she* ate fish, he and everyone else must eat fish. He must consent to stay up all night and go to bed at dawn. If he shared her bed he might realize, sadly, as various former lovers have admitted, that sex in itself gave her no satisfaction. At this stage of life Edith, with increasing rheumatism and digestive troubles, was unlikely to change. But in the meantime she had to be amused for her emotional life was not only empty, she began to fear that no one would ever love her again: men were deceivers ever: 'I realized one day that someone was pretending to love me in order to succeed, out of self-interest. The first time, in 1957, I heard the man who said he loved me telling friends: "Edith has allowed me to succeed in a few weeks, without her it would have taken years." That day I realized that I had grown old, and that is a terrible day for a woman.'

She wrote this in her last confession, which was to be published only after her death. And it was then, she said, that she began to fear not so much death, but the thought of dying alone. She was forty-two.

Few performers sang more about sad endings and rejection than Piaf, and few people laughed more loudly and more often in real life. Her laugh was unmistakable and according to one

Paris journalist it could dominate a party of 200 people, while after the 1940s there are few social photographs of her where she is *not* laughing; she liked a surrounding crowd, not only to keep away darkness and depression but also for two-way amusement. No wonder Marcel Blistène, the film director, suggested that her laughter was a clown's reaction to the grimness of life. She was particularly fond of Ginette Richer because she was cheerful and carefree – she liked her to be there when she woke up. She loved practical jokes, which hardly improved her image, but at least they act as a corrective to the worship that still surrounds her. Sometimes Edith's own songs supplied the jokes, such as the unrepeatable, fortunately untranslatable words she would sing when the moment was right to that splendid melodrama *Mon Légionnaire*, and among all her lost songs who does not regret one that is more lost than most, the fiercely funny anti-men song that she and Marguerite Monnot were reported to sing in the small hours, provided of course that all the men had left.

But of course most men stayed. Roland Avellys stayed because he was, in a sense, Edith's court jester. His name is unknown outside France except to those who relish the gossip-loud byways of the music-hall world. He was known as *Le Chanteur sans Nom*, the singer without a name, and it was often added, without a voice. He had no obvious means of support and so became a sponger about whom even Edith complained, but she did not banish him from the court. Officially he acted as one of her secretaries for a time and his work did nothing to reduce the chaos of life in the boulevard Lannes apartment. His worst joke was played in a provincial theatre where Edith came on stage as usual and then, to everyone's amazement, signalled 'curtain'. She was bent double, not with stomach cramps but with helpless laughter. The prompter's box in the front of the stage framed a remarkable sight: somebody's bare bottom, the cheeks holding, if that is the right word, a pipe. Nobody, of course, was going to identify the owner of the bottom, but Roland Avellys seemed to be the only candidate. Edith had her laugh and eventually the show began.

The unfortunate Avellys was a diabetic, and later became so ill that with financial help from Edith, Aznavour and others, he was sent to a home for impoverished theatrical survivors.

There had never been any absence of men acting in varying capacities. Claude Figus was there as a secretary, and even boasted that Edith had let him make love to her, just once. He had been a hopeful fan since the age of fourteen, and did mad things in an attempt to amuse Edith. So mad that he had even been sent to prison for frying eggs over the 'eternal flame' at the Arc de Triomphe. One man who could have been a lover years earlier but never found the right time, now contributed something new to her life that was to last longer than a love affair. The man was the legendary actor, Pierre Brasseur, one of the sacred monsters of the French stage and cinema who never did anything by halves. His contribution to Edith's career was the scenario for the film *Les Amants de demain*, directed by Marcel Blistène and first shown in Paris in 1959. Brasseur, a powerful actor, was the sort of man who could get violently drunk very quickly and attack anyone who did not agree with him, or just anyone, come to that. He once had such a row with André Schoeller about the stupidity of abstract art and the value of various films in which he himself had appeared that even Edith was alarmed. *Les Amants de demain* was not a great film but it was moving in a near sentimental way, with violence for those who wanted thrills, and good performances by several people in what seems to us now an old-fashioned typically French atmosphere, almost cosy because we recognize all the elements. A composer, Pierre, has killed his wife, and on a dramatically rainy Christmas Eve a car breakdown forces him to stop at a hotel restaurant, *Les Géraniums*, only to find even more drama. The highly *macho* Louis is unfaithful to his wife, Simone, played by Piaf, and treats her so badly that she has taken to drink. There is much breaking of china, Pierre falls in love with her, she responds and even finds the strength to kill her husband. The ending would surely bring tears to many eyes, even if their owners are flinty-hearted; the lovers walk down the stairs together towards the waiting police, to the accompaniment of the title song. Marguerite Monnot had composed the music for three other songs with words by Henri Contet, not great works but all part of the Piaf *œuvre*.

Since the early 1950s Edith had had small film parts, mainly singing parts, and this was the last film in which she appeared. It is sad to reflect that some of the violent unhappy scenes were reminiscent of those in her own life. The revue *Films français* described this film in 1959 as a 'realistic drama' in *demi-teintes* adding that 'certain passages' had a 'certain sensitivity', while Piaf's performance revealed 'emotion and touching sincerity'. Another French reviewer described how Brasseur's scenario brought out the star's 'undeniable dramatic talent', and how she acted with 'intense emotion', her expression *dramatiquement bouleversé*: a phrase that recalls Piaf the singer. If she had outlived her own voice would she have been able to start a new life on the large and small screens? One can only speculate. Marcel Blistène was amazed to discover that Piaf was not considered good box-office at the time, and believed that if she had had the chance to make more films she could have become a star comparable to Italy's Anna Magnani. Later critics disagree with this opinion and have not seen her as a potentially great actress. She herself preferred the music-hall stage to the studio, for there she could do more or less as she wished and would not be 'directed' or 'produced' by anyone, although she always appreciated her accompanists and especially her conductor Robert Chauvigny.

But 'realistic drama' continued in life as on the screen. As Cocteau was so fond of saying, *le hasard fait bien les choses*; but if one does not believe in *le hasard* it may be safer to say 'destiny' rather than 'chance'.

As Louis Barrier and those close to her knew so well Edith had to have a lover, she had to be in love, otherwise she was tiresome.

When she first saw him Edith remarked that Georges Moustaki looked like a Greek shepherd boy, but he had in fact been born in Alexandria, Egypt, in 1934, studied French, worked in Paris as a journalist, ran a bar with a piano, played the guitar and was soon writing successful songs. He met the gypsy musician Henri Crolla, a cousin of Django Reinhardt, and a collaborator with the poet Jacques Prévert. Crolla, also a guitarist, introduced him to Piaf. He was young, broad-shouldered, smiling: she responded to him immediately but apparently told Ginette Richer to see that he took a bath. This was discreetly arranged, but the slippery bath earned him a dislocated shoulder, a possible hint of trouble to come. He accepted the challenge nonetheless: he went to Sweden with Edith in 1958 as guitarist and lover.

At first he was resilient enough to cope with everything, including the all-night rehearsals and the violent rows which Edith enjoyed. He, in turn, enjoyed giving orders to her entourage, and soon realized that at all costs he must stop her from drinking.

Naturally he had not anticipated the complexities of life with Piaf: being made to sing one passage of one song no less than thirty times was only half the story. After ten days in Sweden, so the story goes, Edith announced that the food was bad for her, cancelled her next appearance and chartered a DC4 to take the whole party – seven people – to Paris for a decent meal, which at all costs had to include Camembert cheese. It was a typical Piaf *coup de tête*, more expensive even than usual.

This story may have been apocryphal, but there was another incident at the end of Edith's second tour of Scandinavia in 1958. It was successful professionally but nobody could have been proud of the way it ended. In Stockhom Edith suddenly complained of stomach pains and had to cancel the performance she was about to give, if in fact she had not already begun it. She was admitted to hospital and even received advice and help from the doctors who looked after the royal family. She was told she was likely to have an intestinal blockage and the surgeons would have to operate the next morning. But Edith was nervous; she decided that if surgery was essential she would rather go back to Paris where she had more faith in the medical experts, who after all knew her only too well. She told Danielle Bonel in the hospital that evening that in any case she was now feeling better and insisted on going back to her hotel. So, like naughty children, they crept secretly out of the hospital during the night. A plane was found that would take her back to Paris in the early morning, the long suffering Louis Barrier met her at the airport accompanied by a doctor and took her to hospital. She had no surgery but a long expensive rest. Danielle did not forget the end of the story: for her first meal back home in the boulevard Lannes Edith asked for smoked herrings and garlic mayonnaise. It could all be described as a typical Piaf story.

Edith's total poverty when young might have made her careful with money when it came her way, but not so: money was for spending and giving away, never for keeping or spending on dull things, in itself it did not interest her in the slightest. The contrast with Mistinguett and Maurice Chevalier is amusing, both those performers being famous for their devotion to *le fric*. Edith's harassed agent, Louis Barrier was not pleased at this latest episode, but at least he knew that another US tour was due, and that would surely remedy the eternally desperate financial situation. Moustaki was learning fast, seeing that Edith had to keep the expensive crowd of people round her because she could not bear to be alone.

He loved her for a time and made her promise not to drink. He told her that her promise was the symbol of her love, and she, after her fashion, loved him for a time in return. This did not stop her from being unkind to him in public, and once, thinking she had overdone it, she invented a particularly cruel explanation.

'Tell him I'm pregnant', she apparently said to Ginou, 'that's why I've been so horrible'. The embarrassed girl told him and reported that he wept with emotion. Needless to say, soon afterwards he had to be told of her miscarriage. He wept again.

In one sense, fortunately, Piaf and Moustaki had some progeny. Who, even today, has not heard *Milord*? In 1960 her recording of it stood at number seventeen in the British Top Twenty charts for two weeks, unusual for a continental star. The melody can crop up in a totally unrelated British TV dancing show, performed, so to speak, by girls who may never have heard of the song or the people who created it. The song has a lengthy history going back, apparently (again according to Auguste Le Breton) to Piaf's younger days. Once, standing outside the Paris Opéra as the notables emerged after a gala première, she saw Leslie Howard, the British film star, coming down the staircase. He at least looked like a 'milord', and was wearing a long white elegant scarf with his evening dress, as men did in the 1930s. Edith recounted her memory to Moustaki, and so in his song the girl in the waterfront café invites the unhappy rich man to share his troubles with her. She had seen him looking proud, like a king, wearing his long silk scarf, but now he was weeping and she would never have believed that possible: *Ça, je ne l'aurais jamais cru*. Moustaki compressed the whole story into two stanzas, and Marguerite Monnot devised the music in a fox-trot tempo with a melody that lingers easily in the head and allows of surprising variations in timing and interpretation. Oddly, Moustaki sang this song himself before Edith did, but never with success. That had to wait for her recording of 1959.

Moustaki wrote both words and music for three other songs, *Le Gitan et la fille*, which is a high-drama love-song by a gypsy ready to go to prison for his girl; *Un Etranger*, based apparently on melodies from Greek folklore, and *Les Orgues de Barbarie*, a nostalgic reminder of the barrel-organs which Edith had so often heard in the streets when she was young.

Who could have expected such a talented man as Moustaki to devote himself for long to a tyrant twenty years older than himself? Like Eddie Constantine, André Pousse and the others, full of admiration mingled with varying percentages of love, affection and even pity, he could not stand it for long, especially when Edith began to drink again. It was his bad luck to be driving her back from her country house when the car skidded as he tried to avoid a lorry. She was not seriously hurt but facial injuries had to be patched up before a trip to New York. Moustaki felt guilty. Unbelievably, they later had a second minor accident at the same spot, a hamlet called A la Grâce de Dieu. Saint Thérèse had been watching, but Moustaki realized enough was enough. Edith then found out, or chose to believe, that he had been unfaithful to her with the girl who was looking after his little daughter.

Unwillingly, persuaded by the diplomacy of Louis Barrier, Moustaki went with Edith to the US in January 1959. The agent had told Moustaki that if he did not go with her, she would have refused to go to the Waldorf Astoria, where she was to appear and they would demand compensation. She was enormously successful until her drink–drug excesses caught up with her. She collapsed on stage in New York and was taken to the Presbyterian Hospital. There she survived a four-hour operation for stomach ulcers and internal haemorrhage. She was incredibly tough, and she still mattered enough to Moustaki for him to come back from a trip to Florida.

'Do you love me?' she asked.

He could not say yes, and friendship would not do. In Edith's emotional life there was no room for half-measures. A few years later she made two journalists watch as she threw some splendid jewellery into the lavatory and flushed it away, saying it reminded her of a man who had let her down. Since 1959 Moustaki, later long-haired and grey-bearded, has tended to become identified with his own moving song, *Le Métèque*, the outcast.

He has sung and composed, and who, listening, for example, to Serge Reggiani's interpretation of his song *Les Gestes* with its sensuous accompaniment, could possibly deny Moustaki's individual quality?

In 1959 however Edith was unrelenting. She condescended to keep *Milord* in her repertoire for her audiences wanted it, but Moustaki's other songs, *Le Gitan et la fille*, *Un Etranger*, *Les Orgues de Barbarie*, were removed. Fortunately she had recorded them all in 1958, but she recalled later that her astrologer had warned her that the man in her life at that time would make her unhappy. He would have to go.

In 1984 Moustaki, then aged fifty, remembered Edith, who had left the scene twenty years earlier but was still there, with her laughter, her anger, her gestures, her glance, her voice. Only death, he believed, brought her some rest from her rage to live, to love and to sing. 'There is no "after Piaf". She is *l'amour-chanson*, *l'amour de la chanson*, *la chanson d'amour*.' The words love and song were inseparable when speaking of her.

De mortuis nil nisi bonum. And the editor of *Témoignages sur Edith et Chansons de Piaf* added: 'Between Piaf et Moustaki, between *Milord* et *Le Métèque* much water has passed under the bridges of the Ile de Saint-Louis, where he lives.'

From this period onwards there are literally hundreds of photographs showing Piaf in hospital, usually with her hair well set, and nearly always being kissed by some admirer. Immediately now there *was* a new admirer, and for once she had not known he was there already waiting in the wings.

It could have been some teenage romance. He came from Atlanta, adored Piaf the singer, and had taken to visiting the hospital in New York merely to have news of her progress. He had even left bunches of violets for her. Those close to Edith used to say that the endless flowers she received did not interest her in the slightest, but this time she noticed them and asked to see the man who brought them. Douglas Davis, soon to become Doug, was introduced, and since he was a good-looking painter of twenty-three, his immediate future at least was predictable. He had been in France as a GI and then studied painting in Paris. He was the perfect partner for Edith. Fortunately he was at hand when she had a relapse and needed a second operation. At least he was there to see her through it.

Of course he came back to Paris with her, but her run of bad luck was not over. He too crashed her car – or rather, the car she had given him – and she as usual suffered more than the other passenger, Michel Rivgauche in this case. Again she had broken ribs, again she insisted on singing and did so, after the inevitable and destructive pain-killing injections.

Douglas Davis has gone down in the photographic records as Piaf's swimming instructor. A few years earlier Jacques Pills had persuaded her to try swimming – normally no exercise of any sort interested her – and she had even bought elegant swim suits from a Paris couturier. But as usual *plaisir d'amour ne dure qu'un moment*, Doug was allowed no time to paint, to meet Picasso, or visit the nearby places where Van Gogh and Cézanne had painted. The Mediterranean light had revolutionized his vision, he wanted to translate it on to canvas but Edith did not see things his way. She was, of course, glad enough to sit for her own portrait, and the few that Doug had time to paint are immensely striking, highly tragic and, to those who only know the obvious publicity pictures, unrelated to all the photographs taken over the years. But Douglas Davis had seen the true deep sadness within Piaf, he was more of a prophet than he knew and perhaps he foresaw tragedy. The tragedy was not limited to Edith. In September that year, 1959, she had yet another serious operation, this time for pancreatitis from which many sufferers never recover. Saint Thérèse had been at work, the doctors could hardly believe it, Edith was soon home and soon on the road.

There was a great row in Biarritz, and by the time the couple had reached Bordeaux in December Doug had had enough.

One legend recounts that he fled during the night, promising to telephone. Another says that when Edith realized he had gone she rushed to the station by taxi only to see the Paris train pulling out. Edith had told him that if he left her she would kill herself. But she didn't even try. Two years later Douglas Davis left Orly airport for the US; his plane crashed shortly after take-off. There were no survivors.

Despite the quasi-romantic episodes of these few years Edith was not making herself any happier or healthier, and recorded only three songs in 1959, one of them, *Milord*, marked *Tempo di fox moderato*. A surprisingly large number of her songs in fact are marked *moderato*, a way she never behaved in life. At this stage of existence the indication could have been *rallentando*, and if the collapses on stage, the operations in New York and Paris, only increased the despair of the doctors and the devotion of her fans, theatrical managers became slightly nervous and newspaper reporters would lurk about, hoping, if that is the word, for even more drama.

Part Three

Tempo di Slow

9

No regrets

The reason Piaf's life has been so much publicized, and still is nearly half a century after her death, is of course the unique quality of her singing. Listening to her songs is a fascinating experience but it grows immensely richer when absorbed against the background of her life, for nearly all her lovers and friends had contributed in some way to her songs and their performance. Her early experiences shaped her career and she then chose to spend the rest of her life as she thought she wanted to, allowing her lovers to condition her and conditioning them in return. At the same time she was more than a singer, she was an actress and lyric writer: she wrote the words for about eighty songs and she knew instinctively more about the public relations business than many highly trained specialists.

Anyone who is intrigued by Piaf's contribution to her repertoire as a creator and not solely as a performer will enjoy studying the texts she wrote for her own songs. It should be said that some people even quite close to her have denied that she actually wrote them: some say she merely 'inspired' them, but in any case there is never any guarantee that a lyric will be the same at the completion of a song as it was at the start, and she always worked closely with her musicians. The lyrics themselves are obviously revealing, even if the range of imagery is as restricted as the note-span. There is a touch of fantasy in *Le Vagabond* of 1941 but *La Vie en rose*, for thousands of people the one identifiable Piaf song, is set to a very short lyric of no particular value which still contains two ordinary phrases of interest to anyone looking at the whole of Edith's writing: '*Il me dit des mots d'amour*', a phrase which supplies the title for a later song – *Les Mots d'amour*, 1960 – and recalls the remark by one of her lovers that she sang more words of love than she ever spoke; then comes '*Des mots de tous les jours*', which of course supplies an easy rhyme but also recalls the words used by Raymond Asso in his last song for her, *On danse sur ma chanson* (*They're dancing to my song*). It also goes right to the heart of all those people who can use no other words, for 'everyday words' are the only ones they know, or perhaps need to know.

In 1958 another simple phrase seemed to haunt her, for in *C'est l'amour qui fait qu'on s'aime* comes a mention of '*le droit d'aimer*', again a phrase which supplied a title for the song written in 1962 by Robert Neyl and Francis Laï. The same song links, as so often with Piaf, love and grief, for the singer has paid with *tant de larmes*, so many tears, for the 'right to love'.

And in 1962, so close to the end of her life, came *Les Amants du Dimanche*. It was copyrighted but does not seem to have been professionally recorded. It expresses yet again the sadness which permeates so many of her songs, a feeling that love, if it has been found at all, is always in the past: something which the novels of Françoise Sagan (the first, *Bonjour Tristesse*, was published in 1954) had been saying also, in their different way, for several years. Edith had written these words to Francis Laï's music. It was given a first performance by Claude Figus, that unhappy obsessed young man who had finally succeeded in impressing Edith before taking his own life shortly before she died.

Only her own behaviour had left her as she was in 1960, ill, loveless and uncreative, having made no concessions to anyone, and following a path of self-destruction equalled only by the rock singers of the 1970s and the heroin addicts of the next decade. Writing about her sadly in the late 1960s the journalist

Jean Noli subtitled his book 'Three years to die'. When he first met her he obviously did not know this, but things looked so bleak that he might have been forgiven for seeing an even shorter future for her.

His description of his first meeting with Piaf is worth quoting because it is neither melodramatic nor ecstatic, merely realistic. She had consented to see him at noon, therefore, naïve as he was, he arrived at noon and waited in the salon where the curtains were drawn and the shutters closed. Two eminent people joined him, Marguerite Monnot, the composer, and Bruno Coquatrix, director of the Olympia, the big Paris music-hall. The wait continued, tea and other refreshments were offered from time to time, various other associates of Edith arrived, including Michel Rivgauche, the librettist, and Claude Leveillé, the Canadian composer. Finally Jean Noli's colleague Hugues Vassal appeared. He was Edith's favourite photographer, for he always amused her, and at this moment the two men were working closely together for the newspaper *France-Dimanche*, whose sensational reportages were world-famous. They were hoping for a good series of articles about Edith. The wait continued until 9 o'clock.

Then a door opened. Edith Piaf appeared and walked with hesitant steps across the salon. She wore a pale blue dressing-gown, none too clean, over a crumpled nightdress. Her thin red-dyed hair was untidy, her face looked orange and swollen, without expression. She neither spoke nor smiled, she merely sniffed and sat down on the divan 'as carefully as an elderly cat'. Noli also noticed her transparent fingers and twisted rheumatic hands.

She had appeared to announce bad news. Having promised Coquatrix that she would sing at the Olympia that autumn, she now felt so ill that she would have to say no. Coquatrix had been banking on her appearance as the only way to save his music-hall, for attendance and receipts had been falling, the cinema was more popular. Now he was shattered. Noli was not so much shattered as repulsed by Edith's appearance, and he did not warm to her, although he was impressed by her speaking voice. It was 2 a.m. when he finally left the apartment, accompanied by Vassal. He found himself agreeing to come back that same afternoon, and did not know when he arrived that an historic meeting was taking place round the drawing-room piano.

Edith's entourage, from her cook to her agent, from her maid to her secretary, were by now despondent about her, the great star, one of the most highly paid in the world, who had deteriorated into a prematurely old woman, her ailments uncured, perhaps beyond cure, by doctors or drugs or will-power; was there any future for her, or indeed for them? She did not even have an admirer or lover, old or new, whom she could admire and love in return, and preferably build up into a star. There was, of course, that hanger-on Claude Figus, a kind of secretary but principally a jester and a supplier of drugs when necessary. He was no escort for Edith and his attempts to sing had not yet got him very far.

Edith herself, however, had been recording that year, and singing in public, or attempting to do so. Preferring as usual to forget the warnings of doctors, surgeons and friends, she had insisted, earlier in the year, on undertaking what has always been called the 'suicide tour'. Operations and pain-killing drugs had left her very weak. This tour took place in the north of France including towns such as Maubeuge, where Edith only reached the end of the programme with a great struggle, and Dreux, where she sang only a few songs and then collapsed on the stage. By now the tales of her fragile health, together with her insistence on singing, had turned far too many journalists into inquisitive ghouls. There was one question that nobody dared ask at the time, an obvious one in France. Was she going to die on stage, or at least in the theatre, like the great Molière in the seventeenth century? Everyone knew she would never retire, and she herself had always said she did not want to be old.

So more and more journalists pursued her round the provincial theatres, hoping for a drama of some sort.

Saint Thérèse had not performed any obvious miracles recently, and nobody reported a sudden unexplained scent of roses, usually associated with the saint, as had happened in New York once; but various forces, notably of course Piaf's own insistence on living, at least took her through various kinds of medical treatment, including a deep sleep cure.

But where do miracles begin? When Guillaume Hanoteau in 1975 decided to write a book about a man named Lucien Vaimber he called it *Les Doigts du miracle* (*Miraculous Fingers*), for the subject was a chiropractor whose treatments were causing a surprising number of people to take up their beds and walk. He was used to hopeless cases, and if none seemed more hopeless than that of Edith Piaf he was called in by Dr Fernand Laly after the disaster at Dreux, to see if he could help. At first Vaimber was not too keen to treat her, for he knew she disobeyed doctors, and ill-treated them as much as she did herself. In the end he relented. On his first examination of her he found that her spine – the crucial starting-point for this kind of treatment – was a disaster, so many vertebrae were blocked. Gradually he succeeded in unblocking the nervous system, and as soon as possible he concentrated on those parts of the spine which affect the hepatic system. Like all the orthodox doctors who tried to help Edith at this stage of her life, he could not understand how she was still alive. Yet her will to live and sing, or sing and live, was so strong that she accepted the inevitable pain at the start of the treatment, for at first Vaimber had to touch inflamed muscles. She responded, she promised to take no pills – always the chiropractor's enemy – and no alcohol. She had been in such poor form that her voice had almost faded away, and as she gradually recovered it was still hoarse.

The subtleties of Vaimber's treatment enabled the nerves controlling the voice to become unblocked, and as she continued to improve Edith became one of his most devoted patients; she paid him the great compliment of telephoning him only during the daytime and not in the small hours of the night, the time she usually preferred for most such conversations. She also asked him to help the ageing Marie Dubas, who had impressed her so much when she was young; Marie was ill with Parkinson's disease and short of money now, and in fact it was too late, but at least Vaimber was able to make her more comfortable.

The chiropractor was hardly impressed by the sycophants of the boulevard Lannes, and wondered if they did not imagine things were even worse than they appeared, in order to give themselves more importance. When Edith was at her worst he was reminded of the corridors of Versailles in the seventeenth century, filled with gossiping courtiers as the king lay dying. Edith was soon far from dying, but she wanted a positive reason for living. Nobody was going to forget what Vaimber called the 'Waterloo of the café-concert', that disastrous northern tour; he himself never talked about the miracle cures, and the problem now was to sustain his difficult patient's improvement.

If her physical body had been rescued from crumbling, she still had not recovered her emotional drive, there was no man close to her who could concentrate her thoughts before she translated them into her singing, and then projected them directly on to her audience. One miracle was not enough, something else had to happen and it could not be anything obvious. *Je cherche un millionnaire*, Mistinguett had sung for several decades. Although Piaf as usual owed thousands, if not millions, of francs, as she almost always did, she was not looking for any material solution, but for something much more difficult, an end to emotional loneliness. Piaf, surrounded with people, laughter and gossip, was intensely, incurably lonely. That day in 1960 when Noli and Vassal arrived at her apartment, they were told she was dead tired and in a very bad mood, so things did not look hopeful. The two men were sent to wait in the kitchen.

In the drawing-room that day in September 1960 was a composer whom Edith had been turning away literally for years. She had been more than cool, almost hostile, to Charles Dumont, who was still a young man. He had been born in Cahors, in south-western France thirty-one years earlier and had been first drawn to the world of professional music by his schoolboy admiration for Louis Armstrong. He had successfully studied the trumpet at the Toulouse Conservatoire, but owing to an operation he had to give up playing it. Then came three more years of piano study in Paris, mainly in the hope of progressing to the organ. He met the writer Francis Carco and set some of his poems to music, but he still had to struggle to earn his living, and at one stage even did clerical work in a car factory. He also sang a little. He was given a chance by that splendid lady of French music publishing, Madame Raoul Breton, and he had composed for several of the well-known *chanteurs de charme* including Tino Rossi, Sacha Distel and others. He had various successes; he won, ironically enough, the Prix Edith Piaf, with *Offrande* at Deauville, and in 1959 the Coq d'Or prize with *Lorsque Sophie dansait* – but Piaf remained supremely uninterested. She had always refused prize-winning songs, she had always wanted to create all the songs in her repertoire herself.

It was not a miracle, nor was it luck, that brought Dumont, along with his friend Michel Vaucaire, to the boulevard Lannes. It was sheer persistence. The helpful Vaucaire was an experienced librettist who had supplied lyrics for Jean Sablon, Fréhel and that splendid quartet Les Frères Jacques. Edith liked him, but she did not like Dumont. She thought he was too fat. She had even tried to cancel the appointment. However, she received the two men, scowled and said, 'One song only'. She heard the song through and then asked Dumont to play and sing it again. Then she stopped him halfway through.

'*Formidable*', she said. She asked him what the title was.

171

'*Non, je ne regrette rien*'. 'No Regrets'. It was an inspiration, perfect for Edith, because of course the words exactly fitted her own attitude to life and people, and instinctively in those few minutes she sensed that it would reach out to vast audiences directly and immediately. It would reach those who felt, or thought they felt, the same way, and more particularly those who wished they dared to. Its range, musically, was suitably narrow and low.

In the edition published by S.E.M.I. in Paris *Non, je ne regrette rien* is marked *Tempo di slow* (i.e. slow fox trot), and is set in assertive C major, based on blocks of quavers in triplets throughout. Neither words nor music waste any time:

> I regret nothing, good or bad,
> All is forgotten, I don't care about the past,
> I've lit a fire with my memories,
> Old loves are swept away,
> I'm beginning again . . .

and here, in the last four words, the important personal note:

> It begins with you.

Edith had fallen in love many times and now she was in love again, with a song rather than with a man. But no song composes itself and Charles Dumont after his years of rejection was now identified with this one. That night he had to play and sing the song not once or twice but endless times, for everyone in the Piaf entourage had to hear it after she had first given her unexpected approval.

Charles Dumont left the boulevard Lannes exhausted, wondering how Edith would find the strength to sing the song, but surely pleased, not knowing of course that nobody could be accepted by Edith Piaf and remain on the fringe of her existence.

As usual with her it was all or nothing, and now it was all. That very night he was summoned back to the apartment at 3 a.m. – Claude Figus had the task of issuing these instructions by telephone because Edith wanted Bruno Coquatrix to hear the song at once.

Why could it not wait? Because the day before, Edith had broken Coquatrix's heart, and in fact he was literally having heart trouble, such were his financial problems. His Olympia, of course, was no ordinary music-hall, its nearest equivalent in Britain being the London Palladium where the most prestigious of international stars have always appeared. Bruno Coquatrix had become inseparably identified with the Olympia which is in the boulevard des Capucines, not very far from the famous, oppressively pseudo-classical church of La Madeleine. The complex history of the Olympia, dating from 1893, forms a colourful chapter in the history of Parisian entertainment, and in 1954 Coquatrix had rescued it from its reduced existence as a cinema, earning himself enthusiastic popularity. The Olympia with its 2,000 seats, its boxes, and its red and gold décor, had a soul; it was a link with the past like those older vanished music-halls such as the Eldorado, so beloved by Cocteau and his generation, where Mistinguett had appeared when she was young. But the scene was changing quickly yet again and the rival A.B.C. had given in, accepting finally a new life as a cinema.

Coquatrix himself had all-round experience, he had composed more than 300 songs and several operettas, acted as an impresario, and directed the Bobino music-hall. He was now identified with the Olympia, it was a show in itself – it must go on. The programme for the year 1960, looked at nearly fifty years later, had no shortage of big names: Georges Brassens, Colette Renard, Josephine Baker, Gilbert Bécaud, Judy Garland, while Edith had originally been billed for three months, opening in late December. She had now been cured by song, she improved visibly every day, but there was still a vast amount of work to do. The date was put off until the very end of the month, and during that autumn Edith continued her cure by forcing herself to work several hours a day, in the late afternoon or the early hours of the morning. As she got better her entourage got worse, she pushed them all to the point of collapse, but none of them, composers, pianists, journalists, domestic staff, were allowed any human rights whatsoever. They had become objects, they were no longer people. She subjected them to a kind of house arrest. Everyone had to be ready at 5 p.m. when she got up, and then there would be three hours or so of intensive rehearsal. The so-called relaxation granted to the prisoners was worse than work. She-who-must-be-obeyed would decree what play or film they were going to see, and according to Edith's usual practice nothing was to be seen just once. If Ionesco's celebrated play *Les Chaises* was wonderfully entertaining the first time it was something of a stale joke by the eleventh visit. The same was true of that classic film *The Third Man*.

Even dinner had to be eaten under Edith's personal martial law: everyone had to eat the same thing, something nourishing such as calves' liver with boiled rice. Not only had the guests to eat the same thing day after day, but they must never dare to say that they did not enjoy it. Gilbert Bécaud once disobeyed orders in a restaurant, which did him no good. Alcohol was forbidden. Lucien Vaimber helped to keep Edith on the path to recovery by recommending home movies, and lent his own. Edith, he remembers, was particularly fond of the great Pagnol films.

Charles Dumont produced song after song, while the unfortunate Marguerite Monnot, brilliant composer and lifelong friend, saw her titles gradually excised from the planned programme, for Edith maintained she must at all costs sing something new. With her all-or-nothing outlook she now thought only of Dumont, who of course had to be there practically non-stop. Fortunately he was able to preserve his personal identity – he was ready to compose and manage, and escort, but no more. If Edith was a survivor, so was he, and he even weathered her attempts to break his spirit – such as making him listen in on the telephone to other composers attacking his work during her personally conducted opinion polls.

Since she had not sung to a large discriminating Paris audience for a long time her agent arranged for a few appearances in the provinces so that she could test out the new songs, and notably her new self. She was to sing in Rheims ten days before the Olympia, everyone was expected to go with her and give moral support. Marguerite Monnot did not go. She was hurt at finding that nearly all her songs had been cut from the programme, while Charles Dumont, Edith's golden boy, had taken over. Dumont had enormous respect for Marguerite Monnot's talent, but of course he was in the hands of the dictator. Lucien Vaimber had not wanted to go but he was persuaded to do so in the end, following a plea from Edith.

'No pills, no stimulants', he said.

'I must have them', she replied. 'I can't go on without them.' She would have terrible stage fright, she added, she wouldn't be able to sing. So he went with her, and so did far too many journalists who made no secret of their ambition: they wanted to be in at the 'death'.

The chiropractor worked on her neck until she was sufficiently relaxed to start. To his horror, and that of everyone else, she broke down as soon as she began to sing. She looked to Vaimber for help and he gave her a glass of Evian water, nothing more. She then sang fifteen songs without trouble. The audience acclaimed her to such an extent that all the mirrors in her dressing-room were broken in the rush of admirers, and she had to sign autographs until 2 a.m.

The next stop was Nancy, 200 kilometres away. The roads were so wintry that Claude Figus had an accident, his small car turned over, but he was unhurt. Edith's driver fortunately encountered no problems. The final rehearsal before the

Olympia took place at a cinema in Versailles on the evening of Christmas Day. Marlene Dietrich sent a telegram. There was even a song intended to please Edith's chiropractor; a song with his name in it: *Mon vieux Lucien*, telling the story of the man who is saved from suicide by an old friend. It had been improvised by Dumont and Michel Rivgauche, and Edith had learnt it in three days, almost, for she sang a few bars and then dried up. Fortunately the words came back to her almost at once, and she began again to loud applause.

Then came the Olympia. Edith got up at 5 p.m., her usual time, and when the moment came to dress there was a great scene. How could she possibly wear a brand new dress and new shoes, she told Danielle her helper that, she must have known that new fabric rubbed her skin and new shoes pinched her feet. She wore an old one, and old shoes. She had, of course, arranged every detail of the stage presentation herself, especially the lighting, but her entourage lived through a few hours of total hell. When she appeared on stage the ovation lasted for sixteen minutes and at the end there were twenty-two curtain calls. It was an unforgettable evening. Fortunately, the performance on 29 December was recorded, and again Edith forgot the words of *Mon vieux Lucien*. She told her audience it had happened before, and she would start again now because otherwise she would never sing this song. Inevitably she was greeted with typically wild applause. She would not allow this hold-up to be removed from the recording: it happened, she said, that's what I did, and sales of that unique record reached a million.

If Marguerite Monnot had complained about her banishment from the repertoire she surely could not complain about the last item on this recorded programme: her song *Les Blouses blanches*, one of Edith's most terrifying performances, terrifying because it is about a woman in a mental hospital who remembers the day when she wore *une petite robe blanche avec des fleurs*, and the hand that held hers. 'I'm not mad, I'm not mad', she cries, surrounded by the white-coated staff. Edith did not so much sing as act. Where did she learn those intonations, those half-whispered words, that mad laughter? If there has been a good deal of talk in France about Piaf the tragedian, then this piece alone can justify it.

Dumont had supplied her with a prolific new range of songs – *Les Mots d'amour, Les Flons–flons du bal, Mon Dieu, La Belle Histoire d'amour*, are just a few titles that literally kept her alive and led her into a range of interpretation that she had never known before. She made more recordings during 1961 than any other year, and night after night she sang at the Olympia. Not content with her decisive comeback, she found another means of terrorizing her entourage. She told Bruno Coquatrix that she would extend her performances by a whole month until mid-April. Her confidence had never faltered and her records were selling in thousands. At the same time the cost to herself was mounting. Even if she had spoken on the radio in praise of Lucien Vaimber, she did not honour her part of the contract, and soon she was going on stage only after an injection of coramine, a drug which at least allowed her to stand for the necessary time. But her voice was clearly not what it had been in late December and she continued to ignore everyone's good advice.

After the Olympia season Edith's entourage, from her agent to the ever-present Charles Dumont, thought that she would surely have a rest, but they were mistaken. *They* needed a rest, they wanted a little normal life, they wanted to see the daylight, the sunshine. Edith, on the other hand, as though intent on using every hour twice over, not only wanted but insisted on taking up a contract with L'Ancienne Belgique, an expensive night-spot in Brussels. Believing that she could, must, cope with any health problems whatsoever, convinced that the round of drugs and injections – she used several doctors independently to keep her going – would buoy her up for ever, to Belgium she went and of course everyone else went too.

The Belgian audience were entertained and Edith's agent was paid, but everyone, including Edith, suffered. In the first place the audience at L'Ancienne Belgique were in the habit of eating, talking and drinking during any performance at their expensive old-fashioned café-concert type of establishment. This hardly suited Edith, but as Charles Dumont has recounted since, nobody could be certain any evening that there would be a performance at all, for Edith had become by now so unco-ordinated that sometimes she could hardly speak. Dumont and Barrier would escort her to her dressing-room in what appeared to be a sub-human condition, she would sit and wait for her miracle-injection which was given to her twenty minutes before she went on stage. Then she took her stimulants, far too many, and sang as though practically normal. She was supposed to sing eleven songs but stopped after nine. She insisted on late supper after the show, was of course wide awake until 6 or 7 in the morning, and could not be left alone. Everyone else was on the point of collapse, even the highly resistant Charles Dumont who was not merely composer and escort, he had to sing at least one song with Edith, *Les Amants*, his own composition to words she had written herself. This is a particularly moving song, but ideally needed two voices. When Dumont asked who would sing it with her she replied, 'You will'. He did as he was told and was to realize later that Edith had brought him back to singing, telling him also, inevitably, how to conduct himself on stage and how to get the best out of a song. This one opens in *Tempo Barcarolle*:

Quand les amants entendront cette chanson
C'est sûr, ma belle, c'est sûr qu'ils pleureront
Ils écouteront les mots d'amour que tu disais
Ils entendront ta voix d'amour quand tu m'aimais
Quand tu croyais
Que tu m'aimais

Que je t'aimais
Que l'on s'aimait . . .

As the refrain returns after, of course, love is known to be over, syncopation and 'Tempo de Slow Rock' enter the song. Edith's words were simple and near-sentimental, expressing a simple and near-sentimental situation which, of course, set to Dumont's deceptively simple music, made the song a huge success. Everyone in the audience from the age of sixteen to sixty would have experienced, or thought they had experienced, such a situation.

After the tour, Dumont had had enough. He insisted that Edith should go to a clinic to be cured of her drug abuse. Such was his authority – it seemed to be lasting well – that she did so, for she was terrified that he and his music would go out of her life. She emerged in early June, better but weak, and was persuaded to spend a convalescent summer at Louis Barrier's house at Richebourg near Houdan where she hardly ever went outside, avoided the sun, but held court in the afternoons. The faithful, Charles Dumont, Jean Noli and the photographer Hugues Vassal, still attached to Edith on behalf of *France-Dimanche*, drove over from Paris; they had to be *there*. Dumont made his first and much publicized mistake – he tried to persuade Edith to go to the mountains later in the year for winter sports. He started the propaganda early for he knew he would have to work hard at the idea. Unconsciously Edith, clearly helped by Lucien Vaimber, also summoned to Houdan, as her health slowly improved, was beginning to look for a man who would be more to her than a composer. She appreciated Dumont, but she wanted a more intimate companion – she had never been without one before. She was not well enough to sing in public although she had succeeded in recording a dozen or so songs early in the year. The range of these, again, was amazingly wide and many remain, or should remain, Piaf classics, if they were better known. In *Le bruit des villes* (Dumont) the accompaniment is loud, but it was meant to be, and the orchestration is complex and dissonant. *Carmen's Story* (Dumont and Rivgauche) is a drama in four verses telling the story of a violent lovers' quarrel during the making of a 'Carmen' film. *Marie-Trottoir* is the portrait of the classic prostitute: *Marie qui vend du rêve à ceux qui ont envie d'espoir*, Marie who sells dreams to those who want hope – while *Exodus*, the theme from the film, proves that even when Edith accepted music very different from her usual repertoire she was immensely moving because she sang with her whole being: she sang as though she genuinely, deeply cared about the plight of the people concerned – she who hardly spent any time thinking about events outside her own immediate theatrical world.

Charles Dumont, longing for some mountain air, duly made all arrangements for Edith and her essential staff to leave on a ski-ing holiday in January. At the last moment Edith summoned him to her at 2 a.m. and told him she would not go. Charles was given to understand that if he went he need not bother to come back. He went. When Edith telephoned this to Jean Noli, he went to the apartment and found Edith in a rage, knitting furiously. He then listened to a tirade of violent anti-Dumont complaints: he wanted all the advantages of *le métier d'artiste*, and none of the drawbacks: he was never there when she wanted him, etc, etc. Edith did not know the word 'unfair', it was a grey word, she knew only black or white.

So she was not there or strictly not available when Dumont telephoned or called on his return. He did not enjoy his excommunication, but he never lost his sense of humour. One day he was told, against the deafening sound of the record-player, that Madame was asleep.

'Tell her to turn the sound down', he replied, 'or she'll wake herself up'.

He had become unpopular at the boulevard Lannes, for he had acquired too much power, and the irritating panderlike

Claude Figus had been exiled, although sometimes he would creep back and eat secretly in the kitchen. Now he was reinstated and liked to think that power had returned to him.

In a way, so it had.

Figus still adored Edith but away from the boulevard Lannes he had found other ways of passing his time. He was lost briefly in the wilds of Saint-Germain-des-Prés where he made some new friends, including a good-looking Greek boy called Theophanis Lamboukas, whose parents kept a hairdressing establishment in the suburb to the south of Paris, La Frette-sur-Seine. He had been trained as a hairdresser himself and was so likable that he had a busy social life. The story goes that he knew someone who knew Brigitte Bardot and when Figus told Edith about this she said she wanted to meet her. Theophanis, known as Théo, was present at the resulting dinner and was soon invited again.

Edith needed to be constantly amused, for her health was far from good. For someone remembered by all her friends for her tremendous laughter it is sad that illness dogged her so persistently – but of course much of it was her own fault. She always maintained that the air of Paris was all that mattered to her – no sea-breeze, no mountain glow could interest her – but at this point the un-French habit of sleeping with the bedroom window open did not help, for she developed bronchial pneumonia, was sent to a clinic at once, and placed under an oxygen tent. If Piaf was ill there could be news, so the *France-Dimanche* reporting team was instructed to find out where she was. Her staff, without bribery, disclosed the secret to these trusted men who regarded themselves as the *grognards*, the old guard.

So off they went to Neuilly, and having mistakenly gone to a maternity clinic first, they found her because of the noise. They could hear it on the ground floor, she was clearly better, clearly not alone, and the staff were furious. Noli and Vassal found a cheerful, convalescent Piaf and, sitting cross-legged on the narrow metal bed were Claude Figus and Théo. Everyone was happy, and Edith wore that seraphic smile which meant that she was falling in love. She had already decreed that Théo's surname should be 'Sarapo', her adaptation of the Greek word meaning 'I love you'.

She was too preoccupied that day to allow any photographs. 'Come back tomorrow', she said. 'I'll ask to be put back under the oxygen tent'. There was no tomorrow at the hospital for Edith was so much better that once again she was ready to bite the hand that fed her, and instead of showing any gratitude to the staff, or consideration for the other patients, she found an opportunity for pure devilment.

Claude Figus knew, or at least tried, all ways to her heart, and he was now clever enough to find her a new musician, Francis Laï, a brilliant young accordionist and composer who was delighted to play to her, even if he were not used to playing in a medical establishment, as he was now summoned to do. Nobody else was delighted, and Edith in her malicious enjoyment even told him to play more loudly. Complaints from the patients, let alone the anger of the nurses, could have only one result: Edith was asked to leave.

That indefatigable team, Noli and Vassal, then deserted Edith briefly – good news of her meant no news for their paper, although they were personally pleased. What they could not bear was Edith the culture-vulture. She had always tried to improve herself, but when she decided to improve everyone else the results were devastating. 'She treated us with disgust', said Jean Noli, 'as though we were illiterate. She had decreed that we must all read, understand and learn by heart, Teilhard de Chardin. Edith sat upright on her divan like a primary schoolteacher and droned out *Le Phénomène humain*'. We can feel sorry for that audience who might have thought they had suffered enough. 'The horror we felt when she brought us together in a half-circle for these cultural sessions is indescribable. We had to listen, go into ecstasies, and ask for more. Nobody understood one word of these esoteric texts which Edith read to us with no regard for punctuation'. Martial law forbade yawning or drowsiness.

Edith once said during an interview that she had been deeply impressed when young by Jack London's novel *Martin Eden*, which is about the struggles of a man who decides to educate himself. Like the hero, she never really learnt where to start.

During another period when all seemed quiet on the boulevard Lannes front, Noli and Vassal were sent on other expeditions of the sort known to fascinate readers of *France-Dimanche*. But they began to yearn for that diminutive Lorelei again. 'The boulevard Lannes was the end of the world, the salon was a separate planet where everything gravitated round her … War could rage in Algeria or Vietnam, Cuba could threaten peace, earthquakes, strikes, derailments, wage demands, racism could increase … everything left us unmoved. Unconsciously we reacted only to the rhythm of her pulse, we were upset only by her heartaches.' She was irresistible – lovers, would-be lovers, or non-lovers, journalists, hangers-on, friends, admirers, people who queued for tickets, or went into record shops, they could not keep away.

There was no lover at this moment. Were there still would-be lovers, apart from Claude Figus, whose sexuality in any case was considered ambiguous? But Figus was surely conscious of his power, and even ready to abdicate from his own aspirations when he saw Edith and Théo draw inexplicably closer to each other, the twenty-year age gap between them being apparently irrelevant. Figus amused Edith, but Théo had a kind of grace which attracted not only her but everyone who met him. At the same time he was no male chauvinist – he was not interested in telling every woman what to do, he was usually ready to take orders from them. So fate surely decreed he should meet Edith Piaf, who may have been aged by illness but at the same time never grew up.

10

'You are the last, you are the first'

Sarapo's promotion was rapid, even if Edith would sometimes find him too obedient, too ready to accept everything from her. In the past she had loved a fight, she had even loved being beaten, especially, so the story goes, in the days of Paul Meurisse.

In 1962, in an interview published in the magazine *Marie-Claire* she made no secret of her predilection for what is now called *machismo*. She liked to rely on men, she wanted to please them and not displease them, while a lover should do all he could to keep what he had. In the United States, she felt, this type of man hardly ever existed, and in France it had almost disappeared. He was more easily found in Italy, Spain or Greece. 'These men make many demands on a woman', she said, 'but at the same time they protect her'. They were also jealous, and a man who was not jealous did not really care. The primitive Piaf of the Pigalle days had not changed; the feminists would find her old-fashioned, while many psychotherapists would probably consider her to be quite right. But of course she wanted it both ways: men must protect her and she must dominate them.

Now she had plans for Théo. She was not too ill or too old to transform him into a new personality, he was temptingly ready for shaping, like modelling clay. So of course he must become a singer. In a strange way this was her style of motherhood, the sort of motherhood that needed no partnership with a father, and that suited her perfectly. Other women had children, she bred singers. The eldest had been Yves Montand, the youngest Félix Marten who had escaped from home very early, and Charles Dumont who had broken the rules at least once.

She laid her plans carefully. First of all Théo must lose some weight, so his diet was regulated by martial law – no fried food, no fat, nothing sweet. She took his future so seriously that she even asked Lucien Vaimber to check his health, and of course it was perfect. She was in love with Théo now, after her fashion, as the journalists had suspected, or she would not have decided that he had a voice, for he had not been aware of it himself. Among his predecessors perhaps only Aznavour, who loved Edith but was not her lover, had ever worked so hard. Théo was in any case acting as the second secretary now and opened the letters, about fifty of them a day, while Claude Figus was in charge of the telephone and appointments generally, which usually involved changing arrangements as fast as they were made.

Théo was also Edith's hairdresser, her official escort, and her lover. But her lover had to have a personality of his own, a *raison d'être*, and that is why he had to work hard, and become a singer. Reports by those who saw and heard Edith's training sessions bring tears to the eyes. How could anyone possibly stand it? How could Théo stand it? Presumably because he loved her, because he had entered the magic circle and could no longer escape. Also, of course, he needed direction, he was twenty-seven, something must fill the future, something more than hairdressing or the friendship of the deceptive Claude Figus, who was all smiles and laughter and defeated the doctors by constantly finding forbidden drugs when Edith wanted them. The most wearing of the singing lessons took place during the second summer break at Louis Barrier's house, when Edith had decreed that she did not want to see any green grass.

The musical scene had changed. The unfortunate Marguerite Monnot was now at a distance. Charles Dumont had been forgiven, his exile had in fact only lasted a few months. Edith needed him but he was no longer the only composer in her life. Francis Laï was already producing songs, there was a new pianist, Noël Commaret, who had again been procured by Figus. But Jean Noli reported, to his amazement, that somehow in the end Théo had become a singer, a good singer. How did she do it? Through being a dictator and a bully and somehow remaining a fascinating woman. Not only did she make him work ten hours a day, but she would come into his bedroom in the middle of the night, wake him up, and go on talking about songs. Yet when she could not sleep she would call him and he would obediently make tea for her and wait beside her bed until she went to sleep again.

Edith wanted to be quite certain that all the world still loved a lover, as they had done in the past. She had to be reassured that her public, whose opinion was the only one she cared about, would not be shocked by the twenty-year age gap between her and the secretary-escort who had become a lover. She manoeuvred Jean Noli into suggesting a newspaper article which would produce a reaction, a plebiscite so to speak. He wrote the article, she received several thousand letters of approval. All was well.

Events had moved incredibly fast. Claude Figus had probably met Théo Sarapo in January 1962. During the same month and during February, Edith was well enough to make some recordings after a silence of seven months in 1961, and she also went with Théo to hear Figus sing Chez Patachou in Montmartre. It was more than fortunate that Charles Dumont was back in favour, for he was never short of ideas and the new group of songs that he produced at this point, if not among the best remembered today, were all perfectly 'right' for Edith: *Ça fait drôle* (words by Jacques Plante), about finding love again when it no longer seemed possible, a theme topical enough for her life then; *Fallait-il* (words by Vaucaire), *Emporte-moi* (Plante), all on the typical Piaf theme of *la difficulté d'aimer*, then *On cherche un auguste* (words by Robert Gall), on the problem of being a clown.

But it was Michel Emer who composed both words and music for one of the best-known songs of that year, *A quoi ça sert l'amour*. His contribution to Edith's repertoire had not been prolific but it had been crucial: *L'Accordéoniste*, twenty-two years ago in the dark days of 1940, then *De l'autre côté de la rue*, and *Le Disque usé* soon afterwards in 1942. There are twelve short verses in *A quoi ça sert l'amour* and if the recording lasts only two minutes thirty-five seconds there is a whole life story within it. Part of the message recalls *La Goualante du pauvre Jean*: without the joys and sufferings of love, life is meaningless. In the tenth verse there is a strong new personal note, for Edith sang this song with her new heaven-sent partner, Théo:

Mais oui, regarde-moi . . .

Mais toi, t'es le dernier,
Mais toi, t'es le premier.
Avant toi, y avait rien.
Avec toi, je suis bien.

C'est toi que je voulais,
C'est toi qu'il me fallait,
Toi que j'aimerai toujours,
Ça sert à ça, l'amour.

Edith, with much, not a little, help from her friends, had been able to stage-manage the last show of her life and had created the partner she needed. In the past her partner had rarely been on stage with her as a singer, apart from Eddie Constantine and Jacques Pills, but now she needed support from a physical presence, someone must be onstage with her, at least part of the time. 'You are the last', she sang, 'you are the first. Before you there was nothing, with you I'm fine'.

It was a song for Edith and Théo, and of course a song for everyone. Did it matter if her voice was older? Did it matter if

Théo's voice was not the perfect voice? Of course not. The miracle was that the two voices, the two people, were there at all.

And this was far from being the only song. Francis Laï, who had played his accordion to Edith in the Neuilly clinic, composed several songs for her now – *Musique à tout va*, and *Le Rendez-vous*, both with words by René Rouzaud who had written *La Goualante du pauvre Jean* in 1954. But there was one new song from this present year, 1962, which is one of the most memorable from her later repertoire. Laï and Robert Neyl produced *Le Droit d'aimer* in which the singer asserts the 'right to love', just as most of the human population of the world at that time were demanding their 'rights' in one way or another. It was one of those 'all or nothing' songs that suited Edith so well: 'The sunrise can be red or grey, time goes by and hours pass', but:

> *A la face des hommes*
> *Au mépris de leurs lois*
> *Jamais rien ni personne*
> *Ne m'empêchera*
> *D'aimer . . .*

'I have the right to love … I have won this right through the fear of losing everything, at the risk of destroying myself, to keep love alive, I have paid for this right …'

It sounded in fact like her own story. She herself wrote the lyrics for at least two songs composed by Laï, and if *Roulez tambours* appears to announce some quasi-military number reminiscent of her early days, this is far from the case: the drums have sounded in the past for Napoleon and for so many wars, let them sound now for those who die every day,

> *Pour ceux qui pleurent dans les faubourgs*
> *Pour Hiroshima, Pearl Harbour . . .*

and when will they sound for love, for the boy who's going to love me, for my friends who are suffering? These words, which show Edith at least accepted, seem to show that she was ready to think not just about herself but for once looking out into the world.

But all this activity was not merely a personal miracle, not just a good moment for the nostalgic record-collector, Edith might be better in health, and in love which was essential for her, but the point of her recovery and her new songs was performance. Louis Barrier had nervously arranged a summer tour along the Mediterranean coastal resorts, refusing to say in advance whether he believed that Théo would be professionally ready or not. Again it was Jean Noli who gave the definitive account of developments.

Edith's headquarters in 1962 was to be a suite at the Hôtel Majestic in Cannes. Again martial law was in force: the shutters were closed and the curtains drawn. The only light came from a small table lamp, and the heat was of course stifling: sunshine was dangerous. Edith disapproved of sun-tan and hated the inescapable sound of outboard motors from the distant harbour.

Gradually a dark plot came to light. In its search for news during the August 'silly season' that successful newspaper *France-Dimanche* looked to the inventive Vassal-Noli team for a new idea. All that was happening in the outside world at the moment was boring. It was Vassal who said it first: 'If Edith could get married ...' His editor looked no further. The team had been instructed to bring back a vital document: no political scandal, no international treaty, simply a note from Edith announcing her marriage to Sarapo. This was all the more important because a rival newspaper seemed to have had the same idea. There was no need to talk her into it, she had been her own skilled publicist for years. She was quite ready to sign the announcement written out by Théo. Jean Noli noticed that she was forced to hold the pen in a strange way for her wrist was so misshapen by rheumatism. She laughed that problem off as profoundly idiotic, hoped that her statement, which Théo also signed, would sell the paper, but at the same time she was genuinely happy.

On their way out Noli and Vassal were able to laugh – silently – at something else, for Francis Laï, Noël Commaret and Edith's essential companion Danielle were playing truant from darkness. They had boldly raised the Venetian blind a little and let the sunshine, real warm sunshine, fall on their calves and feet. Despite the heat, which she disliked, Edith sang in Nice and Monaco as well as in Cannes, with Théo. She watched him from the wings, he looked to her for encouragement. It was vital to sing well enough for her, if she approved the audience would surely follow her. He survived, he was applauded, especially when he sang without a shirt. The duet *A quoi ça sert l'amour* was always applauded, and if Edith's voice and expression brought tears to many eyes this, according to Noli, could well have been part of her plan.

The announcement of Edith's marriage made news across the English Channel. The romantic novelist Denise Robins gave her a good deal of advice in the columns of the *Daily Sketch*, explaining how she too had married a man younger (twelve years younger) than herself. Her advice was sensationally unoriginal, for she told her not to be jealous, make him feel free, be natural.

Edith condescended to give an interview to Victor Newson of the *Daily Express*, the first British journalist she had spoken to since her marriage plans were announced because, as she said, 'I don't think the British understand about falling in love'. She then went on with the remarks that could have been expected: 'In love age does not matter. It's how you feel in your heart. And a woman knows from her heart when she is in love. I am a logical woman (sic) and I know I am in love'. She then went on to say that one older partner in a marriage can help the other, through his or her longer experience of life. She described how they had met, how she liked to have young people around her, the members of her orchestra were young. And of course, she added that she did not care what people thought about the marriage, and 'His parents have given our love their approval'. After their quiet wedding they were going to give concerts together in the US; in any case, concluded the *Daily Express* writer, 'this is a love affair that France loves'.

That, after all, had been the object of the campaign conducted ostensibly by *France-Dimanche*, but indirectly of course by Edith herself.

The wedding was planned for October for there was a short engagement at the Olympia first. Since Edith and Théo were themselves officially 'engaged' Théo wanted to civilize the neglected boulevard Lannes apartment, but he was perhaps unaware that she had no money to spare at the time. If she had known, she would not have cared, for she was not interested in having money, only in spending it or, preferably, giving it away. The couple moved into the Hôtel Georges V for a few weeks while the work was carried out, or at least begun, in the salon and the library. Noli viewed the 'improvements' with a cold eye: 'a somewhat hybrid ensemble with English and Danish furniture, dark-red silk wall coverings, white shelving and cupboards, big pouffes and armchairs covered in black velvet, and a green fitted carpet'. As a wedding present Théo asked for, and received, an electric train set where the background even included a model of La Frette, his home suburb. Another gift was a white exercise bicycle, while he persuaded Edith, who was still impressed by other people's culture, to buy French classic authors in rare editions and fine bindings: Balzac, Victor Hugo and Baudelaire. He pointed out that they were objects of beauty and also a financial investment.

In September Edith still found the energy to make a few recordings, and on the 25th she sang at the Eiffel Tower during a gala organized to launch the film *The Longest Day*, about the American landings in France on 6 June 1944. The writer Joseph

Kessel, who had heard Edith sing at Gerny's in the pre-Piaf days, was delighted to present her to the public.

There followed the two-week season at the Olympia, where she was kept alive as before by injections and pills, and also of course by applause. After the show she was always in a state of collapse, but somehow she carried out the contract.

The next 'contract' was her marriage, and it had been arranged for 9 October – as announced in Cannes – at the Mairie of the 16th arrondissement where ten years before she had married Jacques Pills. The house of Chanel is said to have designed a cream-coloured suit for the occasion, but in the event Edith wore black velvet. Vast crowds came to gaze at the happy couple – '*les petits fiancés de Paris*'. Her audience never let her down.

That day was almost as much of a strain for her as any theatre performance, for at 2 p.m there was a party at boulevard Lannes, and at 5 p.m. the religious marriage, which took place at the Greek Orthodox Church in the rue Daru, a much-photographed occasion complete with simple crowns for the bridal pair and much scattering of rose petals; as part of the theatrical-style ceremony the bridal pair had to walk three times round the altar.

These two 'matinée' performances might have tired a much younger, much healthier woman, and nobody knew until later that Edith had very nearly called the whole thing off, partly from exhaustion and partly because she suddenly thought she was too old to marry such a young man. Various people close to her had even suspected she might be slightly bored with the devoted Théo, but as usual she gave her audience what they wanted. The reason she did so was apparently because she had for the first time a different kind of stage-manager, the nurse Simone Margantin, appointed on the insistence of one of Edith's doctors to keep close watch over the patient.

When Edith seemed ready to behave like a perverse child Simone reminded her of something ultra-important: she must think of her public. How could she threaten to cancel the marriage? What would *they* think? That settled it. This was Simone Margantin's first success and she needed it, for Edith promised to be the most difficult patient in Paris. The entourage did not at first respond to a person so alien – as they thought – to themselves, but they soon came to appreciate her deeply, as Edith did, for her devotion was total; she would, of course, threaten to leave when her patient overdid her perversity and disobeyed all the rules. But then everyone close to Edith had done the same for years, and no one had ever disappeared for good. Typically, Edith the bully came to respect anyone who stood up to her.

At this moment the patient had no chance to be a newly wed; she went into a coma and had to submit to another *cure de désintoxication*; then, unbelievably she left for a tour of Belgium and Holland, accompanied of course by Théo. She was well enough to watch every minute of his every performance, she was more critical, more cruel than ever, she found Théo sub-professional, she would subject him and everyone else to violent tirades on the necessity to work twenty-four hours a day – which he did more or less. For once she even noticed and mentioned what was happening in the outside show-biz world. Singers were now launched far too quickly, she said, and for that reason lasted five minutes.

Théo was not the only one to receive rough treatment. Before leaving for Brussels Edith had told Charles Dumont that she intended to remove *Non, je ne regrette rien* from the programme and substitute *Le Droit d'aimer*. She enjoyed perpetrating such minor cruelties, and made it clear that she would sing it at L'Ancienne Belgique, where they had created *Les Amants* together. Then two days later she summoned him to her apartment and showed him the words for a new song she had written. He was ordered to compose the music and come to Brussels. This was *Le Chant d'amour*:

193

Si vous voulez bien écouter
Je vais chanter
Un chant d'amour
Les paroles sont banales à souhait
Il y a deux amants qui s'adoraient …

Dumont found the words moved him to tears. She sang the song in Brussels, the first and last time he heard it in the theatre. It was the last song she wrote, the last he set for her, and he felt there was some deeper significance in the occasion. However the audience at Brussels, at the end of the show, demanded *Non, je ne regrette rien*. She had not anticipated this, but she sang it, and never omitted it from any show again.

Edith could not, obviously dared not, rest. Simone Margantin gave her vitamin injections now, but knew that her patient could not live on nervous energy alone. The patient succeeded all the same in giving a series of performances at Bobino, the famous old music-hall in the rue de la Gaîté. Her success, despite the huskiness of her voice and her avoidance of long-held high notes, even brought her an offer for a tour in the US, Canada and Japan, while Théo was at last well received by the Paris public, despite criticisms that his singing voice was too nasal.

'War, earthquakes, strikes, derailments' and the like were still nothing compared to the crises at the boulevard Lannes, especially when the news leaked out that Théo was a patient at the Ambroise Paré clinic. Not possible! Whatever was the matter with him? He had a boil. Nobody believed that, or that Edith was at his bedside. Eventually the real news was discovered, not only by the *France-Dimanche* writers but by most Parisian journalists, who had also nosed out a good story. The patient of course was not Théo but Edith who had caught a chill by refusing to keep warm after leaving the stage – her mink coat was too heavy, she said – and soon developed pneumonia, accompanied by more liver trouble. Fortunately her heart was strong enough.

But her stage life came to a cruel end after a performance at the Lille opera house : 31 October 1962. She had a cold and the theatre was half full.

Théo decided to take his ailing but still tyrannical wife away from Paris and the hangers-on. He rented a villa with twenty-four rooms near Cap Ferrat on the Mediterranean coast. It turned out to be too big, even though the entourage took up residence. The swimming-pool was tempting, but Théo was soon forbidden to swim in case he drowned, just as he had been forbidden to fly when Edith had heard about Douglas Davis's death in an air crash.

If Edith herself could no longer impose martial law Simone Margantin organized each day into a strict convalescent home routine – sleep, food, relaxation such as Scrabble, which Edith loved, especially if she found a chance to cheat. Sometimes she seemed incredibly well and even sang a little, including even *L'Hymne à l'amour*, which was not easy. Members of Théo's family came to stay and all might have continued in quiet convalescence if a certain visiting musician had not tried to take over the situation, for he told Edith she could certainly eat what she liked. He destroyed all Simone Margantin's careful work and after Edith had eaten an omelette and a paella she went into a hepatic coma. Everyone was prepared for disaster, but once again a miracle happened and she recovered. A little later Edith spent a short time in a local clinic and then the whole group moved to a smaller house near Mougins, La Gatounière, unsuitably situated opposite a petrol station, boasting only four bedrooms, but that at least deterred unwelcome hangers-on. It was also further away from the humid sea air, something that Edith had to avoid. Unfortunately a local doctor gave her an unsuitable drug for another problem and again she had to spend some time in a nearby nursing home. The small party stayed only a month at La Gatounière and then moved on. They were constantly short of money now for there were no more performance fees for Edith, only royalties from record sales, which could not cover medical fees, rent, and salaries for her staff, although the latter were all devoted and far from grasping.

The group were much more comfortable in a village called Plascassier near Grasse. A rough narrow road led to the house, L'Enclos de la Rourre, which Edith had seen and approved. 'A gravel path led to the baroque edifice which was a cross between a house in Normandy and a chalet in Savoy, a strange building which still called itself a *mas provençal*. There was a small swimming-pool opposite the house; dead leaves floated on the stagnant dirty water; shrubs and trees surrounded the property'. The Côte d'Azur landscape only looks 'right' in brilliant weather, and in a sunless autumn there is no more depressing place. However, Edith could occasionally go for short walks in the grounds and Sophie, the toy black poodle that Théo had given her, and known as *la Boule noire*, enjoyed playing with the fruit that fell off the persimmon tree.

The stage lights began to grow dim for Edith. She was alive only because her old, good friends came or telephoned, Aznavour and Dumont especially, in addition to Noli and Vassal. Cocteau was ill at Milly-la-Forêt, near Paris, but telephoned regularly. Edith was not told that Claude Figus had died mysteriously, probably due to a drug overdose, in Saint-Tropez.

Théo came down from Paris at least every weekend. He was trying to make a stage and film career for himself and Edith, his self-constituted publicist, encouraged every journalist to support him. She now decided that she would study the history of France and advised a student who was supposed to help in the house to study Racine's *Andromaque* instead. She became so convinced of her own recovery that she began to plan the programme for a gala at the Palais de Chaillot – the proceeds were to go to medical research, for just as she had always given money away she was now intent on helping the specialist who had helped her.

In the meantime Danielle hired old films to amuse Edith, games of canasta and Scrabble continued, but it was becoming apparent that she now seemed bored even by the faithful Théo. At the same time she seemed to be living partly in the past and even suggested that the chauffeur, Christian, could be a singer, he must record some songs on the tape-recorder. Did she see herself as a Pygmalion figure again?

Visitors found their way to Plascassier, including Edith's half-sister Denise Gassion, who had left Canada and was living fairly nearby. But Edith did not want to see her, or her children.

Raymond Asso, the more than helpful figure from the early days before 1940, now over sixty, came more than once. On his last visit he talked to her alone for quite some time. A few years later he remembered his early association with Edith and in particular the conversation at Plascassier. He had never been able to accept her entourage and now described it as 'a band of pitiful evil clowns'. He went on: 'She took me aside and, slowly, talking as she had done in 1936, choosing her words carefully, she said, "Raymond, I'm in a very bad way. This time I think it's the end. Perhaps I've got one more chance. You, since you're free, when I'm back in Paris, come and live with me and get rid of everything that's doing me harm; all these people around me." She made only one exception, Louis Barrier, her devoted agent'.

Did Raymond Asso hear what he wanted to hear? Had she lost touch with reality? He wished he had had the strength to take her away. Théo Sarapo, on hearing of this, later, threatened legal action. 'I am not a clown', he told the press. But Edith's staff had begun to suspect she was no longer interested in him.

If sometimes Edith was incapable of speech at other times she talked about her friends from the past and said she had an idea for a song. 'It will be the story of an abandoned soul whom passion does not rescue from solitude …' Charles Dumont and Francis Laï would write the music. She talked of reincarnation, the Rosicrucians. She added significantly that she would like to

197

come back to earth when life was over, reminiscent of words Cocteau had written years before: 'I shall disturb after my death'.

She was already disturbing everyone now. She began to resemble Norma Desmond, the heroine of *Sunset Boulevard*, playing the ghost of herself. On bad days she told everyone to listen to her records, saying that she would never sing again, but she also said that Charles Dumont really had written a song for her. Dumont, talking to the singer Jacques Brel in a Marseilles bar, had mentioned Edith. On hearing how ill she was Brel suggested that they should write a song for her. He began that moment and Dumont never forgot the evening. He was overwhelmed by Brel's affection for Edith and by the quality of the song, which he believed to be near genius. The words had an immense relevance: 'for life and laughter, I rely on you'. Next day Dumont read them to her over the telephone: *Formidable*, she said, but wanted to be better before she saw him.

Simone Berteaut telephoned, Edith refused to speak to her. Then the so-called 'sister' of her early days, *sa frangine*, arrived at the house, with her schoolgirl daughter; Edith refused to see them, but Simone Margantin persuaded her to allow them in. Edith deliberately had lost touch with her and had in the end been angry about her behaviour vis-à-vis Cerdan. She insisted that Simone Margantin should stay in the room. There was a very brief conversation and Edith advised the daughter to work hard, 'study's the only thing'. She then made it clear that the visitors must go and later snapped at Danielle Bonel for having allowed them in. Margantin's plain report of this short visit sets the record straight, for a few years later Simone Berteaut was to write an embroidered, dramatic account of her visit, as far from the truth apparently as a chapter in any *vie romancée*.

In the small hours of 10 October Simone Margantin realized that Edith was suffering from an internal haemorrhage. She administered the necessary serum and installed a drip-feed. The doctor came at 5 a.m. but he could do nothing. Later that day, as the wind outside rose in a storm, just after one o'clock, Simone told Danielle to telephone for a priest. At ten minutes past the hour Edith's eyes opened brightly, then closed.

The music grew loud, the lights were finally out.

The house lights of course came up at once. The singer had left the stage but the audience were still in the theatre, waiting for more. They hoped for a curtain call, and in fact they had more than one.

The radio announced that Edith Piaf had died in Paris, which was a lie, but how could Edith Piaf, *la môme Piaf*, die in some unheard-of village in Provence? Her body was taken to Paris overnight by ambulance, accompanied by Théo and Simone Margantin and so she 'died' officially at the boulevard Lannes apartment, as the plaque on the wall there still witnesses. Edith's friends appeared at once, so did her audience, in thousands, and the heartbroken Théo eventually allowed them to file through the apartment and pay their last respects. A rose and an orchid had been placed in Edith's hands. Kiffer drew her portrait.

Lucien Vaimber came. 'Death', he said, 'had made her beautiful'. He noticed that the new curtains hung lamentably at the windows, for ever unfinished.

The tributes in the press and over the airways were more emotional than usual. How could they have been otherwise? Everyone had expected another miracle, another resurrection, for after all Piaf was 'different', and she was only forty-seven. Michel Emer wondered for whom he could write songs now. Félix Marten said he owed her everything, he would have given his life for her. Norbert Glanzberg, the composer, an intimate from the days of the German Occupation, likened her to an Indian fakir who could make you believe in an invisible rope, her genius could transform a mediocre song into a minor masterpiece. And Yves Montand remembered how they had laughed together.

Jean Cocteau had died on the same day as Edith, having mistakenly agreed to give a radio interview about her. The news of her death had struck a final blow. The burial at the cemetery of Père Lachaise was the last theatrical event, on a mild day, with a blue sky. The vast crowds were practically out of control, and there were many other stars on parade, Aznavour for instance, and notably Marlene Dietrich, who had been aware that she had abandoned this 'poor lost child', as she destroyed herself with drugs. The Catholic church would not allow a religious ceremony since Piaf had remarried after divorce. The writer Colette had received similar treatment. However, a chaplain was permitted to give a blessing and a detachment from the Foreign Legion sent a wreath. There was general chaos and the unfortunate Bruno Coquatrix was pushed into the grave. The evening papers sold well that day and the photographer Hugues Vassal remarked on how much Edith would have enjoyed the show.

Marlene Dietrich, as though on tour, went on to Cocteau's funeral at Milly-la-Forêt.

Edith had joined her father and her daughter, whose names are engraved on the expensive tomb. It is well marked on the Père Lachaise map; Oscar Wilde and Modigliani are not far away.

Seven years after Edith's death, her young second husband, Théo Sarapo, correctly Theophanis Lamboukas, joined her. Any memory of him perpetuated the same aspect of her life and nothing expresses it better than the ninth verse of the song they had sung together:

En somm' si j'ai compris,
Sans amour dans la vie,
Sans ses joies, ses chagrins,
On a vécu pour rien.

(If I've got it right,
Without love in your life,

200

Without its joy and sorrow,
There's no today or tomorrow).

The tomb in Père Lachaise is rarely deserted, for people of all ages come from all over the world to pay their respects. It is maintained by Théo Sarapo's sisters and Les Amis d'Edith Piaf.

Many Parisians, including Jacques Chirac, mayor of the city at the time, had earlier believed that Marcel Cerdan, Edith's ideal love, should be reburied in the Père Lachaise Cemetery. Cerdan's son Marcel thought so too, but his widow, did not agree. There was no need to perpetuate that story, *La belle histoire d'amour*, in such obvious fashion.

Cerdan's remains have been transferred from Casablanca to Perpignan, where several members of his family now live.

After Edith's funeral the then president of the S.A.C.E.M., Jacques Enoch, remarked sadly that with her death a 'a form of French song has disappeared'. The *chanson* does not die, it survives in different modes, it lives on, and 'all the lonely people' will always be remembered. Edith cannot come back to earth, as she had hoped, for she did not die, she is immortal. She took *la chanson* into new adventures but never forgot how it had developed among 'the poor people of Paris', even if these latter may not have been aware of the provincial background which was so important in its history.

Coda

The funeral may have constituted Piaf's last appearance but there was little chance of her being forgotten. Almost immediately *La Semaine-Radio-TV* published the story of her life in eleven instalments with strip-style drawings, and the French press in general canonized her. The obituaries published in Britain preferred to concentrate on what they presumably saw as straightforward interpretations of *la chanteuse réaliste*: Philip Hope-Wallace in the *Guardian* quoted an earlier description: she looked like a little woman who had 'been ironing shirts for the wrong guy for a great deal too long', while the *Sunday Times* wrote that her voice sounded like 'a cracked church bell and sometimes as if it were torn out of her entrails'. The paper went on to say that she, 'without any personal reticence or even humour, but with staggering sincerity, thundered her demand that the wretched, middle-class and ugly should be able to live on a Cleopatra's diet of wine, roses and love'.

In 1965 her autobiography of 1958 was published in Britain as *The Wheel of Fortune*, while four years later Simone Berteaut scored an international bestseller success with her book *Piaf*. This led to many complaints and legal actions in France, all of which came to nothing; the author said in an interview that she had been aware of Edith's presence with her after her death and that as she wrote the book Edith had brought *her* back to life. She later wrote her own autobiography, *Momone*. She moved to a little house near Chartres where she lived with a homosexual friend. He left her and a few months later she died alone, in poverty.

Edith had left incalculable debts. The widowed Théo made a valiant attempt to settle them and gave various theatre performances outside France in order to earn untaxed money. Franju's film *Judex* in which he had appeared was not a success in France, although British critics received it more kindly. On Christmas Eve, 1963, two months after Edith's death, the bailiff went to the boulevard Lannes apartment and drew up a list of the items which could be sold: they were few. André Schoeller bought back the Lanskoy painting and sold it to the owner of a well-known store in Paris. In 1970 Théo himself was badly injured in a car crash near Limoges and died before reaching hospital. Jacques Pills died of a heart attack a few weeks later. Marguerite Monnot had faded from Edith's life and then from life itself in 1961, due to undiagnosed peritonitis. The sixty or so songs she wrote for Piaf and her brilliant music for *Irma la Douce* are her true memorial. Charles Dumont found himself in the cold for a few years but made a brilliant comeback as composer and singer.

The record companies in France naturally prolonged Edith's life; they continued, and still continue, to bring out records and cassettes, some released, they say, for the first time, re-recorded and all on well-edited CDs. Occasionally amateur recordings of 'lost' songs are found, but never of course enough to satisfy the devoted fans.

In 1965 French television viewers saw and heard an unusual work, *La Voix*, which owed a great deal to Piaf. Five years earlier, despite illness, she had still possessed enough energy to think of staging something new for her, a *comédie-ballet*, initiated by the dancer-choreographer Pierre Lacotte. According to Michel Rivgauche, who wrote the dialogue and lyrics, Edith worked for three months on this idea with the librettist, the composer

Claude Leveillé and the designer Pierre Clayette. A young man hears a voice in his dreams, the girl who loves him pretends she is the owner of the voice and finally convinces him that reality can sometimes be as attractive as dreams. Twelve songs were composed for Edith, who was to sing them without appearing. By chance one day she sang three of them – *Non, la vie n'est pas triste, Le kiosque à journaux, Le métro de Paris* – and by chance an amateur recorded them, fortunately. The remainder were sung in performance by a chorus, for the creators did not want any other solo voice. The title *La Voix*, The Voice, and the themes of the songs Piaf recorded, were a true reflection of this essentially Parisian work which sadly she never saw in its final state.

Jane Lapotaire's committed acting in Pam Gems' play *Piaf* (1978) also prolonged the singer's reputation and increased her audiences among a new generation, even if the French, predictably, could not accept the dramatist's approach. In 1983 Claude Lelouch, a film director admired by many, made *Edith et Marcel*, in which the rôle of Cerdan was played by his son Marcel Cerdan Junior, because the actor originally chosen for the part had committed suicide. The son's resemblance to his father was one of the few noteworthy aspects of the film.

In September 1981 Jacques Chirac, mayor of Paris, inaugurated the place Edith Piaf, situated at the crossing of the rue du Capitaine Ferber and the rue Belgrand, in the 20th arrondissement close to her birthplace. Monsieur Chirac recalled Baudelaire's phrase, '*Fourmillante cité, cité pleine de rêves*' – 'Seething city, city full of dreams', so well expressed in Piaf's repertoire. Her songs evoked the crowds and the noise of city life, the crushing brutality of the modern world: but all this is transformed by the anguished search for love and its consolations. On the same day the mayor also inaugurated a square not far away in honour of *le gars de Ménilmontant*, the Man in the Straw Hat, Maurice Chevalier, who had always given the highest possible praise to Edith's professionalism. There is a plaque commemorating her on the building that once housed Gerny's Club.

If in her last months she did regret something, the many ways in which she had ruined her health, it is worth recalling a remark she had made much earlier when being questioned about her career: 'I have never been disappointed.' If she could see how far the French and gradually the whole world care about her, she would surely have said the same thing again.

It is possible to 'situate' Edith Piaf, not perhaps to explain her. Before she was a teenager, no more than a child in fact, she was in the midst of a tradition, although of course she was unaware of it at the time. In various ways her earlier experiences were not unique: Rachel, the great nineteenth-century tragic actress, had been discovered when singing in the streets of Lyons at the age of ten. The extraordinary Eugénie Buffet, born in Algeria in 1866, somehow transformed herself from a maid and a kind of camp-follower into a minor performer in Marseilles and then into a singer so popular in Paris that the police had to barricade the streets when she sang to raise money for the poor – one of her main preoccupations, when not demonstrating in various odd ways for political parties of right-wing or royalist tendencies. In spite of world tours and great success she ended her life as poor as the people she had sung for. Her song *La Sérénade du pavé* (later sung by Piaf in the 1954 film *French Can-can*), was as famous as *Le Fiacre* interpreted by Yvette Guilbert who revitalized French popular song at the end of the nineteenth century and later sent it on a new course. All these women singers had to fight for their careers, not one of them had an easy time, they had to support themselves and quite often various members of their family, and of course they had to deal with hostile, noisy audiences. Several of them went into the music-hall because they had been forced to give up the theatre or could not find any other work. They usually had to start by singing the songs that everyone knew and then, when they had built up some reputation, they could find or arrange their own songs in their own style. They had never heard of feminism. They had to compete with men, usually without much success when it came to money, but of course their competition was indirect in some ways because the men and women sang different types of song. Any woman who dared to appear before a café-concert or early music-hall audience had to be tough, especially if she happened to be flat-chested, like Yvette Guilbert, for the men showed no mercy. Any successful song heard in these places was soon heard outside, for economic conditions meant that a great number of people were forced to earn money, or at least extra money, by singing in the streets, just as people were doing in 1985 in Paris and London and New York, even if they preferred the forbidden but warmer corridors of the métro, the Underground or the subway.

Piaf may have sung the *Ça ira*, the famous song from the French Revolution, with her usual total commitment, she may have sung 'Hitler, I can't stand him', but she would never have committed herself to any social or political movement, she was no La Pasionaria, no Joan Baëz, she sang only about the individual, even if occasionally she saw individuals within a crowd, as in *La Foule*, or *Roulez Tambours*, or sang the theme from *Exodus* in a totally committed way. Her individual people however all seemed to have the same problems, which might have led her to see some collective solution, but she didn't: every man, and more particularly, every woman, must look after themselves. Nobody else would even try. General de Gaulle is said to have known her songs, but she herself apparently hardly ever knew or remembered the name of the President of France or the Prime Minister. However, she made one unexpected indirect contribution to the political scene. When the Algerian war ended in 1962, after many painful years, the members of the OAS, as they drove out of the country and back to the transport ships waiting to take them home, sang not *La Marseillaise* but *Non, je ne regrette rien*.

Class and class distinctions meant nothing to her, except in one way: the high class of supreme professionalism meant a great deal to her: Marcel Cerdan could be the ideal lover, Marlene Dietrich a close friend, Lena Horne a valued acquaintance because they had all 'risen' to celebrity and the top of the bill in one way or another. Edith Piaf had a deep respect for star quality.

Religion played a much larger part in her existence than the later generations of her admirers might realize. It was natural for someone whose entire life was lived by instinct to absorb the religious atmosphere of France in the 1920s and 1930s: orthodox Roman Catholicism with no established church but an accepted social framework and a helpful, comforting hierarchy of saints. Since Edith had had no formal education she absorbed the elements of religious observance that were in the air, and so of course her instinctive nature left her superstitious. She knelt down every night to say her prayers, lit endless candles either in hope or gratitude, wore hardly any jewellery except a crucifix, wanted and obtained two church weddings, though she did not go to Mass herself. She also respected the religion of other people and once, when she had a Jewish composer-lover during the war, she apparently even contemplated conversion to the Jewish faith.

The many priests who have talked about her have always stressed her capacity for love, while her generosity – if that is the word – became legendary. It always seems a pity to destroy a good legend but it appears most unlikely that Saint Thérèse cured her of blindness. However, Edith always believed that the saint was on her side and in the last year of her life she urged her entourage to light extra candles for Saint Rita, the patron saint of lost causes. It is sad that when her nurse realized she was dying it was too late for a priest to come to her. Her secretary tried to contact one but significantly could not get through on the telephone. An element of religiosity appeared in several of her songs, especially when Robert Chauvigny, who orches-

210

trated and arranged many of them brilliantly, introduced choirs, whose voices, added to hers, always seemed to aspire towards heaven.

Since the source of all her strength was instinct, and since it was not curbed or controlled by any training of an intellectual kind, she was naturally drawn to the esoteric. It seems hard for us to accept that she believed in those messages from the other world which are supposed to have reached her through the table, but she needed and wanted to believe them. Once, in the US, she is said to have foreseen that a certain plane would crash and forbade her party to take the flight. It *did* crash.

Towards the end of her life she became a Rosicrucian and would spend some time each day in meditation. *Toujours avec nous* – Always with us – is the phrase constantly used by Les Amis d'Edith Piaf, the association formed in Paris in 1967 by a group of young admirers, supporters and previous associates who work with extreme dedication to preserve and further her reputation worldwide. One person with strong evidence of Edith's continued presence is Ginette Richer, who was in fact close to her for a long time and literally gave Edith several years of her life. Ginette always arranged for Mass to be said for her on the anniversary of her death. On the thirteenth anniversary she unaccountably forgot, but on that day the gold chain given to her by Edith clawed at her neck, fell on the table and broke. There were thirteen links in it. The next year, according to the writer Auguste Le Breton, there were fourteen, and the year after that, fifteen ...

Again it is the predominance of instinct in Edith's nature that makes her accessible and understandable to practitioners of the 'alternative' sciences. She holds no mystery for them: Patricia Marne, the British graphologist, was startled when she analysed Piaf's writing and found evidence that she had handled a gun. She also found intelligence, good observation, emotional jealousy and aggression, while Edith emerges as restless, prone to morbid depression and, as everyone knew, possessed of strong manipulating ability.

In the same way the astrologer John Wilson studied her background and her ascendancy carefully, finding evidence that corresponds with amazing accuracy to Edith's life-story and life-style. He has discerned for instance that her mother was probably so unwillingly pregnant and so violent that she may even have tried to abort herself, all of which could partly explain why she abandoned Edith as a small child. Edith's own incapacity for love was only too obvious, only matched by the intensity of her search for it. She could not be submissive and constantly failed in the essential of a relationship with a man. She always looked for a man who would have something of the father-figure about him, which is surely why Raymond Asso meant so much to her for a comparatively long time. Yet she had to have freedom, was extremely obstinate and much better at transforming others than herself.

Edith's whole life was a long attempt to assert her tyranny, her lovers being the first to suffer, even though she believed she wanted protective men. Much of her unhappiness came from this conflict, obviously destined to remain unsolved. The tyranny extended to women as well. She obviously mesmerized Simone Berteaut, even if at the time of their closest association she needed a continuous presence because she lacked confidence as a woman. Her life-long attempt to compensate this lack with dedication to her career was never entirely successful either. And she was terrified of being alone, so there had to be *une frangine*, a kind of sister. This was not *une amitié amoureuse*, love that is more than friendship but less than sexual love. The same is true of the relationship with Ginette Richer who left her husband for Edith. There was no lesbian element in the association but Ginette found herself impelled to live for a time in Edith's orbit, there was no escape.

212

Piaf was of course a living paradox, and her background had been full of violent contrasts in every aspect. Belleville, where she was born, had once been a beautiful village and the rue de Belleville in fact follows the line of the old village street. But Piaf knew it only as a built-up, working-class district and all her life she wanted streets and squares, she had an agoraphobic reaction to open space, greenness and emptiness. There was even a paradox about her physical appearance. Shortly after the Second World War the Canadian journalist Marjory Whitelaw saw Piaf at L'Etoile in Paris: 'All the men in the audience leaned forward in their seats as though they wanted to take her in their arms.' Small and thin she appeared to be, but a closer look at photographs will show a solid neck and, before her last illnesses, a solid stance, which had already been noticed at the start of her career. This was the physical basis of her style and the power of her voice.

And was she sad, or not sad? Noël Coward thought she overdid the drama and tragedy. 'Piaf in her dusty black dress', he wrote in his diary in 1956, 'is still singing sad songs about bereft tarts longing for their lovers to come back and still, we must face it, singing them beautifully, but I do so wish she would pop in a couple of cheerful ones just for the hell of it'. At that period of her career of course she was not singing many of the few cheerful ones that she had sung in the past, and her comic talent always remained unrealized. She laughed a lot as a form of escape, she liked to be amused, she enjoyed practical jokes, often of doubtful taste, and yet she wrote a group of sad little lyrics for songs: *les paroles sont banales à souhait*, to quote *Les Amants*: 'the words are perfectly banal', and sad to the point of hopelessness. She would have liked to be more like Marie Dubas; she once told her: 'You can make people laugh, I can only make them cry.'

If her style was based on instinct it was of course built up through extreme application of technique into what seemed a totally synthetic result, composers being limited to the narrow range of her voice and librettists by her insistence on a particular kind of mini-drama. Yet the preponderance of songs about unhappy individuals and couples reflects a kind of pervasive sadness that had its roots in the France of the 1920s and 1930s with its moral decline and the state of society that had given the young Edith Gassion such a tough start in life. Her repertoire, in its individual way, is the equivalent of the songs that came out of the depressed years in America.

Why, in the end, was Piaf so different in performance, with a difference that can even come through on a studio recording? Other singers have had bad times, bad health, have been unlucky in love. Others have sung with what is nearly always called 'total commitment', as they moved their audiences to tears. Piaf had little on her side beyond her voice – she had none of that obvious but ultimately boring 'glamour' that a great stage star is expected to have. She might look 'glamorous' for the occasional publicity photograph, but this was not her true image. She had one gift that nobody could ever learn: she lived and sang entirely through her instincts, she never let her intelligence interfere with them but used this intelligence to obtain a paradoxical result: if her songs went straight to the heart, beginning with her own, everything about her stage presentation had the high technology which led to total simplicity. She relied on a minimum number of props: the plain black dress for herself, a wineglass for the song *Les Amants d'un jour*, broken at the end, a movement of the arms or hands to conjure up the accordionist or the clown, or the flow of the crowd along the street. In her own way she had the indefinable gift of the choreographer: she worked so closely with her writers and composers that she seemed to be creating the songs with them: Henri Contet was particularly aware of this. In a sense she dominated them by this intensity, just as she inevitably tried to dominate her lovers. And if her education for the music-hall started in the street, surrounded with rivals and a drifting audience who might only stand to listen for a few minutes, then she knew that only intense concentration would hold them, as the ancient mariner had once discovered. Before songs can hold a street audience they must be basically simple, and they must be sung with simplicity. Edith was probably not aware how close her technique came to that so admired by Cocteau: the acrobat who works without a safety net, the skill that must not look like skill: the complex theatrical minutiae, from orchestral arrangements to lighting, from the management of repeated phrases to the order of songs in a programme: it must all look or sound as though it had never been thought out, it must be 'invisible'.

To those unaware of theatrical artifice Piaf always made a direct appeal, as though she were in fact still singing in the street, and looking into their faces. At the same time she has always appealed to the more sophisticated, those who may relish artifice for its own sake, because she has selected and controlled all aspects of technique and technical aids, while somehow giving the impression that she has done nothing unusual: she has just come on to the stage and sung a song made up of everyday words, telling an everyday, usually sad little story. And an audience of intellectual élite are suddenly full of nostalgia for that distant country of emotion and instinct from where they emigrated so long ago.

In the 1950s a French reviewer appreciated the new songs she was then singing, such as *Bravo pour le clown* – disliked by the writer Boris Vian as melodramatic – but pointed out that she hardly renewed herself or her style. How could she? he asked, her singing reflected an age-old heredity, nothing could change it. If some outside influences crept into her later work she was one of the last in a particular line of French singers, and there were no successors. The new audiences who might once have been happy, if that is the right adjective, with those three-minute songs in which every word can be clearly heard, were no longer interested in dead legionnaires or lonely sailors or 'bereft tarts': if you have lost your love, the new policy seemed to be, then go and find a new one. Saint-Germain-des-Prés or the Cavern in Liverpool had brought a new sound and a new way of thinking. The times they were a'changin'.

Piaf was not the only singer to destroy herself as she sang of the destruction of love: Billie Holiday, Judy Garland, Janis Joplin belonged to the same family-without-a-family. Did they not love themselves or life enough? In one way Piaf was more successful than they were. Despite all her illnesses and drug dependence she was always ready to laugh at something or tease someone the moment she realized she was not dying. Her reactions are surely preferable to those of the successful and eternally healthy celebrities described by Noël Coward in the 1950s, sparked off by a performance by Marlene Dietrich at the London Café de Paris: 'She was very good indeed … but afterwards … she was fairly tiresome. She was grumbling about some bad press notices and being lonely. Poor darling glamorous stars everywhere, their lives are so lonely and wretched and frustrated. Nothing but applause, flowers, Rolls-Royces, expensive hotel suites, constant adulation. It's too pathetic and wrings the heart …' Piaf's last year or so can wring the heart, but truly so, and without irony on our part; if she regretted nothing, or very little, neither did she blame anybody else for anything that happened to her. There had been poor press notices sometimes, written usually by young people who had not, so to speak, grown up with her, but these did not worry Edith, she knew her real audience would always accept and forgive her.

She suffered indeed from the death of the heart, for with her, love had died early. Her life was spent in the search for an emotional happiness she never found, but the search led to an intense professionalism in the creative interpretation of 200 dramatic songs, a search that has prolonged her existence and continues to enrich the lives of her worldwide audience.

Postlude

Admirers of Edith Piaf outside her home country will remember that the French were said to approach her, 'like a religious ceremony'. In the autumn of 1983, twenty years after her death in October 1963 Parisians and others indeed honoured her memory with serious devotion. A representative of Les Amis d'Edith Piaf and the deputy mayor of the 20th arrondissement took flowers to the tomb in the Père Lachaise cemetery, where Théo Sarapo's parents were present at an informal ceremony. The recording companies sent representatives too, while other members of Les Amis came from several European countries and from Canada. On 9 October a Mass with Gregorian chant was sung at the church of Saint-Roch, three of Edith's best-known songs were played on the organ and after the Mass, *La Foule*, which had come from Peru, was sung by a group, Les Machocambos, whose name recalled its origin. Edith's brother, Herbert Gassion, was among those present, so too were Michel Rivgauche, Marc Bonel, Jacques Liébrard, plus many show-business people and admirers of all ages.

Two days later, at the church of Saint-Eustache in the 1st arrondissement, there followed a concert in memory of Piaf and Jean Cocteau, who had died on the same day. The song of 1960, *Mon Dieu*, composed by Charles Dumont, was given a stirring performance by 200 choristers, eighty musicians and an out-standing trumpet soloist, followed by Bach's Mass in B minor.

Memorial services were also held in Brussels, Edith's last film *Les Amants de Demain* of 1950 was shown at the Centre Pompidou, while tributes broadcast on radio and television, along with newspaper and magazine articles, were legion. And, as this is written, they continue.

In 1988 a street in Bernay, Normandy, was named after her and on that occasion, in the town cinema, the 'Piaf', Charles Dumont gave a recital of songs she had sung. A school in the French provinces has recently been named after her, so has a cabaret-restaurant in Los Angeles.

Also in the late 1980s, the French magazine *Paris-Match* chose four people, two men and two women whose legendary lives, in their view, had reflected twenty years of French history, from the 1930s to the 1950s – the men: Jean Gabin, André Malraux; the women: Gabrielle Chanel, Edith Piaf . . .

The Prix Edith Piaf was inaugurated in 1969. One of the most successful prize-winners has been Cassita, to be heard singing sometimes at Le Lapin agile in Montmartre, thereby maintaining a link with the past when the Impressionist painters went there.

In her lifetime Edith received endless tributes of flowers but the only flower she really cared for was mimosa, which had been a favourite with Louis Leplée. Once a record company sent her flowers. From them came the sound of birdsong. The company had imprisoned a sparrow, *un piaf*, among the flowers. Edith, predictably, immediately let it fly away.

Bibliography

Achard, Marcel, *La P'tite Lili*, Paris Théâtre, 1951

Amis d'Edith Piaf, Les, *Circulaires*, 1983–5, 5 rue Crespin-du-Gast, 75011 Paris

Aznavour, Charles, *Yesterday When I Was Young*, W. H. Allen, 1979

Beaumont, Cyril, *Ballets of Today*, Putnam, 1954

Berteaut, Simone, *Piaf*, W. H. Allen, 1970 (Laffont, 1969) (Extracts from this text appeared also in the album *Edith Piaf*, Wise Publications, 1976)

Billy, Madame, *La Maîtresse de 'Maison'*, La Table Ronde, 1980

Blanchard, Claude, *Le Parisien de Paris*, Preface by Jean Galtier Boissière, La Jeune Parque, 1946

Blistène, Marcel, *Au revoir, Edith*, Editions du Gerfaut, 1963

Boissonnade, Euloge, *Piaf et Cerdan, L'Amour foudroyé*, Editions France-Empire, 1983

Bonel, Marc & Danielle, *Edith Piaf, Le Temps d'une vie*, Editions de Fallois, 1993

Bret, David, *The Piaf Legend*, Robson Books, 1988

Brunschwig, C., Calvet, L.-J., Klein, J. C., *Cent ans de chanson française*, Seuil, 1981

Cerdan, Marcel jnr [with Gilles Durieux], *Piaf et moi*, Flammarion, 2000

Chevalier, Maurice, *The Man in the Straw Hat: My Story* (Paris 1949), Thomas Y. Crowell Co, n.d.

Cocteau, Jean, *Le Passé défini*, I 1951–1952, Gallimard, 1983

—— *Lettres à Jean Marais*, Albin Michel, 1987

Costaz, Gilles, *Edith Piaf*, Poésie et Chansons, Seghers, 1974

Coward, Noël, ed., Graham Payne & Sheridan Morley, *The Noël Coward Diaries*, 1982

Delarue-Mardrus, Lucie, *La Petite Fille comme ça*, J. Ferenczy et fils, 1927

Dietrich, Marlene, *ABC meines Lebens*, Blanvalet, 1963

—— *Marlene D.*, Grasset, 1984

Duclos, Pierre & Martin, Georges, *Piaf*, Editions du Seuil, 1993

Dureau, Christian, *Edith Piaf 20 Ans après*, Editions SIPE, 1982

Fildier, André, ed., *Edith Piaf 1915–1963*, Collection Im. Phot., Editions Fildier Cartophilie, 1981

Flanner, Janet, *Paris Was Yesterday, 1925–1939*, ed. by Irving Drutman, Popular Library Edition, 1972

Gassion, Denise, *Piaf ma Sœur*, Guy Authier, 1977

Gems, Pam, *Piaf*, Amber Lane Plays, Amber Lane Press, 1979

Gillett, Charlie, ed., *Rock File*, Pictorial Presentations Ltd in association with NEL, 1972

Grimault, Dominique & Mahé, Patrick, *Piaf-Cerdan, Un hymne à l'amour, 1946–1949*, Laffont, 1983

Guedalla, Philip, *The Hundredth Year (1936)*, Thornton Butterworth Ltd, 1940

Guilbert, Yvette, *La Chanson de ma vie (Mes mémoires)*, Grasset, 1927

Hanoteau, Guillaume, *Les Doigts du miracle* (about Lucien Vaimber), La Table Ronde, 1975

Harding, James, *Maurice Chevalier: His Life 1888–1972*, Secker & Warburg, 1982

Henry, Gilles, '*D'où venait cette voix? Les origines d'Edith Piaf*', in *Gé. magazine La Généalogie aujourd'hui*, no. 6, April 1983

Hiégel, Pierre, *Pierre Hiégel présente Edith Piaf*, Sélection du Readers' Digest S.A., 1975

Hillairet, Jacques, *Connaissance du vieux-Paris*, Les Villages, Editions Gonthier, 1963

Jünger, Ernst, *Premier Journal Parisien, Second Journal Parisien*, Christian Bourgois, 1980, Livre de Poche, 1984

Lange, Monique, *Histoire de Piaf*, Editions Ramsay, 1979

Laroche, Robert de, with Bellair, François, *Marie Dubas*, Candeau, 1980

Larue, André, *Edith Piaf: L'Amour toujours*, preface by Liza Minnelli, Editions Carrère, Michel Lafon, 1983

Laurent, William, *Edith Piaf*, Collection Numéro 1, Editions Franklin Loufrani, 1983

Le Boterf, Hervé, *La Vie parisienne pendant l'Occupation*, Vols I and II, Editions France Empire, 1974, 1975

Le Breton, Auguste, *La Môme Piaf*, Hachette Littéraire, 1980

Lesley, Cole, *The Life of Noël Coward*, Jonathan Cape, 1976

London, Jack, *Martin Eden*, Heinemann, 1910

Mercier, Jacques, *Charles Dumont: Un chant d'amour*, Editions Labor, Editions Carrère, Michel Lafon, 1984

Monserrat, Joëlle, *Edith Piaf et la chanson*, preface by Jacques Lorcey, Editions PAC, 1983

Noli, Jean, *Edith Piaf: Trois ans pour mourir*, Presses Pocket, Stock, 1973

Paul, Elliott, *A Narrow Street (The Last Time I Saw Paris)*, Penguin, 1947

Piaf, Edith, *The Wheel of Fortune*, preface by Jean Cocteau, Peter Owen, 1965 (*Au Bal de la chance*, Jeheber, 1958)

Piaf, Edith, *Ma vie: Texte recueilli par Jean Noli*, Union Générale d'Editions; 1978

—— *My Life* [translated by M. Crosland], Peter Owen Ltd, 1990

Prasteau, Jean, *La Merveilleu Aventure du Casino de Paris*, Denoël, 1975

Ribert, Pierre, ed., *Témoignages sur Edith et Chansons de Piaf*, preface by Louis Amade, Editions Métropolitaines, 1984

Rouff, Maurice, *Cerdan mon ami*, Mengès, 1983

Rudorff, Raymond, *The Myth of France*, Hamish Hamilton, 1970

Searle, Ronald & Webb, Kaye, *Paris Sketchbook*, Saturn Press, 1950

Shaw, Irwin & Searle, Ronald, *Paris! Paris!*, Weidenfeld & Nicolson, 1977, NEL, 1978

Shipman, David, *The Story of the Cinema*, Vols 1 & 2, Hodder & Stoughton, 1982, 1984

Signoret, Simone, *La Nostalgie n'est plus ce qu'elle était*, Seuil, 1976

Thérèse of Lisieux, Saint, *The Story of a Soul*, Burns Oates, 1951

Vernillat, France & Charpentreau, Jacques, *La Chanson française (Que sais-je?)*, Presses Universitaires de France, 1971

Webster, Paul & Powell, Nicholas, *Saint-Germain-des-Prés*, Constable, 1984

Sheet music and Songbooks published by Paul Beuscher, Editions Intersong, Editions Salabert, Editions S.E.M.I., Paris

The recorded repertoire of
Edith Piaf
and her contemporaries

Edith Piaf made her first published recordings on 18 December 1935 between 2 and 5 p.m. in Studio 2 of the Polydor company, 74 bis Boulevard de la Gare, Paris 13e. Some tests had been carried out the previous 5 November in the same studio, but neither the titles nor the accompaniments are now known.

Recordings come to light, principally at radio stations, and previous information is revised and corrected, so that discographies of this artist in particular soon become out of date. The most recent is currently being published in the *Bulletins* of the Association française des détenteurs de documents audiovisuels et sonores (11 quai François Mauriac, 75706 Paris Cedex 13). It began with No 17 (Autumn 2000). The information here is as detailed and accurate as can be expected to be found. Our purpose is to draw the attention of readers to five Edith Piaf collections readily available in the United Kingdom. Her recording career spanned nearly thirty years with two principal contracts. From 1935 to 1944 Edith was with Polydor, later Polygram, now Vivendi, and from 1946 with the EMI group, known in France at that time as Pathé-Marconi. All the Polydor recordings as well as the early Pathés on the Columbia label are now in the public domain. A selection from both contracts is now found on *Edith Piaf: La Vie en rose. Twenty-two classics 1935–1947* on ASV Living Era CDAJA5307.

The Edith Piaf everyone knows from recordings blossomed when she signed with EMI. *Edith Piaf: L'Immortelle* has twenty-four of these tracks: *La Vie en rose; Les trois cloches; Hymne à l'amour; Mon Dieu; Jézébel; Le Noël de la Rue; Padam, padam; La Chanson de Catherine; Bravo pour le clown; Johnny, tu n'es pas un ange; Heureuse; LaÇoualante du pauvre Jean; Enfin le printemps; L'Accordéoniste; Le Chant d'amour; C'est à Hambourg; Les Amants d'un jour; La Foule; Mon manège à moi; Milord; La ville inconnue; A quoi ça sert l'amour; Le diable de la Bastille; Non, je ne regrette rien.* (UK CDEMC 3674).

A similar selection, but with enough difference to make it worthwhile owning both is found on *Edith Piaf* in EMI's digi-pak series *Legends of the 20th Century*:

Non, je ne regrette rien; La Vie en rose; La Goualante du pauvre Jean; Bal dans ma rue; Le Chemin des forains; Les trois cloches; Le Diable de la Bastille; L'Accordéoniste; Padam, padam; La Sérénade du pavé; C'est à Hambourg; Les Amants d'un jour; L'Hymne à l'amour; Bravo pour le clown; Au Bal de la chance; Boulevard du crime; La Foule; Enfin l'printemps; Milord; Mon vieux Lucien; Carmen's story; A quoi ça sert l'amour; Mon manège à moi; Les Flons-flons du bal; No regrets: EMI-UK 520142.2.

Edith Piaf at the Paris Olympia covers 'live' recordings from shows in 1962, 1955, 1956, 1958 and some tracks from the 1961 performance, often considered her finest recording:

Milord; Heureuse; Avec ce soleil; C'est à Hambourg; Légende; Enfin le printemps; Padam, padam; Hymne à l'amour; L'Accordéoniste; Mon manège à moi; Bravo pour le clown; Les Mots d'amour; Les Flons-flons du bal; T'es l'homme qu'il me faut; Mon Dieu; Mon vieux Lucien; Non, je ne regrette rien; La Ville inconnue; La belle histoire d'amour; Les blouses blanches: EMI 7944465.2.

Edith Piaf Hymn to Love. Greatest hits in English. Edith Piaf learned English in the United States very quickly indeed. She was able not only to produce English sounds phonetically as many French singers do, but to sing English in such a way that it was clear she understood it and was able to interpret it in the way she wanted.

Hymn to love (*Hymne à l'amour*); *One little man* (*Un petit homme*); *La Vie en rose* (English version); *Chante-moi* (English version); *Simply a waltz* (*Simplement une valse*); *My God* (*Mon Dieu*); *Don't cry* (*C'est de la faute à tes yeux*); *Autumn Leaves* (*Les feuilles mortes*); *I shouldn't care* (*J'm'en fous pas mal*); *The Three Bells* (*Les Trois Cloches*); '*Cause I love you* (*Du matin jusqu'au soir*); *My lost melody* (*Je n'en connais pas la fin*); *Heaven have mercy* (*Miséricorde*); *No regrets* (*Non, je ne regrette rien*); *Lovers for a day* (*Les Amants d'un jour*); *Heureuse* (English version) Recorded 'live' at Carnegie Hall, New York: EMI PRMCD4.

A number of French series cover Edith Piaf's forebears and contemporaries in great detail, notably Chansophone, the productions of Frémeaux Associates, EPM and 'Piaf and her contemporaries' EMI. Information on most of these may be obtained from the Internet. A number of compilations have been released in the UK by ASV Living Era (pre-1950 material) and EMI. Three of the latter are bestsellers:

Paris after dark: with Charles Trenet, Edith Piaf, Tino Rossi, Josephine Baker, Maurice Chevalier, Mistinguett, Lucienne Delyle, Georges Ulmer, Lys Gauty, Les Compagnons de la Chanson; Lucienne Boyer, Jean Sablon, Fréhel: EMI CDP 7906672.

Paris by Night: Edith Piaf, Charles Trenet, Maurice Alexander, Lucienne Delyle, Tino Rossi, Léo Marjane, Charles Aznavour, Mireille, Jean Sablon, Les Compagnons de la Chanson, Lys Gauty, Fréhel, Maurice Chevalier, Eva Busch, Django Reinhardt, Damia, Line Renaud: EMI CDP 7944782.

Paris is for Lovers: Jean-Claude Pascal, Yvette Giraud, Yves Duteil, Lucienne Boyer; Charles Trénet, Lys Gauty, Franck Pourcel, Jean Sablon, Cora Vaucaire, Georges Guétary, Germaine Montero, Paul Bonneau, Enrico Macias, Line Renaud, Charles Dumont, Danielle Darrieux, Elyane Embrun, Bourvil, Mathé Altéry André Claveau and Jacques Hélian: EMI 530 608 2

R.H.

Checklist of songs

Guide to the recorded songs of Edith Piaf, composers, lyric-writers and recording issuing companies (EMI, PM Ph, POL, CBS, and DEC). Dates refer to the year of issue.

L'Accordéoniste Michel Emer	POL/Ph	1940
L'Accordéoniste Michel Emer	PM/EMI	1955
L'Accordéoniste Michel Emer	CBS	1956
Adieu, mon coeur Marguerite Monnot, Henri Contet	PM	1946
A l'enseigne de la fille sans coeur Gilles	PM	1951
Les Amants Charles Dumont, Edith Piaf	PM	1961
Les Amants de demain Marguerite Monnot, Henri Contet	PM	1958
Les Amants de Paris Léo Ferré, Eddie Marnay	PM	1948
Les Amants de Téruel Mikis Theodorakis, Jacques Plante	PM	1962
Les Amants de Venise Marguerite Monnot, Jacques Plante	PM	1953
Les Amants d'un jour Marguerite Monnot, Edith Delécluse, Senlis	PM/EMI	1956
Les Amants merveilleux Florence Véran, Robert Gall	PM	1960
L'Amour du mois de mai Wal-Berg, Jacques Larue	DEC/MUS/ RCA	1945
A quoi ça sert l'amour Michel Emer	PM/EMI	1962
Au bal de la chance Norbert Glanzberg, Jacques Larue	PM	1952
Autumn Leaves Joseph Kosma, Jacques Prévert, Johnny Mercer	PM/EMI	1956

Autumn Leaves Joseph Kosma, Jacques Prévert, Johnny Mercer	CBS	1956
Avant l'heure [operetta *La P'tite Lili*] Marguerite Monnot, Marcel Achard	PM	1951
Avant nous Marguerite Monnot, René Rouzaud	PM	1956
Avec ce soleil Philippe-Gérard, Jacques Larue	PM	1954
Bal dans ma rue Michel Emer	PM/EMI	1949
Le Ballet des cœurs Norbert Glanzberg, Michel Rivgauche	PM	1958
Le Bel indifférent Play by Jean Cocteau	PM	1953
La Belle Histoire d'amour Charles Dumont, Edith Piaf	PM	1960
Le Billard électrique Charles Dumont, Louis Poterat	PM	1961
Les Bleuets d'azur Guy Magenta, Jacques Larue	PM	1961
Les Blouses blanches Marguerite Monnot, Michel Rivgauche	PM	1960
Boulevard du crime Claude Leveillé, Michel Rivgauche	PM	1960
Bravo pour le clown Louiguy, Henri Contet	PM/EMI	1953
Browning Jean Villard, Raymond Asso	POL/Ph	1937
Le Bruit des villes Charles Dumont, Louis Poterat	PM	1961
Le Brun et le blond Marguerite Monnot, Henri Contet	POL/Ph	1943
Ça fait drôle Charles Dumont, Jacques Plante	PM	1962
Ça gueule ça, Madame Gilbert Bécaud, Edith Piaf	PM	1952
Le 'Ça ira' Bécourt, Ladré, arr. Jean Françaix	PM	1954
Carmen's Story Charles Dumont, Michel Rivgauche	PM	1961
'Cause I Love You Eddie Constantine, Edith Piaf	PM	1956
'Cause I Love You Eddie Constantine, Edith Piaf	CBS	1956
Céline Trad. arr. Louis Liébard, Marc Herrand	PM	1946
Celui qui ne savait pas pleurer Ch. Normand, Henri Contet	POL/Ph	1938
C'est à Hambourg Marguerite Monnot. Edith Delécluse, Senlis	PM/EMI	1955
C'est de la faute à tes yeux (*Don't cry*) Edith Piaf, Robert Chauvigny	PM	1950
C'est de la faute à tes yeux Edith Piaf, Robert Chauvigny	CBS	1956

C'est la moindre des choses Paul Misraki	POL/Ph	1940
C'est l'amour Marguerite Monnot, Edith Piaf	PM/EMI	1960
C'est lui que mon cœur a choisi Max d'Yresne, Raymond Asso	POL/Ph	1938
C'est merveilleux [film *Etoile sans lumière*] Marguerite Monnot, Henri Contet	PM/EMI	1946
C'est peut-être ça Charles Dumont, Michel Vaucaire	PM	1961
C'est pour ça [film *Neuf garçons, un cœur*] Marguerite Monnot, Henri Contet	PM	1947
C'est toi [operetta *La P'tite Lili*] Robert Chauvigny, Edith Piaf	PM	1951
C'est toi le plus fort René Cloërec, Raymond Asso	POL/Ph	1937
C'est toujours la même histoire Daniel White, Henri Contet	POL	1942
C'est un gars Pierre Roche, Charles Aznavour	PM/EMI	1950
C'est un homme terrible Jean-Pierre Moulin	PM	1958
C'est un monsieur très distingué Louiguy, Edith Piaf	POL/Ph	1941
C'était pas moi Francis Laï, Robert Gall	PM	1963
C'était une histoire d'amour Jean Hal, Henri Contet	POL/Ph	1942
C'était un jour de fête Marguerite Monnot, Edith Piaf	POL/Ph	1941
Le Chacal Robert Juel, Raymond Asso, Charles Seider	POL/Ph	1938
'Chand d'habits R. Alfred, Jacques Bourgeat	POL/Ph	1936
La Chanson bleue Marguerite Monnot, Edith Piaf	PM	1951
La Chanson de Catherine P. Damine, C. Youri, A. Jourmiaux	PM/EMI	1951
Le Chant d'amour Charles Dumont, Edith Piaf	PM/EMI	1963
Le Chant du pirate [film *Etoile sans lumière*] Marguerite Monnot, Henri Contet	PM	1946
Chante-moi Edith Piaf	PM	1946
Chante-moi [in English] Edith Piaf, Mack David	CBS	1956
Le Chasseur de l'hôtel Henri Bourtayre, Henri Contet	POL/Ph	1942
Le Chemin des forains Henri Sauguet, Jean Dréjac	PM	1955
Le Chevalier de Paris Philippe-Gérard	PM	1950
Le Ciel est fermé Marguerite Monnot, Henri Contet	PM	1950
Les Cloches sonnent Marguerite Monnot, Edith Piaf	DEC/MUS/ RCA	1945

Comme moi Marguerite Monnot, Edith Delécluse, Senlis	PM/EMI	1957
Le Contrebandier Jean Villard, Raymond Asso	POL/Ph	1937
Corréqu' et reguyer P. Maye, Marc Hély	POL/Ph	1937
Coup de grisou Louiguy, Henri Contet	POL/Ph	1942
Cousu de fil blanc Michel Emer	DEC/MUS/ RCA	1945
Cri du cœur Henri Crolla, Jacques Prévert	PM/EMI	1960
Les Croix Gilbert Bécaud, Louis Amade	PM	1946
Dans les prisons de Nantes Trad. arr. Marc Herrand	PM	1946
Dans leur baiser Charles Dumont, Michel Vaucaire	PM	1961
Dans un bouge du vieux port A. Liaunet, A. Deltour	POL/Ph	1939
Dany Marguerite Monnot, Edith Piaf	PM	1949
De l'autre côté de la rue Michel Emer	POL/Ph	1943
Demain il fera jour Marguerite Monnot, Marcel Achard	PM	1951
Des histoires Charles Dumont, Michel Vaucaire	PM	1960
Les deux copains Raymond Asso, Borel-Clerc	POL/Ph	1939
Les deux ménétriers L. Durand, Jean Richepin	POL/Ph	1936
Les deux rengaines Henri Bourtayre, Henri Contet	POL/Ph	1943
Le Diable de la Bastille Charles Dumont, Pierre Delanoë	PM	1962
Ding, din, don Raymond Asso, P. Dreyfus	POL/Ph	1938
Le Disque usé Michel Emer	POL/Ph	1939
Don't Cry Edith Piaf, Eddie Constantine	PM	1956
Le Droit d'aimer Francis Laï, Robert Nyel	PM/EMI	1962
Du matin jusqu'au soir [operetta *La P'tite Lili*] Edith Piaf, Marcel Achard	PM	1951
Du matin jusqu'au soir [*see* 'Cause I Love You]		
Eden blues Georges Moustaki	PM	1958
L'Effet que tu me fais Marc Heyral, Edith Piaf	PM	1953
Elle a dit Gilbert Bécaud, Edith Piaf	PM	1952
Elle fréquentait la rue Pigalle Louis Maîtrier, Raymond Asso	POL/Ph	1938
Embrasse-moi Wal-Berg, Jacques Prévert	POL/Ph	1940
Emporte-moi Francis Laï, Jacques Plante	PM	1962
Enfin l'printemps Marguerite Monnot, René Rouzaud	PM/EMI	1954
Entre Saint-Ouen et Clignancourt Adelmar Sablon, André Mauprey	POL/Ph	1937

Escale Marguerite Monnot, Jean Marèze	POL/Ph	1940
Et moi Michel Emer	PM	1953
Et pourtant Michel Emer, Pierre Brasseur	PM	1956
L'Etranger Marguerite Monnot, Robert Juel, R. Malleron	POL/Ph	1936
Exodus [film *Exodus*] Ernest Gold, Eddy Marney	PM/EMI	1961
Fais comme si Marguerite Monnot, Michel Rivgauche	PM	1958
Fais-moi valser Borel-Clerc	POL/Ph	1936
Fallait-il Charles Dumont, Michel Vaucaire	PM	1962
Le Fanion de la Légion Marguerite Monnot, Raymond Asso	POL/Ph	1937/38
Faut pas qu'il se figure Charles Dumont, Michel Rivgauche	PM	1961
La Fête continue Michel Emer	PM/EMI	1950
Les Feuilles mortes [*see also Autumn Leaves*] Joseph Kosma, Jacques Prévert	CBS	1956
La Fille et le chien Borel-Clerc, Jacques-Charles, Charles Pothier	POL/Ph	1936
Les Flons-flons du bal Charles Dumont, Michel Vaucaire	PM/EMI	1960
La Foule A. Cabral, Michel Rivgauche	PM/EMI	1957
Les Gars qui marchaient Marguerite Monnot, Henri Contet	POL/Ph	1942
Les Gens Francis Laï, Michel Vendôme	PM/EMI	1963
Le Geste Michel Emer	DEC/MUS/ RCA	1945
Le Gitan et la fille Georges Moustaki	PM	1958
La Goualante du pauvre Jean Marguerite Monnot, René Rouzaud	PM/EMI	1954
Le Grand Voyage du pauvre nègre René Cloërec, Pierre Delanoë	POL/Ph	1940
Les Grognards Hubert Giraud, Pierre Delanoë	PM	1957
Heaven Have Mercy (*Miséricorde*) Philippe-Gérard, Rich French	PM	1956
Heureuse Marguerite Monnot, René Rouzaud	PM/EMI	1953
Les Hiboux P. Dalbret, E. Joullot	POL/Ph	1936+ 1942
Histoire de cœur Marguerite Monnot, Henri Contet	POL	1942

232

L'Homme à la moto [*Black denim trousers & motor-cycle boots*] Jerry Leiber, Mike Stoller, Jean Dréjac	PM/EMI	1956
L'Homme au piano H. Henning, Jean-Claude Darnal, Terningsohn	PM	1954
L'Homme de Berlin Francis Laï, Michael Vendôme	PM	1963
L'Homme que j'aimerai [operetta *La P'tite Lili*] Marguerite Monnot, Marcel Achard	PM	1951
L'Homme des bars [first published 1982] Marguerite Monnot, Edith Piaf	Ph	1982
Hymne à l'amour Marguerite Monnot, Edith Piaf	PM/EMI	1950
Hymne à l'amour (If You Love Me) Marguerite Monnot, Edith Piaf	CBS	1956
Hymn to *Love* Marguerite Monnot, Eddie Constantine	PM	1950
Il a chanté Marguerite Monnot, Cécile Didier	PM	1948
Il fait bon t'aimer Norbert Glanzberg, Jacques Plante	PM	1950
Il n'attend plus rien [According to a list supplied by Pathé-Marconi in 1960 this title was in their archives. It is not in the present 'Intégrale']	PM	
Il n'est pas distingué P. Maye, Marc Hély	POL/Ph	1936
Il pleut Pierre Roche, Charles Aznavour	PM	1948
Il riait Bartholé, Henri Contet	POL/Ph	1942
Il y avait Charles Aznavour, Pierre Roche	PM	1950
Inconnu excepté de Dieu Charles Dumont, Louis Amade	PM	1962
I Shouldn't Care Michel Emer, Rich French	PM	1956
J'ai dansé avec l'amour Marguerite Monnot, Edith Piaf	POL/Ph	1941
J'ai qu'à l'regarder Alex Siniavine, Edith Piaf	POL/Ph	1943
La Java de cézigue Eblinger, Groffe	POL/Ph	1936
La Java en mineur Léo Poll, Marcel Delmas, Raymond Asso	Private	1938
[Private recording (Collection François Bellair) recorded at the home of singer Marie Dubas. Broadcast by Radio France (France-Inter) in *Les Cinglés du Music-Hall* No. 645 on 25.6.1981. Illustrates Piaf's natural humour.]		
La Java en mineur [from collection Bellair]	Ph	1981
Jean et Martine Michel Emer	PM	1953

Je hais les dimanches Florence Véran, Charles		
Aznavour	PM	1951
Je me souviens d'une chanson Jean-Pierre Moulin,		
Félix Marten	PM	1957
Je m'imagine Marguerite Monnot, Nita Raya	PM	1960
J'm'en fous pas mal Michel Emer, Rich French	PM/EMI	1946
J'm'en fous pas mal Michel Emer, Rich French	CBS	
J'en ai tant vu Michel Emer, René Rouzaud	PM	1963
Je n'en connais pas la fin Marguerite Monnot,		
Raymond Asso	POL/Ph	1939
J'entends la sirène Marguerite Monnot, Raymond		
Asso	POL/Ph	1938
Jérusalem Jo Moutet, Robert Chabrier	PM	1960
Je sais comment J. Bouquet, Robert Chauvigny	PM/EMI	1958
Je suis à toi J. Bouquet	PM	1960
Je t'ai dans la peau [film *Boum sur Paris*] Gilbert		
Bécaud, Jacques Pills	PM/EMI	1952
Jezebel Wayne Shanklin Snr., Charles Aznavour	PM	1951
Jimmy Brown Song [*See The Three Bells*]		
Jimmy, c'est lui Wal-Berg, Kamke	POL/Ph	1940
Johnny, tu n'es pas un ange [*Johnny is the boy for me*]		
Trad. Rumanian, arr. Les Paul, Marcel Stellman,		
Paddy Roberts, Francis Lemarque	PM/EMI	1953
J'suis mordue Jean Lenoir, L. Carol, R. Delamare	POL/Ph	1936
La Julie jolie Léo Daniderff, Gaston Conté	POL/Ph	1936
Kiosque à journaux [ballet *La Voix*] Michel		
Rivgauche, Pierre Lacotte, Claude Leveillé	PM	1960
Légende Gilbert Bécaud, Edith Piaf	PM	1955
Le Long des quais [*See also* II n'attend plus rien]	PM	?
Madeleine qu'avait du cœur Max d'Yresne,		
Raymond Asso	POL/Ph	1938
Margot cœur gros Florence Véran, Michel Vendôme	PM	1963
Mariage [film *Etoile sans lumière*] Marguerite Monnot,		
Henri Contet	PM	1946
Marie la Française Philippe-Gérard, Jacques Larue	PM	1956
Marie-Trottoir Charles Dumont, Michel Vaucaire	PM/EMI	1961
Les Marins ça fait des voyages Mitty Goldin,		
Raymond Asso	POL/Ph	1938
Le Mauvais Matelot P. Dreyfus, Raymond Asso	POL/Ph	1938

Mea culpa Hubert Giraud, Michel Rivgauche	PM/EMI	1954
Le Métro de Paris [ballet *La Voix*] Claude Leveillé, Michel Rivgauche, Pierre Lacotte	PM	1960
Milord Marguerite Monnot, Georges Moustaki	PM/EMI	1959
Miséricorde [See also *Heaven Have Mercy*] Philippe-Gérard, Jacques Larue	PM	1955
Les Mômes de la cloche Vincent Scotto, Decaye [not a Piaf 'creation' as often stated. *See* Mimi Pinson, Pathé Catalogue, 1915]	POL/Ph	1936
Mon amant de la Coloniale Juel, Raymond Asso	POL/Ph	1936
Mon ami m'a donné Claude Valéry, Raymond Asso	PM	1952
Mon apéro Robert Juel, R. Malleron	POL/Ph	1936
Mon cœur est au coin de la rue Albert Lasry, H. Coste	POI/Ph	1937
Mon Dieu Charles Dumont, Michel Vaucaire	PM/EMI	1960
Mon Dieu Charles Dumont, Michel Vaucaire [in English]	PM	1961
Mon Légionnaire Marguerite Monnot, Raymond Asso	POL/Ph	1937
Mon manège à moi Norbert Glanzberg, Jean Constantin	PM/EMI	1958
Monsieur Ernest a réussi Michel Emer	DEC/MUS/ RCA	1945
Monsieur et Madame Michel Emer	PM	1952
Monsieur Incognito R. Gall, Florence Véran	PM	1963
Monsieur Lenoble Michel Emer	PM	1948
Monsieur Saint-Pierre J. Hess, Henri Contet	POL/Ph	1942
Monsieur X Roger Goze, Michel Emer	DEC/MUS/ RCA	1945
Mon vieux Lucien Charles Dumont, Michel Rivgauche	PM	1961
Les Mots d'amour Charles Dumont, Michel Rivgauche	PM/EMI	1960
Musique à tout va Francis Laï, René Rouzaud	PM	1962
My Lost Melody Marguerite Monnot, Harold Rome [in English]	PM	1956
Les Neiges de Finlande Marguerite Monnot, Henri Contet	PM	1958
Ne m'écris pas René Cloërec, L. Lagarde, Jean Rodor	POL/Ph	1937
Le Noël de la rue Marc Heyral, Henri Contet	PM	1951

Non, je ne regrette rien Charles Dumont, Michel Vaucaire	PM/EMI	1960
Non, la vie n'est pas triste [ballet *La Voix*] Claude Leveillé, Edith Piaf	PM	1960
No regrets Charles Dumont, Michel Vaucaire, Hal Davis [in English]	PM/EMI	1961
[in German]	PM	1961
Notre-Dame de Paris Marc Heyral, Eddy Marnay	PM	1952
N'y vas pas, Manuel Michel Emer	PM/EMI	1953
On cherche un auguste Charles Dumont, Robert Gall	PM	1962
On danse sur ma chanson Raymond Asso, Léo Poll	POL/Ph	1940
One Little Man [See also *Le Petit Homme*] Philippe-Gérard, Rich French	PM	1956
Opinion publique Marguerite Monnot, Henri Contet	PM	1957
L'Orgue des amoureux André Varel, Charly Bailly, Francis Carco	PM	1949
Les Orgues de barbarie Georges Moustaki	PM	1958
Où sont-ils, mes p'tits copains? Marguerite Monnot, Edith Piaf	POL/Ph	1941
Ouragan Claude Leveillé, Michel Rivgauche	PM	1960
Padam … padam Norbert Glanzberg, Henri Contet	PM/EMI	1951
Padam … padam Norbert Glanzberg, Henri Contet	CBS	
Paris [film *L'Homme aux mains d'argile*] A. Bernheim	PM	1949
Paris-Méditerranée René Cloërec, Raymond Asso	POL/Ph	1939
Partance Léo Poll, Raymond Asso	POL/Ph	1938
Le Petit Brouillard Francis Laï, Jacques Plante	PM	1962
La Petite Boutique O. Hodeige, Roméo Carlès	POL/Ph	1936
La Petite Marie Marguerite Monnot, Edith Piaf	PM	1950
Le Petit Homme [*See also* One Little Man] Marguerite Monnot, Henri Contet	PM	1946
Le Petit Monsieur triste Marguerite Monnot, Raymond Asso	POL/Ph	1939
Pleure pas Aimé Barelli, Henri Contet	PM	1949
Plus bleu que tes yeux Charles Aznavour	PM	1951
Polichinelle Charles Dumont, Jacques Plante	PM	1962
Pour moi tout' seule Guy Lafarge, Flavien Monod, Philippe-Gérard	PM	1949
Pour qu'elle soit jolie, ma chanson [film *Boum sur Paris*] Louiguy, Edith Piaf	PM	1953

Le Prisonnier de la tour Francis Blanche, Gérard Calvi	PM	1949
Les Prisons du roy [Allentown Jail] Irving Gordon, Michel Rivgauche	PM	1957
Quand même Jean Wiener, J. Mario, Louis Poterat	POL/Ph	1936
Quand tu dors C. Verger, Jacques Prévert	PM	1961
Qu'as-tu fait, John? Michel Emer	PM	1947
Quatorze juillet [film *Les Amants de Téruel*] Mikis Theodorakis, Jacques Plante	PM	1962
Qu'il était triste cet Anglais Charles Dumont, Louis Poterat	PM	1961
Regardez-moi toujours comme ça Marguerite Monnot, Henri Contet	POL/Ph	1944
Le rendezvous Francis Laï, René Rouzaud	PM	1962
Reste Will Leardy, Jacques Simonot, P. Bayle	POL/Ph	1936
Retour Jo Heyne, G. Manet, Jean-Marie	PM	1954
Rien de rien Pierre Roche, Charles Aznavour	PM	1951
Le roi a fait battre tambour Trad. arr. Marc Herrand	PM	1946
Roulez tambours Francis Laï, Edith Piaf	PM	1962
La Rue aux chansons Michel Emer	PM	1951
Rue de Siam [see Il n'attend plus rien]	PM	?
Un sale petit brouillard [see Le Petit Brouillard]		
Salle d'attente Marguerite Monnot, Michel Rivgauche	PM	1957
Sérénade du pavé [from film *French Cancan*] Jean Varney	PM	1954
Si le Roi savait ça ... Isabelle [see Le prisonnier de la tour]		
Simple comme bonjour Louiguy, Roméo Carlès	POL/Ph	1942
Simply a waltz Norman Wallace [in English]	PM	1950
Si, si, si [operetta *La P'tite Lili*] Marguerite Monnot, Marcel Achard	PM	1951
Si tu partais Michel Emer	DEC/MUS/ RCA	1945
Sœur Anne Michel Emer	PM	1953
Sophie Norbert Glanzberg, Edith Piaf	DEC/MUS/ RCA	1945
Soudain une vallée [Suddenly there's a valley] Biff Jones, Charles Meyer, Jean Dréjac	PM	1956
Sous le ciel de Paris Hubert Giraud, Jean Dréjac	PM	1954

Sur une colline Paul Misraki	POL/Ph	1940
Les tambours [*see* Il n'attend plus rien]	PM	?
Tant qu'il aura des jours Marguerite Monnot, Michel		
Rivgauche	PM	1958
Tatave Henri Crolla, Albert Simonin	PM	1956
T'as pas profité de ta chance [*see* Monsieur Lenoble]		
Télégramme Michel Emer	PM	1951
T'es beau, tu sais Georges Moustaki, Henri Contet	PM	1959
T'es l'homme qu'il me faut Charles Dumont, Edith		
Piaf	PM	1960
The Three Bells [*see also* Les trois cloches] Jean Villard,		
Bert Reisfield	PM	1950
Tiens, v'là un marin J. Bouquet, B. Labadie	PM	1963
Toi qui sais Michel Emer	PM	1956
Toi, tu l'entends pas Charles Dumont, Pierre Delanoë	PM	1962
Toujours aimer Charles Dumont, Michel Rivgauche	PM	1961
Tous les amoureux chantent Marguerite Monnot, J.		
Jeepy	PM	1950
Tout fout le camp Robert Juel, Raymond Asso	POL/Ph	1938
Traqué Florence Véran, R. Gall	PM	1963
Les trois cloches [*see also The Three Bells*] Jean Villard,		
arr. Marc Herrand	PM/EMI	1946
Tu es partout [film *Montmartre sur Seine*] Marguerite		
Monnot, Edith Piaf	POL/Ph	1942
Un coin tout bleu Marguerite Monnot, Edith Piaf	POL/Ph	1942
Une chanson à trois temps Anna Marly	DEC/MUS/	
	RCA	1945
Une dame Michel Emer	PM	1956
Une enfant Charles Aznavour, Robert Chauvigny	PM	1951
Une enfant Charles Aznavour, Robert Chauvigny	CBS	1956
Un étranger Georges Moustaki, Robert Chauvigny	PM	1958
Un grand amour qui s'achève Marguerite Monnot,		
Edith Piaf	PM	1945
Un homme comme les autres Pierre Roche, Edith Piaf	PM	1947
Un jeune homme chantait Léo Poll, Raymond Asso	POL/Ph	1937
Un monsieur me suit dans la rue Jacques Besse,		
P. Lechanois	POL/Ph	1942
Un refrain courait dans la rue Robert Chauvigny,		
Edith Piat	PM	1946

Une valse Charles Dumont, Jacques Plante	PM	1962
Va danser M. Legay, Gaston Conté	POL/Ph	1936
Le Vagabond Louiguy, Edith Piaf	POL/Ph	1942
La Valse de l'amour Marguerite Monnot, Edith Piaf	PM	1951
La Vie en rose Louiguy, Edith Piaf	PM/EMI	1946
La Vie en rose Louiguy, Edith Piaf, Mack David [in English]	PM	1950
La Vie en rose Louiguy, Edith Piaf, Mack David [in English]	CBS	1956
La Vie, l'amour Robert Chauvigny, Michel Rivgauche	PM	1960
Les Vieux Bateaux Jacques Bourgeat, Jacqueline Batell	DEC/MUS/ RCA	1945
Le Vieux Piano Claude Leveillé, Henri Contet	PM	1960
La Ville inconnue Charles Dumont, Michel Vaucaire	PM	1960
Y'a pas de printemps Marguerite Monnot, Henri Contet	POL/Ph	1943
Y avait du soleil Jean Lenoir	POL/Ph	1936
Y en a un de trop Marguerite Monnot, Edith Piaf	POL/Ph	1940

In addition to the titles listed above it is believed the following may exist on tape or acetate:

Les Amants du dimanche; Black Boy; Blues de février; Blues d'octobre; C'est l'histoire de Jésus; Chanson d'amour; Clair de lune; La Complainte du Roi Renaud; Le Gilet; Moi, je sais qu'on se reverra; Monsieur Lévy; Les Pas; Pas une minute de plus; Le Pauvre Homme; Poker; Pourquoi m'as tu trahi; Le Routier; Sans faire de phrase; Ses mains; Un air d'accordéon; Vol de nuit; Y avait une voix qui se lamentait.

R. H.

Filmography

1936 *La Garçonne* Director: Jean de Limur

Based on the novel by Victor Margueritte. Cast included Marie Bell, Arletty, Suzy Solidor. Piaf, appearing as a young street singer, sang *Quandmême* and *Fais-moi valser*.

1941 *Montmartre-sur-Seine* Director: Georges Lacombe

Love affairs among a group of young people in Montmartre. Cast included Jean-Louis Barrault, Paul Meurisse, Henri Vidal.

Piaf played Lily, a former street singer who gradually becomes a cabaret star. She sang *L'Homme des bars, Un coin tout bleu, Tu es partout, C'est un monsieur très distingué*.

1946 *Etoile sans lumière* Director: Marcel Blistène

Stella, a star of the silent screen, has no voice for sound films, her part is doubled by Madeleine (played by Piaf) who, after the star's death in an accident, hopes to take her place. But she realizes she has not Stella's talent and returns sadly to her former uninteresting life. Cast included Mila Parely, Serge Reggiani and Yves Montand. Piaf's favourite film among those in which she appeared. She sang: *Adieu mon coeur, Mariage, C'est merveilleux, C'était une histoire d'amour, Le Chant du pirate*.

1947 *Neuf garçons, un cœur* Director: Georges Freedland

A client of the cabaret Le Paradis arranges to make dreams come true for Christine (Piaf) and her friends (Les Compagnons de la Chanson), who are penniless singers. Songs: *Les trois cloches, Sophie, Un refrain courait dans la rue, C'est pour ça, La Vie en rose*.

1951 *Paris chante toujours* Director: Pierre Montazel

Two young people compete to obtain the greatest number of autographs by music-hall artists. The winner will inherit the fortune left by their uncle, an eccentric actor. The many stars appearing included Line Renaud, Tino Rossi, Jean Sablon, Yves Montand. Piaf sang *L'Hymne à l'amour*.

1952 *Boum sur Paris* Director: Maurice de Canonge

Bottles of scent have been distributed to music-hall stars at a celebration, but by accident they include one which contains an explosive. The search for this bottle leads to many meetings with famous stars including Charles Trénet, Mouloudji, Juliette Gréco, Les Quatre Barbus. Jacques Pills sang with Piaf *Pourvu qu'elle soit jolie ma chanson*, and she herself sang *Je t'ai dans la peau*.

1953 *Si Versailles m'était conté* Director: Sacha Guitry

The spectacular history of the Château de Versailles, 'a great historical fresco', lasting 165 minutes, with a long cast of famous names, actors and singers, each playing a small rôle. Piaf sang the revolutionary song, *Ça ira*.

1954 *French Can-can* Director: Jean Renoir

The Moulin-Rouge in Montmartre just before the turn of the century, and the story of Nini the laundress whose can-can dance became famous all over the world. A long cast of leading actors and singers included Piaf playing the rôle of Eugénie Buffet and singing *La Sérénade du Pavé*.

1958 *Les Amants de Demain* Director: Marcel Blistène

For the scenario see pp. 154–5. Piaf's last film, in which she sang *Les Neiges de Finlande, Fais comme si, Tant qu'il y aura des jours, Les Amants de demain*.

Piaf contributed the song *Paris* (voice only) to the film *L'Homme aux mains d'argile* (1948), in which Marcel Cerdan appeared.

Appendix 1:
Bal musette to chanson réaliste

La chanson emerged from the disillusion with what remained from the fragile optimism of 'La belle époque', a legacy of a million young Frenchmen, cream of the nation, dead from the War to end Wars and all the human misery that entailed in family life; the constantly frustrated struggle of the proletariat to control its own destiny in the rise and fall of the Popular Front, and an underclass able only to find a voice in artists sympathetic towards it or who knew best how to exploit it.

Male actors supplied the working-class heroes. Jean Gabin was the archetype and he occasionally sang, but those who were deemed to express the 'reality' of the situation were all women. As the 'reality' was almost invariably pessimistic, with rays of hope so rare they might as well not exist, the pessimism tends to be suspect at times. One singer quite openly acknowledged the deception. However, the *chanson réaliste* produced some fine work and nurtured artists whose voices continue to live in their many recordings. It may be no exaggeration to say that the best 'realist' singers were 'born' in an unforgettable way: their songs were almost entirely biographical, at least in the public eye.

One vital aspect of their art is universally ignored. As we can hear most of them now only in recorded form, apart from rare film and television clips and the occasional feature, the musical accompaniments, in part at least, must compensate for the visual encounter. This is why the realist singers made one instrument their own, the instrument that created the typically Parisian 'atmosphere'.

Musette is the name given to a musical style which entered the popular repertoire around the time the scope of this book begins. The word goes back to the thirteenth century when it was a bagpipe or *cornemuse*, little *cornemuse* or (*corne*) *musette*. The court composers at Versailles 400 years later wrote for it and others, not least Jean Sebastian Bach gave the name 'musette' to a dance. In the nineteenth century thousands of land workers and tenant farmers from Auvergne in the volcanic centre of France joined a rural exodus to Paris, driven by crop failures and avaricious landlords to seek a new life in other occupations. The first commercially exploited mine in France, in the Auvergne's Puy-de-Dôme, had begun to produce coal which the Auvergnats brought to Paris where they soon held a monopoly of distribution, together with wood for burning. Their first wood stocks came from the barges – broken into pieces – which had carried the coal to the capital. Other Auvergnat immigrés opened little cafés, the first Parisian bistrots.

In their folk traditions the Auvergnats kept their identity in urban surroundings: at first, dancing at the back of the shop or café, then in dance halls to the sound of the ancient pipes. some became well known: Les Barreaux Verts and Chez Bouscatel. The Auvergnat bagpipe or *cabrette* was made from the skin of a young goat or 'cabris', an instrument from the older generation, called 'musette'.

Together with the hurdy-gurdy (*vielle*), the violin, bells attached to the ankles, and the *cabrette*, also in *chanter* form (that is, without the bag) became the instrument of the *bal musette*.

Then, just prior to 1900, a second wave of immigrants reached Paris from Italy, an estimated 150,000 people. Again, these were economic refugees who settled in those districts (the Bastille, Montreuil ...) where rents were lowest, just as the Auvergnats had. Problems did arise in dance-halls where the

Auvergnat instruments and the Austro-Italian accordion came into conflict with each other. Police were often called to guard places where fights and brawls were likely. In the end, Italian accordionist and composer Charles Peguri married the daughter of the Auvergnat owner of Chez Bouscatel, Monsieur Antoine B. and the dust began to settle. The younger generation of Auvergnats soon realized that their problems of integration were little different from those of the Italians. In any case, the accordion was more adaptable to the 'hits of the day' than the pipe or hurdy-gurdy and the Italian dances, including the popular mazurka (which had originated in Poland), more suited to Parisian taste than the country *bourrées* from Auvergne. The Auvergnat instruments 'retired' from the dance-halls but lived on in people's homes, in the sheet music and record publications of Parisian Auvergnats such as Martin Cayla and later Jean Segurel. The Italian mazurka became the French 'java', a mysterious name giving rise to numerous explanations as to its origins.

One of these maintains that having danced a mazurka with a client, the dance hostess, known as a 'taxi-girl' in the *bal musette*, would say, should she be from Auvergne, 'Cha–Va?' (Ça va? All right?). Hence, the mazurka became known as the 'java', having nothing to do with the largest island in Indonesia or American coffee.

Another explanation is that Auvergnat owners of *bals musette* would greet their customers in the same way: 'Cha–va?' (Ça va?) In any event, the Java became one of the favourite rhythms of the musette song and dance of which there are countless recorded examples from the early 1900s to the present day.

It was neither an Auvergnat nor an Italian who is honoured as being the 'creator' of the *musette* style: Emile Vacher was a Parisian of Breton origin. The tremolos of Vacher's unmiked diatonic accordion, piercing and, above all, pleasing, his incomparable rhythm (*la cadence*), excited and incited the dancers to dance better and longer, adding to their enjoyment, the popularity of the accordionist and income of the 'taxi-boys' and girls. The future 'realist' singers, little-known artists, frequently described as 'vocal refrain' on record labels, sang with the *musette* bands. Many of them sang the better-known 'realist' songs of the day. Jane Chacun with the Emile Vacher trio: black dress, black stole over one arm, became a rôle model for later and much better-known performers.

In the mid-1930s the *musette* accordion was inseparable from working–class political and social aspirations, expressed in films such as the first directed by Marcel Carné: *Nogent: Eldorado du dimanche* (1929), heralding Julien Duvivier's *La belle équipe* (1936, year of the Popular Front) in which accordionists Adolphe Deprince and Victor Marceau accompanied Jean Gabin in (*Quand on s'promène au bord de l'eau* (When we walk along the river bank), expressing newly found freedoms in the countryside at weekends and the belief that social justice and a happy life would soon be the possessions of all.

By 1939 the *musette* style had reached its peak with the whole nation dancing feverishly in celebration of the final days of peace before the outbreak of the Second World War. Those out of earshot of 'live' musicians danced to the 'wireless', notably the Poste Parisien, Radio Cité, Radio Normandie and Radio Luxembourg and the ubiquitous portable gramophone.

In 1940 the authorities closed the dance-halls, as chronicled in the song *Depuis que les bals sont fermés*, fearing they would encourage opposition to the new regimes, the German Occupying Forces and the Pétain Government in Vichy. Many musicians were thrown out of work, though some of the more enterprising skirted the regulations by opening 'dancing schools' where most of the students could dance anyway.

In the more expensive clubs and restaurants frequented by Germans, collaborators and black market moguls the accordion maintained its position with a particular kind of French swing, allegedly free from American influence: 'Swing *musette*' *à la française*. Its principal exponents were Tony Murena and Gus Viseur, 'The Django Reinhardt of the Accordion'.

After the war, as an accompaniment for dancing, the *musette* never quite gained its freshness of the earlier years. Dancing itself had changed: swing, jazz, big band and later *le rock* required different instrumentation.

Even so, accordion musette entered a new phase, some would say 'a more poetic' one. It had already served singers well, especially the *réalistes* throughout the 1930s and 1940s, as an accompanying instrument. Now it was ready to support a new generation of singers with new virtuosi, skilled as accompanists as well as soloists, notably Marcel Azzola. (As Cocteau commented: No one changed poetry into music more than Marcel Azzola.) The names of Edith Piaf, Jacques Brel, Léo Ferré, Juliette Gréco, Barbara and Yves Montand were now filling the halls and the radio programmes. In parenthesis, it is significant that Charles Trenet, whose *ambiance* stands apart from those of others, preferred to use arrangements very sparing of accordion scoring.

The past twenty-five years or so have seen a partial eclipse in the accordion's fortunes, though this may be artificial, for those who direct the media, whatever their pretensions, seem anxious to distance themselves from the world of 'the poor man's piano'.

However, the current accordion renaissance is now bringing the instrument into a new phase as an integral part of France's cultural heritage, and the musette style as 'the only popular music born under the skies of Paris' (Jean-Pierre Beaurenaut: director TV documentary: Paris Musette, 1993).

R.H.

Appendix 2:
The chanteuses réalistes

The native Parisian music described in Appendix 1 has been inseparable from most of the *chanteuses réalistes* apart from those whose style and aims had bordered on the classical *mélodie*. A roughly chronological survey of these singers must surely begin with **EUGENIE BUFFET (1866–1934)**. Daughter of an army officer serving in Algeria, Eugénie Buffet gradually made her way to Paris, after extended stop-overs at theatres in North Africa and Marseilles. Her metropolitan debut was at the Variétés where she sang under the name of Julyani. She became a right-wing militant and in 1889 was imprisoned for insulting a politician. On leaving jail she bought a set of clothes from fellow prisoners and began singing at La Cigale, a caf' conc' in the Boulevard Rochechouart. She drew her repertoire from the Breton bard Théodore Botrel and the bourgeois *réaliste* Aristide Bruant. Eugénie created the costume for a new style of stage performer, the *pierreuse* (from *pierre*, a stone) or 'pavement walker'; a long black cape over a frilly dress or a black skirt, as worn at that time by the professional street-walkers, then called *pierreuses*. This was considered the ideal outfit for delivering the supposedly romantic poetry of the underworld and *les chansons réalistes*.

For many years Eugénie Buffet raised money for service charities by singing in the streets, an occupation never considered degrading in France. *La Sérénade du Pavé* was Eugénie's clarion call. In the early 1920s she toured abroad, on at least one occasion with financial backing from the government, returning in 1924 to three Parisian music-halls: the Empire, the Eldorado and the Parisiana.

Sadly, Eugénie Buffet ended her days penniless in one of the hospitals she had helped to finance by her singing, and her fellow-artists staged benefit concerts to pay her hospital fees. Shortly before her death in 1933 she was decorated with the Legion of Honour. In 1954 Edith Piaf sang *La Sérénade du Pavé* in Jean Renoir's film *French Can-can*.

YVONNE GEORGE (1896–1930) was the professional name of a Belgian-born singer associated with the *chanteuses réalistes*, though the content and often very 'classical' piano accompaniment to many of her songs casts doubts on such a classification. Her contemporaries in the *chanson* of quality may also have had similar misgivings, though most were unqualified in their praise. They named her 'The Muse of Montparnasse' and the 'Queen of The Ox on the Roof', implying a far broader range of poetic feeling than that shown by the *réalistes*.

Paul Franck of the Olympia Music Hall in Paris discovered Yvonne de Knops in Brussels in his search for new artists. Her first night in the Boulevard des Capucines was a disaster. The public booed her and the popular critics considered her 'too intellectual'. Nevertheless, there were influential admirers in the arts and the literary press ready to rush to her defence. Composer Darius Milhaud publicly declared his unconditional support. Journalist, critic and screen-writer Henri Jeanson, later to create the dialogue for the Marcel Carné film *Hôtel du Nord*, rounded on the sceptics: Yvonne George is a very great artist. Get that into your heads! Sentiments shared by Robert Desnos, the future surrealist poet who was unconditional in his praise for the singer.

Most of all, Jean Cocteau encouraged Yvonne George to be an actress by offering her a part in his play *Roméo et Juliette* and it was Cocteau who organized her last concert on 12 June 1928 when so many of the audience came to see her die on the stage, as they did some thirty years later for Edith Piaf. In 1924 Yvonne George had appeared at the first luxury night club established in Paris, Chez Fysher (Rue d'Antin), where her accompanist was the pianist and composer Georges van Parys. In his memoirs, *Les jours comme ils viennent* (The days as they come) (Plon, 1969), van Parys gives us an exquisite picture of the singer. 'Her beautiful eyes were set in an agonized face, its tragedy accentuated by discreet twitches. Occasionally, a slight grin revealed bitter irony, disturbing at first, which exuded from her short, greased-down, ash-blond hair and cadaverous make-up. Then, with all the appearance of an ambushed doe she would come to life, light up and reveal great intelligence, reassuring us that Yvonne George was an exceptional woman'.

Yvonne George steeped herself in traditional songs, which she retained despite unfavourable reactions from undiscerning audiences. *Nous irons à Valparaiso*, recalling the days of sail, was rejected at first because the Parisian public was either unwilling or unable to decipher the English words in the lyric, 'Good-bye, Farewell'. Later, the problem resolved itself.

Yvonne George's most widely accepted song, by Jean Lenoir was *Pars*, in which the singer tells her lover to go, regardless of her true feelings. The most dramatic and 'realist' of all was *La Mort du Bossu*, The Death of the Hunchback whom her father had forced her to marry against her wishes. According to Pierre Saka the accompaniment in the last verse would evoke the steps of a funeral march, the singer miming the funeral procession as she walked towards the wings. Then, turning to the audience, she would break into an avenging, strident hysterical laugh as she took up the march for the last time, exclaiming the words: *Little crooked hunch-back*.

During her all too brief career. Yvonne George sang at the Casino de Paris, the Moulin Rouge, the Bobino and a little-known music-hall, the Apollo. She appeared for a season at the Empire Theatre in London in 1926. During this visit she recorded *J'ai pas su y faire* and 'You know you belong to someone else' for Columbia though at the singer's request these titles were not issued.

Her abuse of opium, cocaine and alcohol, sufficient in itself to gain her a place in the 'realist' camp, and the fact that she was dying of tuberculosis stimulated public interest in her. The great Florenz Ziegfeld who had modelled his Follies on the Folies-Bergère wanted to launch Yvonne George in America, but her health prevented her making the journey. Finally, she left the stage hoping to find a cure in a Swiss sanatorium and in Italy. The French press prematurely reported her death. In the belief she had been cured she sent word to Paris stating that she would shortly be making a come-back. It did not happen.

Yvonne George hated men. Unperturbed, the adoring Desnos was at her bedside in the little hotel in Genoa where she died on 16 May 1930. Towards the close of her career she did come to know what it meant to be accepted by the public, even a goodly number of critics, but it was for far too short a time.

FRÉHEL (1891–1951) ranks second only to Edith Piaf in the roster of the great ladies of popular French song. Born Marguerite Boulc'h in the 17th Arrondissement of Paris, little Marguerite began singing 'professionally', at the age of five, given the name Pervenche (Periwinkle). The tot would stand on zinc tables in cafés singing to the accompaniment of a blind accordionist. The accordion remained her favourite accompaniment. She learned her repertoire from street-singers who sold sheet music to passers-by, in the days before the spread of radio and records. These were the *petits formats*, the only means whereby a song might be published at that time, and then only on a relatively small scale.

La Pervenche would also learn songs by standing within earshot of music shops, in whatever temperature, hot or cold, on uncharitable Parisian pavements. In these ways the young singer's musical ear and prodigious memory for a good title enabled her to build a considerable large mental song book in a reasonably short space of time.

The child's mother would collect the coins her offspring managed to earn and on 'good nights' La petite Pervenche would be forced to sing until 2 or 3 a.m., a good training for the night-life of later years which creased many a hardened trouper. Later, Pervenche rarely spoke of her childhood, and though she complained about being abandoned by her mother and other relatives, and being often beaten, she did say she was always given enough to eat. Everyone regarded this frail-looking child as a great beauty: her Celtic origins seemed to exhale an atmosphere of mystery in the imaginations of the more prosaic Parisians. At the age of fifteen Pervenche entered a short-lived marriage with a middle-class dandy obsessed with the bohemian life-style. Later the singer Damia became his mistress. This was Robert Hollard, known as Roberty, who gave his teenage bride the stage name Fréhel, after the Breton promontory of which she had often spoken with delightful, wistful tenderness. In 1909 'Madame Pervenche Fréhel' made the only recording of her early career.

By her early twenties Fréhel had become recognized as a star with a personal way of life considered eccentric even for those heady days of the French café-concert and music-hall.

Her year-long love affair with Maurice Chevalier was complex, to say the least. Of her many lovers he was the one who haunted her throughout her life. The relationship involved her devastating humiliation of him, in which she manipulated royal and aristocratic suitors to arouse his jealousy. Such suitors, in fact, she despised, though not to the point of refusing their lavish gifts and 'protection'. Maurice, for his part, refused to participate in Fréhel's drug and alcohol culture, though he did fall victim for a while, until he rejected her in favour of the practical, business-like Mistinguett with whom he contrived to promote his career more effectively than with the 'impossible' Fréhel. By early 1914 Fréhel could bear Paris no longer; she made for St Petersburg where Tsarist Society welcomed her with open arms. From Russia she moved to Romania where the Queen was exceptionally kind to her and where she found a Romanian army officer to serve her insatiable sexual needs. In due course he was sent to the Front by a rival of higher rank. The following five years in Constantinople where, said Fréhel, Italian officers made good lovers and other ranks became good friends, proved to be her most tortured. During 1921 and part of 1922 she was said to be taking 15 g of cocaine per day. This drug, together with ether, alcohol and the rest had become Fréhel's way of life.

Yet with drive and determination, almost as if she had learned from Chevalier what it meant to map out a career, Fréhel made up her mind to return to Paris, doubtless with Maurice in mind as well as her work.

Her looks had gone and by this time she was horrendously fat, even ugly, but with the help of the French Foreign Ministry Fréhel left Turkey for France where she was met by ex-husband Roberty and Gaston Braunschwig, known as Montéhus, a singer whose repertoire Fréhel had used a decade previously.

Despite the scepticism from nearly every quarter of the show-business world, Fréhel became a star for the second time. The public still adored her. Under the aegis of Paul Franck at the Olympia she was billed as the 'Unforgettable, unforgotten'. By this time there were not only the stage and records, but the newer media of the radio and the cinema. Fréhel's film parts may have been fictitious, but her audiences knew they were watching the lady herself, as in *Pépé-le-Moko*, directed by Julien Duvivier (1936). Fréhel sings of her world rapidly disappearing, the old houses, the bar on the corner and eating chips from a paper cornet. In *Pépé* Fréhel accentuates the two parts of her life as she sings, *Où sont-ils donc?* Where are they now? to the accompaniment of one of her old records played on an ancient 'wind-up' gramophone with an external horn in the Casbah in Algiers. (A slight anachronism here, *Où sont-ils donc?* was first recorded with the accordionist Maurice Alexander in 1936. No matter!).

Fréhel's repertoire was not entirely 'realist'. She was far too much of a 'good time girl' not to enjoy a laugh. The considerable Fréhel discography, much of which is now on compact disc, is dotted with humorous titles, including The Mermaid's Son (*Le fils de la femme-poisson*), a circus vignette written for Fréhel by Charles Trenet and *Tel qu'il est*, a Vandair-Charlys song with music by Maurice Alexander in tango rhythm in which the singer compares her ideal man with the one she actually has.

Fréhel died in Paris on 3 February 1951. A few days earlier she had sung at a local cinema and her friends had given her a party in a nearby hotel bedroom.

The concept of the 'realist' singer with songs intimately connected with her own life has never been really Anglo-Saxon. In America Ruth Etting came close with 'Ten Cents a dance'. Consequently, very little information about Fréhel has appeared in English. Outstanding, however is the '*Mis-en-Scène of Suffering*: *French 'chanteuses réalistes'* by Ginette Vincendeau (New Formations) and a series of essays, also in English: *La Vie est à nous*: *French Cinema of the Popular Front*. 1935–1938 by Dr Vincendeau and Keith Reader (British Film Institute NFT Dossier No. 3 1986). In 1990, Nicole and the late Alain Lacombe produced a French biography of great insight: *Fréhel*. Fréhel has yet to be 'discovered' outside France: the day that happens the lives of all concerned will be enriched.

SUZY SOLIDOR (1900–83) 'The Girl with the Flaxen Hair' was born Suzanne Rocher in the Breton village of St

Servan-sur-Mer on 18 December 1900. On the opposite side of the street stood the baronial home of the Surcouf family. Robert Surcouf (1773–1827), navigator and privateer, created Baron under the Empire, became immensely rich by capturing English ships in the Indian Ocean. It appears that Suzy did not deny rumours that her mother had been seduced by a titled descendant of the pirate living in the 'big house' who refused to give his name to the baby girl. It would seem that the child knew who her father was but received no recognition from him.

At the age of fifteen Suzy described herself as 'Neither chaste nor flirtatious; rather unsociable and not a little uncouth, yet still free and healthy'. Two years later she qualified to drive an army ambulance in the closing months of the First World War. A well-connected antiquary and trendsetter in fashionable artistic circles, Madame Yvonne Brémond d'Ars launched Suzy, encouraging leading painters to take notice of her discovery with the short flaxen hair, masculine granite-like features, eyes which mirrored the sea and a body worthy of an Amazon.

Painter van Dongen encouraged Suzy in her singing by using her deep baritonal voice described by Jean Cocteau as one 'emerging from sexuality'. In 1932 Suzy Solidor opened an antiques shop of her own, enhancing the preview day with a song recital. Its enormous success prompted her to take up singing professionally. A year later she launched her cabaret, La Vie Parisienne, which attracted everybody who was anybody in Parisian 'Arts' society. At first, her repertoire, concentrating on the sea, ports, sailors and their women, seemed to offer little that was new, until the listener and spectator caught the vibrations of a style unique in its disturbing realism. Suzy Solidor underpinned already existing gossip and innuendo with contrived statements to the press, deliberately intending to provoke until she was heralded as the standard bearer of the lesbian cause, as far as it could be heard outside artistic circles in the Paris of the mid 1930s. At the same time Suzy was courted by the 'strong' sex. Flying hero Jean Mermoz (1901–1936) gave her a jewel, a heart pierced with an arrow in rubies. A year later he disappeared on a routine flight in the South Atlantic.

Suzy Solidor's success continued to rise in fashionable night-spots and surprisingly in the large popular music-halls. She appeared at the Européen, the Théâtre de l'Etoile, the Bobino and in 1938 at the ABC with Charles Trenet. During the second World War her Nordic, 'Strength through Joy' appearance attracted Germans to her performances and at the Liberation she was taken to court accused of 'collaboration'. In the late 1940s Suzy Solidor toured the United States. On returning to France she headed southwards to the Alpes Maritimes where she opened a cabaret at Cagnes-Sur-Mer near Grasse, combining the sale of paintings and antiques with the usual function of a cabaret. Suzy flourished in Cagnes until 1967, singing nightly surrounded by 225 portraits. She selected the best forty of these and donated them to the Cagnes Museum where they may still be seen: the remainder were auctioned after her death.

Suzy Solidor is classified with the 'realist' singers because of the content of her songs. Though she was born in a typically 'realist' situation, to an abandoned and unmarried mother, she always identified herself with the rich, influential and powerful. Her intellectual perception and her skill in emotional manipulation enabled her songs to embody all that was required in poetic realism.

DAMIA (1889–1978) Marie-Louise Damien, known later as Damia, was born in Paris, though like the Bretonnes Fréhel and Suzy Solidor, she too was of provincial origin. The family had come from Lorraine, that part of France which had so often belonged to Germany. It was not uncommon for Marie-Louise to be treated with disdain, most ironically of all by Marlene Dietrich who would refer to her as 'that German'.

Damia's earliest years were restless and disturbed. At the age of fifteen she ran away from her strict home – her father was a police sergeant – having already spent some time in a girls' detention centre. Not without a tongue in her head and possessing plenty of spirit Damia soon found work as an extra at the Châtelet theatre where she was spotted by Monsieur Roberty who gave her singing lessons. It was the same Roberty who had taught, married and separated from the turbulent Fréhel. Now Damia was his protégée and mistress. Roberty instilled into both artists, neither of whom had enjoyed a formal education, a love of words, of poetry and the skill which enabled them to produce impeccable diction.

Damia had more than a good singing voice which she was able to use expressively to a large audience without artificial aids. Her innate sense of drama and ability to project her personality with an apparently total absence of histrionics soon took her to the leading music halls of Paris and she even 'replaced' Mistinguett in London. During the 1914–18 war she was adored by troops on leave who were captured by her beauty as well as by her voice. Her career continued to prosper in the 1920s and 1930s. The intellectual and artistic élite proffered their seals of approval which she graciously accepted, though preferring the adulation of the 'popular', the ordinary people who understood at first hand the joys and sorrows her songs expressed. Their admiration and her acceptance of it link her to Edith Piaf.

The drama of Damia was a drama of restraint totally lacking in any form of self-pity or vulgarity.

Damia's creativity extended to a remarkable stagecraft. She was the first singer to introduce lighting into her act in any premeditated way, by using a spot to accentuate her minutely crafted movements. Her aim was to produce a performance unique to herself, hence the studied, essentially theatrical use of her famous shoulders and outstretched bare arms, her beautiful and characterful face with hair brushed tightly back, lending her the allure of a sensuous goddess of antiquity. Damia enjoyed the billing of 'Tragic Actress of Song'. After all, the Greek word for a song is *tragoudia*.

During the Occupation, Damia's recording manager Jean Bérard steered her away from serious 'realist' repertoire towards lighter things: 'realism' was all too much part of everyday existence. The war over, Damia returned to what she knew best with a triumph at the Salle Pleyel in 1949, again, 'La tragédienne de la chanson'.

In the 1950s, Damia's career moved gently towards its close. In 1953 she enjoyed a wild reception in Japan. French song, so different from its Japanese-Americanized counterpart, is found to be intriguingly exotic in Japan. Forty years after Damia's visit, French artists are still warmly welcomed there.

In 1954, the 'tragic actress of song' appeared at the Olympia with a young Jacques Brel in the first half of the show. A year later she was billed with Marie Dubas and in 1956 made her public farewell on television in Henri Spade's *La Joie de Vivre* (*This is Your Life*). Damia recorded prolifically. Each one of her songs earns our respect for a singer devoted to her craft: many appeal to the emotions through the drama they convey and to some, listeners can eagerly respond with their love.

MARIE DUBAS (1894–1972) Chroniclers of French popular song classify Anne-Marie Dubas with the *chanteuses réalistes* largely on the grounds of a handful of songs, of which *Mon Légionnaire* and *La Prière de la Charlotte* are the most memorable. Personal griefs throughout her life marked the naturally sunny disposition of this passionate and sensitive artist, yet Marie's stage persona was one of unfailing good humour and joy in living. She had been endowed with exceptionally robust health and an unflinching will to work which persisted until her final illness. As a child, little Marie observed everything around her, read voraciously and fell deeply in love with the theatre.

Her serious turn of mind set her firmly against everything she regarded as 'popular' entertainment until she saw the *diseuse* Yvette Guilbert on stage who immediately became her idol. It is quite possible that but for Yvette Guilbert, Marie Dubas may not have been fired with the ambition to become a popular singer. As Marie's ambitions were changing she was growing from being a studious and nervous adolescent into an engaging young woman, full of life, and extrovert enough to face audiences who were not always sympathetic towards a would-be 'artiste' in Montmartre cabarets, Parisian revue theatres and music halls.

Marie Dubas did not conform to the norms required for the background of the *chanteuse réaliste*. She came from an industrious, united, well-disciplined and happy Jewish family and therefore found little difficulty in rejecting the prevalent alcohol and drug subculture of the Parisian entertainment world. Her only drugs were work and more work. The death of a dear friend, Pierre Alin, in a train accident and the passing of her father Isaac, together with what she considered to be unmerited slowness in her career advancement, plus what seemed to her an interminable attack of bronchitis, all brought about such profound nervous depression in this young, talented artist, that taking her own life seemed the only solution. For three years she hardly worked at all, then out of the blue came an offer to appear in a musical comedy or 'operetta' and the critics hailed her as an entirely original *fantaisiste*. André Messager and Reynaldo Hahn, known to us as composers, but possessing welcome influence for Marie as critics, praised her generously until on 23 September 1927 impresario Paul Franck invited her to his Olympia. It was here that Marie Dubas created the *tour de chant*, a formula which still persists in the French music hall. An artist performs upwards of fifteen songs in one appearance, generally as the final item of the evening, or for lesser stars, before the interval. In the late 1920s no one believed such a feat possible, especially for a woman, remembering once again that as yet there was no microphone. Marie Dubas made entertainment and legal history when the Eldorado Music Hall sued her for a 100,000 francs, because she had performed after the Eldorado Show at the late-night cabaret, high society's Chez Fysher.

The judge ruled in Marie's favour. In future, an actor, singer or dancer would have the right to accept other engagements concurrently with his or her principal work, except where the contract stated otherwise.

Marie Dubas had a warm, generous nature. On the night of her mother's death (1928) she made a formal announcement stating the performance would not be cancelled. She added, 'Many of my friends here are paid fees rather than salaries. I must not stop them from earning their living'. When Piaf's father died in 1944, she did the same thing. The show must always go on.

Marie's most lasting success, outrunning all expectations, came with a lyric by Francis Carco, music by Jacques Larmanjat, which she added to her *tour de chant* at the Empire Music Hall on 2 October 1931. This was *Le Doux Caboulot*. It all happened at the very last moment, as Marie painted a canvas in sound to be compared only with the finest paintings Montmartre ever produced. The song tells the story of the dear little wine house covered in lilac blooms. It is impossible to walk past Le Lapin Agile today without those words flooding the mind.

A critic described that October night at the Empire over seventy years ago when the audience, which a moment before had been rolling about with laughter, was suddenly stunned into silence by the sweetness of *Le Doux Caboulot* and 'the incomparable talent of Marie Dubas'.

Now a mature person in her late thirties, Marie had become a pillar of the modern music hall with popular song as the lynch-pin of her performance. She rejected anything trite or obviously ephemeral and year by year consciously and deliberately cemented the loyalty of her public. She renewed her repertoire every six to eight months, including twelve new songs on each occasion.

Hardly the archetypal *chanteuse réaliste*, Marie Dubas was not averse to making parodies of the realist style as in *Le Tango stupéfiant* (*The narcotic tango*) and *Je suis obsédée* (*I am obsessed*) which may be described as 'quasi-Freudian'.

Marie Dubas had the ability not only to select songs which suited her from the vast corpus of music-hall songs already in being, but to spot potential successes for the future likely to come from the pens of struggling young writers such as Raymond Asso. Marie gave Asso part-time secretarial work to enable him to concentrate on his writing. Her generous vision was soon to be rewarded with *Mon Légionnaire* and *Le Fanion de la Légion*, both lyrics inspired by the French Foreign Legion, never failing in their appeal, reaching back to the days of France's colonial empire. With music by Marguerite Monnot, Marie Dubas recorded both these songs for Columbia, on 26 May 1936. Exceptionally they were released on a twelve-inch disc, a format rarely used for popular songs. Within days of its release radio stations were playing both 'A' and 'B' sides several times a day. (for Edith Piaf's association with these songs see pp. 42–3.)

Emmanuel Berl, husband of the composer Mireille who with Jean Nohain, was creating her own particular revolution in the *chanson* that same year, said of Marie Dubas: 'This comic singer is able to become a tragic actress at will. Her song of the Legionnaire reveals pathos equal to any created by Damia and by Yvonne George. Of all the singers of today it is Marie Dubas who, without doubt, exhibits the most intelligence' (*Marianne*, 1936).

The season 1935–6 was the zenith of Marie Dubas' career: she was engaged at the ABC Music Hall five times.

During the Second World War Marie went into voluntary exile in North Africa and South America. On her return to Paris in 1946 she found it hurtful that some critics welcomed her back as an 'Institution', though she was not yet fifty.

Almost as an act of defiance she returned to the ABC with twenty-one songs, fifteen of them new. They ranged in mood from mature humour to deepest anguish and her recital was applauded vociferously in the theatre and in the press.

Yet the ebb and flow of French popular song continued. Paris, though Eternal, is seldom static. The post-war boom was bringing new stars, fresh styles and demands from the public that the music hall had not experienced before. A new jazz age had arrived, ranging from *le be-bop* to revival 'trad'. On the Left Bank cabarets were encouraging singer-song-writers, largely under the aegis of Jacques Canetti, whose wisdom in show-biz matters earned him the nickname Socrates. Rock 'n' roll was rumbling. Radio microphones and recording studios, which Marie Dubas had disliked, if not despised, and had avoided as far as possible were now the *sine qua non* of popular success. 'Live' audiences were on the decrease, though Marie continued to perform 300 times in every year, chiefly on provincial tours. For the first time in years she found she had financial problems and the illness which finally forced her to leave the stage – Parkinson's disease was starting to assert itself. With extraordinary courage she undertook a number of exhausting foreign tours including Quebec Province in French Canada where she was rapturously received. Back in France Marie Dubas found radio and television to be unexpectedly good friends. Surprisingly, too, so was Edith Piaf. Marie was one of the few fellow-artists 'The Sparrow' ever acknowledged in public, paying her warmest tribute to her before the television cameras of *La Joie de Vivre*.

Late in 1959 Marie Dubas accepted a thirteen-week series of ten minutes each for France's largest public service radio station, Paris Inter. She wanted so much to go on working, not resting or taking holidays. 'I find it a nuisance amusing myself. I much prefer to entertain others', she often said.

Marie was to endure Parkinson's disease another thirteen years. Her death in 1972 robbed France of one of the warmest, most human artists it had ever known. Her own description of Edith Piaf might well have been equally applied to herself: 'She is the greatest artist I have ever seen: she astounds me'. And Edith regarded Marie as her model.

MONIQUE MORELLI (1923–93) was one of the last *réalistes* of the post-war generation. A brief career as an actress preceded her singing without a microphone in cellars and cabarets of the Left Bank and Montmartre (Le Vieux Colombier, La Rose Rouge, 1949) and in several large music halls including that dear old 'barn', the Bobino. Monique Morelli's heroines and mentors were Lys Gauty, Edith Piaf and above all, Fréhel to whom she paid tribute in recordings for Ducretet-Thomson and Columbia. On another Ducretet record Monique Morelli reminded old soldiers of their barrack-rooms with four songs by Pierre MacOrlan. Most of all she admired Louis Aragon, a poet whose work she sang extensively on Chant du Monde and Canetti records. When the Red Army invaded Czechoslovakia in the summer of 1968, Aragon wrote *L'Enfant Soldat* (Prague, 1968) in protest. Monique Morelli recorded that song at the request of Madame Ariane Ségal, *grande patronne* of the Arion label.

A 1992 compact disc compilation of older recordings entitled *The twenty-four most beautiful songs of Paris* contains four Aristide Bruant classics recorded by Madame Morelli in superb voice, with a mellow, melodious tone unusual in a *chanteuse réaliste*, reserving the generally more widely employed nasal tones for the more dramatic lines. Monique Morelli was frequently accompanied by the accordionist Charles (Lino) Leonardi. Morelli was a truly poetic interpreter of the 'popular' poets.

BERTHE SYLVA (1886–1941) was the stage name for Berthe Faquet, a 'realist' singer with a marshmallow flavour. In 1910 she launched what became known as, 'the tearful song'. One success followed another: seamstresses in sweat shops, children dying of hunger, others taking white roses to their mothers' graves. Sentimentality upon sentimentality. Yet for many Parisians in the early decades of the century life was hard and sad and people needed to be comforted. For these reasons Berthe Sylva enjoyed immense popularity. She received fan-mail such as no other artist had at that time; audiences slashed seats in theatres where she performed and people bought her records in tens of thousands.

For most members of the French public interested in songs the 'realism' of the *chanteuses réalistes* was more or less at arm's length. 1938 … 1939 … 1940. A new kind of realism which Germaine Montero had experienced in Spain was at the gates of Paris and about to break in … with Occupation and Syncopation.

LYS GAUTY (1908–94) Another singer with a style difficult to classify and a repertoire ranging from the romantic ballad to the 'realist' is Lys Gauty. She was born Alice Gauthier into a family of garage owners at Levallois-Perret in the heroic days of the Panhard et Levassor. Monsieur Gauthier hardly made a fortune: even so he was prepared to make every sacrifice to enable his daughter to receive singing lessons. An enthusiastic, intelligent and devoted student, Alice was soon playing in amateur productions of the more popular Italian operas. In common with many a mechanically minded man of the 1920s Alice's father became a *sans-filiste*, which meant he owned a 'wire-less'. This brought songs of the day into the Gauthier home and Alice soon decided it would be in this direction her career would go. At first amateur, then professional, Alice, now Lys Gauty, began singing in cabaret at the Boîte à matelots (1932), then at her own La Folie de Lys Gauty (1934). Soon she was appearing in the

Parisian music halls: at the Bobino in 1933, the Alhambra (1934) and Mitty Goldin's ABC in 1936.

Lys Gauty's most lasting success was an adaptation into French of an Italian song, *Parlami d'amore, Mario*, under the title *Le Chaland qui passe* (The barge passing by). The same song was also published in English as *Love's last word is spoken chéri* (1934). In the same year, Lys Gauty sang and recorded *A Paris dans chaque faubourg* (In every part of Paris) which René Clair had written (music by Maurice Jaubert) for his film *14 juillet*. Surely this must be amongst the most poetic, atmospheric and 'real' songs about Paris ever written, with its telling street organ and solitary saxophone. Wearing a plain white dress and no jewellery Lys Gauty chose only those titles with lyrics of quality: the 'realist' *Le Bistrot du port*, *Le Bonheur n'est plus un rêve* (Happiness is no more a dream) together with songs by Michel Vaucaire, composed by the Hungarian refugee Joseph Kosma who was the singer's accompanist for a while. Lys Gauty's recordings of songs from Kurt Weill's *Dreigroschenoper* in French translation were awarded a Grand Prix du Disque in 1938. In 1939 she toured South America before returning to France during the war years, when she continued to sing both in Paris and the Provinces. After the War an *épuration* committee decided she should not sing for four years. Though she started again in 1949, her heart was no longer in it. In 1950 Lys Gauty became administrator of Luchon casino and founded her own singing school in Nice. In 1991 the French Government honoured her with membership of the Order of Arts and Letters.

The work of a number of other singers mentioned here impinges on the highly personal world created by those discussed here, though perhaps rather less directly. **CORA VAUCAIRE** (1921–) born Geneviève Collin in Marseilles, though totally Parisian in her sophisticated approach to song, had a theatrical background. Soon after her arrival in Paris she found herself wooed by a literary cabaret (Chez Agnès Capri) where poets and poetry were to her liking, so she felt drawn to 'go it alone'. Francis Carco, Jacques Prévert, Charles Trenet and Pierre MacOrlan would, she thought, constitute a good start. Cora Vaucaire, who a few years ago still enjoyed singing to an audience, confesses to what may be construed as a certain degree of diffidence in her work, in the sense that, if the 'right' songs did not emerge, she would wait until they did. Married to one of France's most successful lyricists, Michel Vaucaire, Madame Vaucaire has possibly found it easier than most to stand back from the intrigues necessary to make a career in show-business. Cora Vaucaire has clearly a great love for her art, revealed in the light and shade of her voice and the dramatic intensity of her presence. In a career spanning forty years Cora Vaucaire assembled an unrivalled song-book which demanded quality as its first criterion of entry; her public though always clamour for *Le temps des cerises, La Complainte de la Butte* and *Les Feuilles mortes*.

GERMAINE MONTERO (1909–2000) commanded a similar loyalty to that of Cora Vaucaire: it stemmed from total integrity. A staunch supporter of the Republican cause Germaine Montero (whose family name was Heygel) made her theatrical debut in Madrid under the direction of Federico Garcia Lorca whose poems she took back to France, making them known in cabaret and on records. The collection of thirteen Spanish songs, *Paseando por España* won the Grand Prix du Disque. Germaine Montero always brought dignity to her performances of French as well as Spanish songs. It was a dignity which originated in a spirit of anger against social injustice and war, but was controlled and channelled into the most effective means of expression of which its own was capable: *canciones* and *chansons*. The French poets Germaine Montero has favoured have included Paul Claudel, Léo Ferré and Jacques Prévert. Her widest popular successes have been in the songs of Pierre MacOrlan, *La Chanson de Margaret* and *La Fille de Londres*.

GEORGETTE PLANA (1918–) tended to resurrect short-lived 'hits' of days gone by rather than look for those with literary or poetic content; at the same time she was totally immersed in the music and life of the Parisian *faubourgs*. She has recorded generous selections from the repertoire of Fréhel with admiration, understanding and panache.

R.H.

Index